WORLD WAR II FROM ORIGINAL SOURCES

THE U-BOAT WAR IN THE ATLANTIC
Volume I : 1939-1941

EDITED BY BOB CARRUTHERS

Pen & Sword
MARITIME

This edition published in 2013 by
Pen & Sword Maritime
An imprint of
Pen & Sword Books Ltd
47 Church Street
Barnsley
South Yorkshire
S70 2AS

First published in Great Britain in 2011 in digital format by
Coda Books Ltd.

Copyright © Coda Books Ltd, 2011
Published under licence by Pen & Sword Books Ltd.

ISBN 978 1 78159 159 8

A CIP catalogue record for this book is
available from the British Library

Printed and bound by CPI Group (UK) Ltd, Croydon, CR0 4YY

Pen & Sword Books Ltd incorporates the Imprints of Pen & Sword Aviation, Pen &
Sword Family History, Pen & Sword Maritime, Pen & Sword Military, Pen & Sword
Discovery, Pen & Sword Politics, Pen & Sword Atlas, Pen & Sword Archaeology,
Wharncliffe Local History, Wharncliffe True Crime, Wharncliffe Transport, Pen &
Sword Select, Pen & Sword Military Classics, Leo Cooper, The Praetorian Press,
Claymore Press, Remember When, Seaforth Publishing and Frontline Publishing

For a complete list of Pen & Sword titles please contact
PEN & SWORD BOOKS LIMITED
47 Church Street, Barnsley, South Yorkshire, S70 2AS, England
E-mail: enquiries@pen-and-sword.co.uk
Website: www.pen-and-sword.co.uk

CONTENTS

CHAPTER 1
OPERATIONS DURING THE FIRST YEAR

RESTRICTIONS IN ATTACK

CHAPTER 2
OPERATIONS BETWEEN ICELAND AND IRELAND (1940 AND 1941)

CHAPTER 3
THE ATLANTIC AND THE MEDITERRANEAN (MAY - DECEMBER, 1941)

NOVEMBER AND DECEMBER, 1941

APPENDICIES

- C H A P T E R   1 -

OPERATIONS DURING THE FIRST YEAR

MOBILISATION

1. U-boat Strength and State of Readiness

At noon on 15th August, 1939, the Naval Staff Operations Division in Berlin called the office of S.O. U-boats in the tender Hecht at Kiel and announced that "an officers' reunion for U-boat officers was to take place on Saturday, 19th August."

This message was a cover for commencing certain U-boat preparations to meet the deteriorating international situation. U-boats fit for Atlantic operations on 19th August were to proceed to waiting positions in the area west of England and the Iberian Peninsula.

In *Fall Weiss* (the sudden and effective destruction of the Polish Armed Forces) the German Navy's task was to cut off the Polish naval forces, to control the merchant shipping and to carry out unobtrusive reconnaissance and defensive operations to prevent enemy forces from penetrating into the Baltic and the Kattegat. The part to be played by the U-boats was defined in a directive issued by the Commander-in-Chief of the Navy, and included the following tasks;

Baltic: Minelaying and patrols off Hela, reconnaissance outside the Gulf of Finland, the Gotland area, the Irben Strait and the Kattegat-by 16 boats (Types II and VII).

North Sea: Seven boats (Type II) to occupy waiting positions east of the English Channel, constituting an unobtrusive defence against possible intervention by the Western Powers. In the event of war these boats were to lay mines off the French and British Channel ports.

Atlantic: All available "Atlantic" U-boats (Types I, VII and IX) were to proceed to waiting positions west of England and the Iberian Peninsula. In the event of war with the Western Powers they were to operate against merchant shipping in accordance with the new Prize Regulations, until the danger areas were announced.

All operational orders for these tasks had been formulated by S.O. U-boats between the end of July and 12th August, and by the 15th August, 56 commissioned boats were available, while another was expected to be commissioned by the end of the month. The distribution of the various types and their state of readiness are shown in the following table:

	Type II -250 Tons- Coastal Boats (30)	Type II -500 Tons- AtlanticBoats (30)	Type II -700 Tons- Large Atlantic Boats (30)
Training boats	9 (U.1, 2, 3, 4, 5, 6, 7, 8, 10)	1 (U.36)	-
Still under training	4 (U.56, 57, 58, 59)	-	-
Still undergoing trials (after commissioning)	2 (U.60, 61)	1 (U.49)	-
Not yet at operational readiness	1 (U.11)	1 (U.51)	2 (U.25, 42)
Ready within 14 days	14	15	6
Total	30	18	8

By including the training boats U.1, 3, 4, 5, 6, 7 and 36 which would shortly be ready for operations and by curtailing the training of U.56-59, ten more Type II boats and one Type VII boat would be conditionally ready for operational service. Thus by the end of August a total of 46 boats, of which 22 were capable of operating in the Atlantic, was ready. They comprised twenty-four Type II, sixteen Type VII and six Types I and IX. The proportion of 46 operational boats out of a total of 56 was exceptionally high. The emergency coincided with a high state of readiness of both boats and crews, with very few boats undergoing training (1)[1].

2. Organisation of the U-boat Command

To meet possible developments with Poland the U-boats were mainly concentrated in the Baltic, and an organisation, previously devised by the Naval Staff for this eventuality, came into force on 18th August, whereby Commodore Dönitz and his staff were embarked in the parent ship Erich Wasmer at Kiel, and the ship proceeded to Swinemiinde on 22nd August. At this time the Commodore was a member of the German Naval Staff, and also in operational control of the U-boats in the Baltic (S.O., U-boats, East) and of the U-boats assembling for Atlantic duties. The operational command of U-boats in the West was vested in Lieut.-Comdr. Ibbecken at Wilhelmshaven. He was then in command of the 2nd U-boat Flotilla, which together with the 1st U-boat Flotilla was assigned to operations in the North Sea and the English Channel.

This organisation remained in force until it became clear that the conflict would not be confined to Poland. Should the situation in the West deteriorate, Dönitz was to proceed to Wilhelmshaven, where he was to take charge of all U-boat operations outside the Baltic.

This change actually occurred on 31st August, when the commitments of the Baltic U-boats had decreased, owing to Germany's non-aggression pact with Russia and because in the meantime the three Polish destroyers had escaped to the West.

By now political relations with the Western Powers had reached a crisis. When Dönitz arrived at Wilhelmshaven he took over as S.O. U-boats (West), leaving Commander Schomburg at Swinemiinde, in charge of Baltic operations.

3. Disposition of the Boats during the Emergency Period

The shifting of concentration to the West can be seen from the following table of dispositions during the emergency period:

---

1 Numbers in brackets refer to the author's notes and sources, which will be found at the end of this volume.

Disposition On 21st August, 1939

Baltic	North Sea	Atlantic
14 Type II 3 Type VII	7 Type II also 4 training boats (to arrive from the Baltic on 30th August)	18 Types VII, I and IX

After the conclusion of the Non-Aggression Pact with Russia on 23rd August, seven boats (Type II), hitherto employed on reconnaissance duties in the Baltic, were released to the North Sea.

Disposition On 23rd August, 1939

Baltic	North Sea	Atlantic
7 Type II 3 Type VII	14 Type II also 4 training boats by 30th August	18 Types VII, I and IX

After the three Polish destroyers had broken out from the Baltic, the three Type VII boats there left for Wilhelmshaven. The four training boats (three Type II, one Type VII) arrived in the North Sea on 30th August.

Disposition On 31st August, 1939

Baltic	North Sea	Atlantic
7 Type II	17 Type II 1 Type VII	21 Types VII, I and IX

4. Mobilisation

On receipt of the warning on 15th August, Commodore Dönitz was on leave in Bad Gastein and returned the following day. The necessary action was taken by Captain Friedeburg, the Chief of Staff, who stopped all training exercises and recalled all boats to their bases to be equipped for war. The Third U-boat Flotilla and the U-boat Training Flotilla were allowed to continue training until 19th and 26th August respectively. As had been expected, the manning and fitting out of the boats and other preparations went according to plan. Difficulties were caused by inadequate stocks of war torpedoes. Prior to 1939 S.O. U-boats had more than once drawn attention to this deficiency.

The excessive number of orders and code-words in the various offices proved a disadvantage. The preparatory plans had foreseen all eventualities, but in the execution these code-words were occasionally disregarded, thereby causing confusion. The change-over from peace to war communications also caused some inaccuracies and delays in transmitting information. For example, a vital order to S.O. U-boats to be ready for action on the evening of 22nd August was received 24 hours late, and then only verbally. It should be recorded that eager as the U-boat crews were to give battle, they felt that the Government would do everything possible to find a peaceful solution to the crisis. An entry in the War Diary of S.O. U-boats for 21st August states:

"The particularly confident attitude of the crews deserves mention. In my opinion it is a sign of the great trust which the majority place in the Government's policy" (2).

PROBLEMS AT THE OUTBREAK OF WAR

5. Survey of the Situation by S.O. U-Boats
When war with Britain and France broke out on 3rd September, the situation could be summed up as follows (3):

"It is evident from the political situation and from Britain's inherent tenacity that this will be a long war.

"Britain is completely dependent on her sea trade for food and raw materials, and above all for building up her military strength. The German Navy's task therefore is to attack the merchant ships carrying these supplies and, if possible, to disrupt them. This means that despite the unfavourable strategic position of our Navy and its considerable inferiority in strength, the battle must be actively waged from the first day.

"No effort on the part of Germany could enable her to catch up with Britain's immense lead in naval construction. Germany cannot hope to compete for naval supremacy. Her only course is to launch a direct attack on enemy sea communications. Apart from the few surface ships fit for long-range operations, only the U-boats are available for this purpose. They alone are capable of penetrating to the main British trade routes in face of the British superiority in surface forces.

"What is the position as regards U-boats? Until the end of 1938 neither the Government nor the Navy had considered Britain as a possible enemy. The Navy had been planned as a homogeneous fleet, and the U-boat arm had been built up within that framework. Thus today at the outbreak of war, the German U-boat tonnage has not even reached the 45 per cent of British tonnage allowed by the Naval Agreement of 1935 (that is, 72 boats) and is far short of the 100 per cent permitted in 1938, which would have given Germany 129 boats of various types, large and small (4). We have today the totally inadequate number of 57 commissioned U-boats, and an inadequate construction programme. Neither the existing forces nor those to be expected from the building programme are sufficient to obtain decisive results against British shipping (see Appendix I).

"Thus three tasks face the U-boat Command:
a. to plan and to carry out large-scale expansion so that it may be possible to disrupt British sea trade during a war expected to be of long duration;
b. to dispose the available forces for maximum results at an early date;
c. the operational control of the available forces."

6. Proposals for a Large-Scale Expansion of the U-boat Arm

On 28th August, during the emergency, S.O. U-boats had submitted to the Commander-in-Chief of the Fleet-Admiral Boehm - proposals for the expansion of the U-boat arm. The Commander-in-Chief gave these proposals his backing in forwarding them to the Naval Staff (5). Envisaging a war between Germany and Britain, Dönitz had urged the raising of the U-boat strength to at least 300 boats of Type VII and Type IX, with the addition of a number of special large boats. The present U-boat programme was totally inadequate. He wanted to establish within the Naval Staff an organisation with far-reaching powers of priority, responsible only to the Commander-in-Chief of the Navy for expanding the U-boat arm.

On 4th September, S.O. U-boats explained his memorandum to Admiral Raeder, Commander-in-Chief of the Navy, at Wilhelmshaven. After reading the plan the Commander-in-Chief confirmed that a large-scale programme of U-boat construction was intended, and he wished to make a senior officer responsible for carrying it out. He asked S.O. U-boats for his opinion on the appointment of Rear Admiral U. Arnauld de la Perriere (retired) to the post, adding that he did not wish Dönitz himself to hold it.

The following is quoted from the minutes of the conference in the War Diary of S.O. U-boats, 9th September, 1939:

"… I replied that I would give my opinion on the following day, as an appointment of this kind would have far-reaching implications. I hold that this post should be occupied by me. As an active service officer I have directed the training of U-boats from the beginning and am known to the personnel. All efforts will be in vain unless we can rapidly build up our numbers, and this task now becomes the most important of all, which should be under the direction of an officer with expert knowledge of the theory and practice of U-boat warfare."

Raeder, however, decided that Dönitz was indispensable for the control of actual operations, and could not be spared for the task in Berlin. Eventually it was decided on Dönitz's recommendation to give Captain Siemens the supervision of the building programme, and this officer also became U-boat Staff Officer on the Naval Staff in Berlin. In the course of the first year of war it became apparent that he was merely Head of a Department, without executive authority, and this was disappointing for the U-boat Command.

Raeder's decision was probably right, for Dönitz was certainly needed to control operations, and his personality was directly responsible for the ultimate achievements of the U-boat War (6).

After consulting S.O. U-boats, the Naval Staff listed their requirements for expansion on 9th September, 1939, and the first wartime building programme was drawn up by the Constructional Office in October.

7. Disposition of U-boats

Type II boats were limited by their radius of action to the North Sea, the east coast of England and the Orkney and Shetland areas. Type VII boats could operate in the area west of England as far as 15° W., including Biscay. Type VIIc boats had sufficient range to operate off the west coast of Spain, as far as Portugal. Type I and Type IX could operate as far as the Azores and Gibraltar and were capable of penetrating into the Mediterranean for short periods.

According to their radius of action, the boats were therefore divided into three groups.

All small Type II boats were to operate in the North Sea and off the English coast, including the Channel. If necessary, Type VII boats could also be sent to this area. This group was under the control of Dönitz, as S.O. U-boats West. In view of their escort duties in the North Sea and on their outward and return journeys, the boats' movements had to be co-ordinated with the operations of the surface forces in Group West's command.

Type VII and Type VIIc boats were to operate on the North Atlantic trade routes; off the North Channel and in the Irish Sea, the St. George's Channel, the English Channel, and the Bay of Biscay.

The few Type I and Type IX boats were to take up more distant positions as far as Gibraltar, on the traffic routes between the Mediterranean and Britain, and Capetown-Sierra Leone-Britain.

8. Objectives

During the critical days before the annexation of Czechoslovakia in 1938 there were so few boats that they could not have had any appreciable effect on shipping. If war with England had resulted, they would have operated only against her naval forces, particularly by minelaying off the British naval ports. But in 1939 the Supreme Command's directive for Fall Weiss stipulated that the first U-boat operations should be against enemy shipping.

Even at that date there were still too few boats to obtain effective results against shipping. The question again arose as to whether in the interest of German surface ship operations it would not pay to use the U-boats against British naval forces. S.O. U-boats answered this question as follows (7):

"Results against the enemy's warships are only possible if these can be lured from their bases. Our weak surface forces cannot be relied upon to achieve this. The German Air Force could raid Scapa and perhaps succeed in driving the main force of the British Fleet (reported to be there) to the open sea. But at present air attacks are not permitted (Section 55).

"In general, U-boat operations against naval forces promise little hope of success. On the surface the U-boat has no margin of speed to haul ahead for attack; enemy escorting aircraft could generally forestall such action. The low underwater speed of the U-boat does not permit attack on fast warships except when the boat is directly in the path of the enemy, and that happens very seldom."

The prospects of Success in support of our own surface forces' operations were generally not encouraging, and so the Naval Staff decided on 7th September that the few ocean-going boats were to operate against shipping.

9. Operational Distribution

At this time all the 22 boats available for Atlantic operations were at sea, with none in reserve. This high figure would not be reached again within the next few months; probably not even within the next year, for the reduction through losses and damage, and the necessary recall of boats for training, could not be compensated by the new boats, which were being commissioned at the rate of about two a month.

The problem arose as to whether it would be more advantageous to distribute the boats equally over the operational area or to concentrate them temporarily in certain regions. If the boats were distributed equally, about one third of the 22 could be sent to the Atlantic at one time. In other words, the Atlantic boats would spend one third of their time refitting, one third proceeding to and from the operational area, and the remainder in that area. Six to eight boats could normally obtain only chance successes; if these boats operated singly, results would be achieved only until Atlantic shipping could be organised into convoys.

"While there are so few boats in the operational area it seems advisable to concentrate them with a view to gaining one major success, such as the destruction of a whole convoy" (8).

At that time nobody could prophesy how the operational situation would develop. The number of boats ready for operations would vary according to the dockyard periods, nature of repairs, special duties, and the health of the crews. Any planned concentration against shipping would only be possible by retaining boats in port prior to the operation. This would necessarily involve a period of inactivity for some boats, with immunity to shipping. Further loss of operational time would occur when the boats returned to base. The simultaneous arrival of many boats in the overburdened dockyards would prolong the refit and delay the next operation. Thus concentrated operations could only be justified if they showed a high degree of success.

U-boat operations can follow no clear-cut mathematical formula. They depend on various factors, such as the weather, visibility, enemy traffic, and enemy defences. Every planned concentration of U-boats must involve an element of risk. But in view of the inevitable variations in numerical strength it seemed right to build up " U-boat waves" for concentrated disposition, by holding back single boats as necessary.

If, however, the strategic objective necessitated the use of a very strong " U-boat wave", then the orders would have to be issued in plenty of time and the interim drop in shipping losses would have to be accepted.

10. Mine or Torpedo?

In the ground mine the Navy possessed an extremely effective weapon. According to the German specialists, the enemy would for some time be unable to counter it. For this reason it should be laid suddenly on a large scale, before the enemy had a chance to learn how to deal with it (9).

The mine could be laid in depths up to 25-30 metres; therefore only in coastal waters. It could be used in narrow approach channels, off the entrances to harbours, against shipping or naval forces-where U-boats could not remain long enough for torpedo operations, because of the strong patrols and the difficulties of navigation. The mines could be laid undetected in one quick sortie, and as shipping had to be confined to set channels, results seemed certain. With luck the harbours could even be blocked. There would be no point in laying the mines against shipping along the coast until it could be learned by careful observation what navigational restrictions had been imposed on coastal traffic.

It would be appropriate to increase minelaying activity in winter, when the long nights and unfavourable weather prejudiced the torpedo-carrying U-boats' chances, and when boats with a small radius of action could not be sure of expending their torpedoes before having to return for fuel. In all minelaying operations it was considered that the boats should also carry a limited number of torpedoes in case of a favourable target. In short, they should combine minelaying with torpedo attacks. But the general principle, even with coastal operations, was that the torpedo remained the main weapon of the U-boat, while mining operations would be ordered from time to time, as occasion arose (10).

11. The Prize Regulations

The German Admiralty's general directive to U-boats was to operate against enemy shipping, while conforming to the terms of the new Prize Regulations. It should here be explained that each U-boat always carried a copy of these Regulations, which laid down the conditions under which shipping could be attacked, and the exact procedure to be adopted in wartime against various categories of ships. These practical instructions for the use of U-boat commanders had only recently been drafted, and were based on the international regulations agreed upon in 1930 by the principal maritime powers, to which Germany had also become a party in 1936.

When war broke out Germany attached importance to the strict observance of these regulations. The circumstances which led to their abrogation are explained in sections 74 to 84 at the end of this chapter.

THE BALTIC

12. Operations
The Navy's task was to cut off the Polish Naval forces, to control merchant shipping, to carry out unobtrusive reconnaissance and to prevent enemy forces from penetrating into the Baltic and the Kattegat. The U-boats had little prospect of action against the few Polish ships.

The operational plans were drawn up by the Naval Staff in conjunction with Naval Group East. They did not altogether meet the views of S.O. U-boats, who, although agreeing to reconnaissance in the northern Baltic, thought that U-boats off the Gulf of Danzig were not needed against the insignificant Polish naval forces.

The following were the individual tasks:
- minelaying with three boats (Type VII) off Hela Peninsula to block the route from the Hela Coast against outward bound Polish forces.
- continuous patrol off Hela by these boats on completion of the minelaying operation.
- reconnaissance to locate Polish naval forces including minelayers and minesweepers.
- reconnaissance patrols in the Baltic by fourteen boats of Type II and Type VII; the areas included the Gulf of Finland, the Irben Strait, Gotland, and Kattegat, in conjunction with aircraft (11).

Should Russian aggression result from our operations against

Poland, a red is position of U-boats in the Baltic was planned, and all boats carried a sealed operational order against this eventuality. It ordered a concentration in the immediate vicinity of the Gulf of Finland.

13. The Emergency Period

By the middle of August all the U-boats detailed for the above operations were ready. They had either completed their dockyard periods or were in the Baltic on maneuvers with their flotillas. The large U-boats, intended for the Atlantic, prepared for war, while in the Baltic similar orders were received as follows:

- on 19th August: by all boats of the Third and Fifth U-boat Flotillas, which were to patrol off the Gulf of Finland, Gotland and Irben Strait;
- on 21st August: by the three U-boats of the Second U-boat Flotilla (Type VII), which were to operate off Hela (minelaying and patrol);
- on 22nd August: by the three U-boats from the U-boat School, which were to patrol the Kattegat.

The boats were to assemble in Mecklenburg Bight and Rugen.

Not all of these measures were carried into effect. The slackening of the tension in the Baltic -the result of the Non-Aggression Pact with Russia-caused the cancellation on 23rd August of the reconnaissance patrols in the Gulf of Finland and the Gotland area, though one boat was left there. Seven Type II boats were transferred to the North Sea under the command of S.O. U-boats West, leaving only ten operational boats in the Baltic. On receipt of the order to prepare for Fall Weiss, these left for their assembly areas early on 24th August.

The original plans provided for an attack on Poland 48 hours after the assembly order. The treaty concluded between Britain and Poland altered the situation, and on the evening of 25th August the *Führer* postponed the starting date, which was to have been at 0430 on 26th August. As a result, the boats were ordered to return to port, excepting two off Irben Strait and Libau, but as the tension persisted, they were sent back to their waiting positions after replenishing. On

30th August U..31, in her waiting position north of Hela, was the first to sight the three Polish destroyers on their way to Britain. They were later spotted several times by aircraft and surface forces, and were last reported by U.6 (Kattegat patrol) leaving the Kattegat on the morning of 31st August.

With the escape of the destroyers-the one valuable element of the Polish Navy-the intended German minelaying operations off Hela became redundant, and the Naval Staff on 31st August ordered the three 500-ton U-boats concerned to be released for operations in the Atlantic. At the same time, Commodore Dönitz turned over the command of U-boats in the Baltic to Commander Schomburg, and himself assumed command in Wilhelmshaven, as S.O. U-boats West.

14. Course of Events after the Outbreak of War

When the war against Poland began on 1st September, 1939, the seven U-boats (Type II) then in the Baltic were disposed as follows: two off the Gulf of Danzig, three near Uiso patrolling the Kattegat, one outside· the Irben Strait and one off Libau. The last two were recalled on the following day to provide relief for the other groups.

Until 7th September there were always two or three boats off the Gulf of Danzig. They lay submerged during the day, ready to attack any Polish submarines which might appear. At night they withdrew northwards to the open sea. Polish submarines were sighted several times; the German boats fired a torpedo on 3rd and again on 7th September, and the commanders reported that in each case a submarine had been destroyed. When the actual positions of the Polish submarines were later established, it was evident that in both cases the German commanders had been mistaken. What they had in the darkness taken to be a hit had been a premature explosion due to failure of the magnetic pistol. These were the first of a series of torpedo failures which were later to handicap U-boat operations for many months.

On 7th September the boats patrolling the Gulf of Danzig were transferred to S.O. U-boats West for operations in the North Sea.

Patrol of the Kattegat from the Läsö area was carried out by two to three boats. Two further boats were placed, one at the north end of the Sound and one at the northern approaches to the Belt. On 10th September all patrols were cancelled, and the boats were released for operations in the North Sea or for training purposes with the U-boat School.

As anticipated, the U-boat operations against Poland ended without any major incidents. The Baltic was free of.enemy naval forces and in the years that followed was used as a U-boat training ground.

WAR IN THE ATLANTIC
AUGUST - OCTOBER, 1939

15. Plans and Dispositions

Eighteen boats were available for the first Atlantic operation. This small number should have been disposed close in to the coast in the approaches to the North Channel, St. George's Channel, the English Channel and Gibraltar, where they would find plenty of traffic. There were, however, objections to this.

In the first phase it was planned to deal sudden and heavy blows at British merchant shipping in widely separated areas, so as to compel Britain immediately to adopt the convoy system (12). Until the danger areas were declared, all boats were expressly ordered" to conduct War on Shipping according to the terms of the revised Prize Regulations"; thus no ship could be sunk without first being stopped for search, and the crews had to be rescued (Section 74).

It could be assumed that when war started the enemy's forces and air patrols would be small and inexperienced; however, to operate U-boats at the approaches to the English coast and Gibraltar, while observing the Prize Regulations, seemed out of the question. In almost all cases, the A/S forces would presumably detect and attack the U-boats in these regions, and it was therefore generally advisable to keep a certain distance from the coast.

The U-boats in coastal waters were to concentrate on ships which the Regulations permitted to be sunk without warning. These included troopships, *i.e.* vessels in which troops' or war material could be observed, or which could be identified in other ways, vessels escorted by enemy warships or aircraft, and vessels participating in enemy actions or directly supporting enemy operations, *e.g.* by transmitting information (13).

For the above reasons, the first U-boat disposition took the form of a very thin wide-meshed network west of England and the Iberian Peninsula. It was anticipated that the convoy system would take several weeks to operate fully. In any case there would be a large number of single vessels still on passage before the system got into full swing, and the open disposition would cope with these. If, however, contrary to expectation, the convoy system should become fully operative at once, it would he possible to form the boats into a southern and a northern group and to appoint to each a *tactical* commander who would be subordinated to S.O. U-boats in Wilhelmshaven. With this in view, the S.O. of the Sixth U-boat Flotilla embarked in U.37 and the S.O. of the Seventh U-boat Flotilla joined U.26.

16. The Question of Tactical Command Afloat

While S.O. U-boats believed in the system of employing U-boat groups against convoys, only war experience would show the value of having a tactical commander afloat. Owing to the hasty development of the U-boat arm, and the geographical position of Germany, it had not been possible in peace to find an answer to the problem of tactical control. Moreover the answer would not be forthcoming until the boats now under construction were fitted with additional radio equipment. In this respect the U-boat Command entered the war with untried theories.

Fourteen boats had put out on 19th August, and four more were to follow before 30th August. While the first boats were outward bound, there were lively discussions between the Naval Staff and S.O. U-boats on the employment bf the remaining four boats and the relief of the first wave (14).

The effective disposition of the U-boats was a problem which concerned the U-boat Command and the Naval Staff. It would have been right for the Naval Staff to instruct S.O. U-boats on the strategic aims and requirements of naval policy and to leave him to deal with the operational and tactical employment of his forces. In practice, however, the Naval Staff became involved in the disposition of *individual* boats, which led to recurring differences with S.O. U-boats. In some cases even the U-boat commanders became aware of inconsistency in their orders.

Discussions between S.O. U-boats and the Naval Staff on such secret matters as intelligence for U-boats, re-fuelling in Spain, etc., took place over the telephone. There was anxiety over the security of the line, particularly as the Naval Staff constantly showed the keenest interest in all details of the U-boat Command, and it was suggested that the headquarters of S.O. U-boats should be moved alongside the Naval Staff in Berlin, but no decision was reached.

17. Ruling on the Distribution of Intelligence

General information on the political, military, and naval situation during the emergency period was transmitted to the Atlantic forces, including U-boats, direct from the Naval Staff. But Dönitz, as S.O. U-boats, wanted to send such information along with his routine orders; by so doing he could maintain closer contact with his forces. As a result of his repeated objections it was decided on 28th August that the Naval Staff was to supply the Atlantic boats with intelligence on the political situation and with Radio Intelligence. S.O. U-boats was free to send other intelligence, on the condition that the Naval Staff was informed. S.O. U-boats alone was authorised to give operational orders to his boats.

But this ruling had its disadvantages. If S.O. U-boats needed to transmit additional information, he first had to ascertain whether this was being done by the Naval Staff, and this caused a delay.

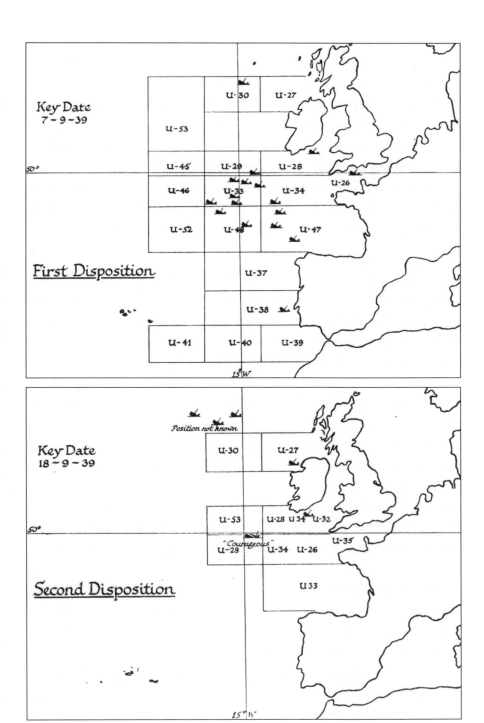

Plan 1. U-boat dispositions at the outbreak of war.

The U-boat arm was a specialised branch of the service, with an outlook of its own. It had been developed and trained in a few years under Dönitz' personal supervision. It had also evolved its own jargon, which a U-boat officer of the First World War found difficult to acquire or understand. Thus it often happened that information issued by the Naval Staff was unintelligible. In such cases S.O. U-boats himself had to clear up the misunderstandings.

Later in the war all information and orders for the boats were passed by S.O. U-boats only. This more satisfactory arrangement upheld the old principle of single control of operations.

18. Initial Measures

When the order was given to commence hostilities against Britain (radio message 1256 / 3rd September, 1939) 18 boats were either in or near their positions. About a week later the number of boats in the operational area was increased to 21; thus all U-boats capable of operating in the Atlantic were at sea.

During the emergency period S.O. U-boats had proposed retaining a few U-boats in harbour to be used as reliefs for the first wave at the end of September. This was turned down in favour of an all-out initial attack against Britain. After the outbreak of war S.O. U-boats again raised the question, and on 7th September ten boats of the modem Sixth and Seventh U-boat Flotillas were recalled, so that they might, after a short refit, resume Atlantic operations at the beginning of October. This decision was influenced by Radio Intercepts and agents' reports, pointing to the probable reduction of British traffic, followed by a large increase in October, with the formation of convoy. A considerable force was to be employed against this traffic. After the recall of the ten U-boats, the remainder were concentrated at the northern entrance to the Irish Sea and at the western end of the English Channel. They were later reinforced by U.31 and U.35. As Flag Officer Commanding U-boats[2] had expected, the boats of the first wave found their targets chiefly in single vessels which they could sink in accordance with the Prize Regulations. Of a total of 21

2 Dönitz was promoted to Rear Admiral on 19th September, 1939.

returning boats, 14 had been successful, attacking one to four ships each. Owing to their premature return, the other boats had spent only four to seven days in the operational area, where they had found little or no traffic. The first two attacks on convoys are worthy of mention. They were made by U.31 and U.3S, each of which sank one ship. The aircraft carrier *Courageous* was sunk by U.29. This success was offset by the loss of two U-boats. The special case of the Athenia is referred to in Sections 74 to 84 (15).

Reports from sea and from returning Commanding officers gave F.O. U-boats the following picture of the situation in the Atlantic: A large proportion of ships was sailing in convoys of four to twenty ships; speed seven to eighteen knots. Very fast convoys were reported from the Mediterranean. Convoys were protected by four to six destroyers, and occasionally by cruisers as well. They were given air cover in the vicinity of the coast. Air patrols around Britain were extensive, judged by contemporary standards. Aircraft carriers had been seen in the Orkneys, west and southwest of Ireland, in the English Channel and in the Gibraltar area. Escort in the coastal areas was provided by patrol vessels and other light forces. U-boats close to the coast and near the English and Bristol Channels were less successful than those in the open sea. The former were apparently hampered by enemy patrols.

19. Prospects of the Operations

The situation corresponded to expectations, particularly regarding enemy defences, but confidence in the U-boat remained unshaken. F.O. U-boats summarised his views in the war diary for 28th September:

"The physical and psychological effect of the U-boat is still far-reaching and impressive less than in the First World War

"It is not true that Britain possesses the means to eliminate the U-boat menace. Experience confirms that British AIS measures are not so effective as claimed. Enemy technique has doubtless improved, but so has the U-boat, which moves more silently. The firing of a torpedo no longer causes a tell-tale splash. The torpedo now has a much higher performance and its track is invisible. (Author's note: the defects in the torpedo had not yet become apparent.) Communications have made such great advances that it is now possible to control the movements of widely dispersed U-boats and to concentrate them as necessary for attacks on convoys. This was proved in the Biscay exercise of 11th to 15th May, 1939 (15a). After careful consideration, I am convinced that the U-boat is still our most effective weapon against Britain, provided sufficient boats are available. We require at least 300 for operations, but more will be needed in order to cover losses and repairs. Given this number, I believe we shall achieve decisive results."

OCTOBER -CHRISTMAS, 1939

20. Planning of Operations

It was evident to the U-boat Command that the high total of 21 boats at sea at one time could not again be reached for some months, and probably not for a year. The effect of the war-time construction programme would not become apparent until 1941. Meanwhile each boat had to be used with maximum effect.

In the first few months the U-boat Command endeavoured-generally in vain-to keep abreast of developments in the enemy's convoy system and A/S measures. Detailed plans for individual operations were prepared, careful consideration being given to their nature-whether torpedo or minelaying-and to the selection of the operational areas and the Commanding Officers.

Special concentrations were also planned, in which all boats leaving harbour during a given period worked together; but towards the end of 1939 it became evident that effective concentration was impossible with the small force available. As long as the urgency of the situation prevented the retention in harbour of an adequate number of boats to build up for planned pack operations, the boats would have to operate singly as they became available. On 1st

October there was only one boat in the Atlantic, and one in the North Sea. Nine were to be ready for Atlantic operations by 15th October. As the British convoys would soon he in full operation, there was no point in scattering these few boats singly over wide areas. The aim must be to intercept convoys and destroy them by a concentrated effort. In view of the difficulty of locating convoys in the open sea, the boats would be sent to areas such as southwest of England, or to Gibraltar, where traffic necessarily becomes constricted. The position southwest of England had the advantage of relative proximity, but the disadvantages of rather strong AIS patrols and, at times, bad weather. The Gibraltar area had neither of these disadvantages, and U-boats going there would pass through the area southwest of England with the possibility of finding targets en route. A sudden concentration on the Gibaltar-England route therefore offered possibilities.

To avoid retaining the boats in harbour unduly, it was planned to assemble them in a limited area southwest of Ireland, where targets had been plentiful. There they were to await orders from F.O. U-boats, or the tactical commander afloat (S.O. Sixth U-boat Flotilla in U.37), to proceed to positions Schwarz (west of Portugal) and Rot (northwest of Spain) in the operational area west of the Iberian Peninsula.

21. First Attempt at a Controlled Pack Operation

So much for the plan. The execution was very different. The dockyard completion dates for two boats (U.34 and U.25) had to be postponed. U.47 (Prien) was designated for a special operation against Scapa Flow. The last of this group (U.40) put out on 10th October; she was to take a short cut through the Channel, but as she did not report leaving the Channel, she was presumed lost.[3]

F.O. U-boats could therefore count on only five boats for the operational area. The Radio Intercept Service confirmed many sin kings resulting from their activity in position Gelb (southwest of Ireland). When reports ceased to come in, the boats were ordered on 16th October to area Schwarz, and were told to report the situation. U.42 and U.45 did not report, so could not be counted on. (U.42 had

---

3 U.40 lost by mining in the Dover Strait on 13th October, 1939.

been sunk by destroyers shortly after her arrival in area Gelb and U.45 was presumably destroyed on 15th or 16th October.)[4]

While proceeding southwards U.46 sighted a northbound convoy, and the remaining two boats joined her to operate against it. When contact was lost, the tactical commander-Lieut.Comdr. Hartman in U.37-ordered a reconnaissance patrol for the morning of 18th October, but contact was regained and the convoy was attacked. About noon the boats were forced to withdraw by the arrival of aircraft. In spite of its short duration this operation had been successful; at least three or four vessels were sunk. Later it was learned that more ships would have been sunk but for torpedo failures.

After the operation one boat, having expended all torpedoes, was ordered to return, one was sent to the Gibraltar and one to the Lisbon area, and for the time being pack operations ceased. Of the original nine boats, only six had been used. Of these, one had been lost on passage, two were lost at the beginning of the operation, which left only three to operate.

This first U-boat operation had shown that the enemy had apparently nothing new or particularly dangerous in the way of A/S measures. If he had achieved little in the long years of peace, it could be assumed that no rapid developments would ensue within the first year of war. But within a short time he could certainly be expected to increase his A/S forces considerably. This would be a serious menace until the U-boats became more numerous, and every effort would have to be made to defeat it. Consideration was therefore given to operating in several widely separated areas without prejudicing the primary object of sinking ships. The enemy would thereby be forced to provide A/S patrols in all areas, and would have to disperse his forces and therefore weaken them in the main operational area. Should his forces become too strong in one place, the U-boats would transfer to another.

---

4 U.45 sunk by destroyers *Inglefield*, *Ivanhoe* and *Icarus*, southwest of Ireland on 14th October, 1939.

22. Thrust into the Mediterranean

In the light of the above considerations and of reports of heavy traffic in the Mediterranean, a thrust into that area was planned. The convoys reported between Gibraltar and Oran were so numerous that, despite the remoteness of the area, and the consequent shortness of operations, it seemed worth carrying out. In the restricted Mediterranean it might not be possible to conform to the Prize Regulations, but there would be legitimate targets which could be sunk without warning. It was considered that the narrowness of the Mediterranean would permit co-operation between a small number of U-boats against the restricted convoy routes. But this theory was disproved within the first few months of the war. Owing to continuous enemy patrols, the boats were frequently unable to make timely sighting reports, or the remaining boats, though only having a few miles to cover, were prevented from reaching a suitable position for attacking.

Of the boats which became ready in the second half of October, three with long range (U.25 and U.26-700 tons, U.53-517 tons) were chosen for this task. U.25 and U.53 had orders to wait southwest of Ireland, to give U.26 a lead of about three days in which to lay mines off Gibraltar. All three boats were then to reach the Mediterranean simultaneously.

Again the execution went astray. From her waiting position southwest of Ireland, U.25 was ordered to attack a northbound convoy, reported some 60 miles northwest of Lisbon by U.40 (a boat of the previous group), but she did not make contact. Proceeding to a new waiting area northwest of Cape Finisterre, U.25 sighted another convoy, attacked it and then had to return with a damaged torpedo hatch, caused by her own gun blast.

When U.26 had gained a sufficient lead, U.53 was ordered to proceed southwards. En route she encountered a northbound convoy off Lisbon, which she reported and shadowed. Coming from the north, three boats of the next group, U.41, 43 and 49 made contact with this convoy. The operation ended 200 miles from the French coast when contact was lost. U.53 had to return for refuelling. She had caused no damage to the convoy despite many opportunities for attack, and the commander was relieved of his post. U.26 ran into a gale off Gibraltar, which prevented her laying her mines. During her short stay in the Mediterranean visibility was poor and traffic scarce, and she returned to base after only one successful attack.

The operation had failed because of inadequate numbers. All targets sighted en route had to be attacked, and owing· to this, two boats had to drop out. The third, after her long passage, could spend only a short time in the operational area and had found no targets. The object of the operation-to force the enemy to take counter-measures-had not been achieved. There would only be results if the boats could remain much longer in that area, for a short visit might easily coincide with a lull in the traffic.

23. Minelaying Operations

Observation of shipping activity on the west coast of England up to October pointed to several places where minelaying would be profitable. While the long nights and bad weather hampered the U-boats' torpedo attacks, they favoured minelaying. A number of operations took place before the end of the year.

It was anticipated that if the British Fleet evacuated Scapa Flow because of our air raids, they would use Loch Ewe as an anchorage. U.31 was sent there, carrying 18 TMB mines. She encountered no A/S forces, but on entering the Loch on 27th October she fouled the net barrage, for she had not spotted the A/S boom until too late. As it seemed impossible to penetrate further, she laid her mines at safe countermining distance across the entrance to the Loch.[5]

U.28, 29 and 33, each carrying 12 TMB mines and six torpedoes, were ordered to mine the Bristol Channel, and later to operate with torpedoes in St. George's Channel and the North Channel. U.28 laid her mines off Swansea on 5th December. U.29 was detected by A/S forces, which prevented her laying mines at Milford Haven. U.33

5 H.M.S. *Nelson* was mined in the entrance to Loch Ewe on 4th December, 1939.

laid 12 mines off The Foreland on 9th November and later sank five trawlers on patrol.

24. Second Attempt at a Pack Operation

The second pack operation was planned on similar lines to the first. It was to be the last for some time, for it also failed owing to the small number of boats, which again had orders to attack anything sighted en route.

U.38, 41, 43, 47 and 49 were to be assembled in November, south of Ireland, and then proceed to an area off Cape Finisterre. Off Ireland, though near the coast and exposed to intensive A/S measures, they ran less risk than at the outbreak of war, because they were now permitted to attack on sight all ships-except liners-which were darkened or which could be clearly identified as enemy.

It became evident that two of the boats would be late in leaving dockyard, and this time Dönitz reluctantly decided on 2nd November to hold back the other boats for a few days, although every day's delay meant fewer sinkings. But plans had to be changed, for at the urgent request of the Naval Staff U.38 had to be sent as relief for U.36, to operate against the Russian timber transports off Kola Bay. U.47 was not yet ready. Thus only three out of the small wave of five boats were available. Because of gales they proceeded direct to a position southwest of Portugal. On 18th November they were ordered to operate against a northbound convoy which U.53 had reported on the previous day off Cape Finisterre. In the course of three days each boat in turn made contact. When the operation ended on 21st November, U.49 had to return as her bow tubes had been damaged by depth charges. The others were ordered to a new area between 48° and 50° N. Once again the original disposition had to be abandoned. U.49 returned without result. U.41 and U.43 each sank three ships. This further comparative failure caused the U-boat Command to defer their attempts at planned concentration and instead to dispatch each boat to the Atlantic whenever it became ready for operations. Not until June, 1940, were pack operations resumed.

25. The Timber and Ore Traffic to Britain

At the beginning of November the Naval Staff requested F.O. U-boats to review the question of attacks on British timber imports from the north Russian ports, which were still reported to be considerable. An interruption of the supply of pit props to Britain was of great importance. It had been intended to send U.36 (the only 500-ton boat available for North Sea operations) to a position east of North Cape. But she was delayed in dockyard, and as the lengthening nights demanded immediate action, U.38, a boat of the previous group, took her place. She layoff West Fjord in bad weather for several days, but sighted no targets, and later found only slight traffic off Kola Bay. She was then ordered to attack the ore traffic from Narvik to Britain, outside the three mile limit at West Fjord. Here and on her return passage along the Norwegian coast she sank three ships.

As time went on, requests by the Naval Staff for similar operations became frequent. Such tasks, which did not materially contribute to the sinking of shipping, were characterised in the U-boat Command as "wild goose chases." Results generally proved agents' reports to be exaggerated, as in the case of the attack on the timber and ore traffic. The U-boats' effectiveness against these special targets had been overrated by inexpert members of the Naval Staff.

26. Operations against British Naval Forces

In September and November the North Sea U-boats operated mainly against enemy naval forces. Apart from the *Royal Oak*, no successful attacks had been made, as the main British units avoided the North Sea. F.O. U-boats then stopped operations in the North Sea and considered attacking the British Fleet in the area west of England. Radio intercepts indicated that the fast ships and several aircraft carriers were hunting packet battleships or escorting particularly important convoys and that the other battleships were apparently based on the *Clyde*.

An attack on this anchorage did not seem promising, as the only approach to these long and narrow waters was protected by a boom.

It would, however, be possible to lay mines at the boom, where the Firth was wider. But as the TMB mine could not be guaranteed to have full effect in such deep water, it was preferable to postpone such an operation until the TMC mine (containing a ton of explosive, for use in water up to 35 metres) became available. Prospects of torpedo attacks seemed good against ships leaving by the northern channel, for here navigational conditions allowed the U-boats to take up position in deep echelon. But the question was-when would the fleet sail northwards?... Possibly only if lured into northern waters by German battleships. A joint operation by surface forces and U-boats for this purpose appeared desirable.

On learning of a proposed northward sortie by the German battleships, F.O. U-boats asked for a postponement for a few days, which would allow eleven U-boats to participate in the *Clyde* operation. This was not granted, and only four U-boats sailed between 16th and 21st November, 0.47 proceeding to the Minch, 0.35 to the Pentland Firth, and U.31 and 48 to the Orkneys. The German big ships had sailed on 22nd November, and two days later the German Radio Intelligence showed that the British were aware of their presence in the North Sea. Nothing was known, however, of any British reaction as the bad weather prevented air reconnaissance. On 25th November the British Fleet was considered to have left the *Clyde*. U.47 was then moved from the Minch to the Pentland Firth, and U.35 from the Pentland Firth to Fair Island Passage. This disposition permitted the boats to proceed at short notice to an intercepting position east of the Shetlands. An unsuccessful attempt was made to locate light naval forces seeking protection from a westerly gale off the east coast of the Orkneys and Shetlands. When German aircraft reported sighting enemy naval forces, the boats were ordered to a patrol line from the Shetlands to the Norwegian coast. As a result U.47 claimed a hit on a *London* class cruiser, which Goebbels' propaganda then reported as sunk. "From the service point of view such inaccuracies and exaggerations are undesirable" (War Diary, 29th November). Later this "hit" was assessed as a premature explosion.

U.31 and U.35, having now insufficient fuel to operate-as originally intended-to the south of Ireland, were dispatched to the east coast of England, and U.47 and U.48 were sent to the western end of the Channel, where they operated successfully.

When, on 19th December, 1939, U.48 passed Fair Island Channel on her return passage, no U-boats remained in the Atlantic.

CHRISTMAS 1939 - MARCH 1940

27. Winter Delays

It was expected that about 12 boats would be ready to sail for the Atlantic during January. The exceptional winter with the attendant ice conditions delayed preparations. Early in the month ice in the fairways of the Baltic caused slight delays and minor damage, in spite of ice escort by old battleships and tugs. Towards the end of the month freezing-up of the dry and floating docks was serious, and led to postponement of torpedo and diving exercises. The U-boat Command had to decide whether to await the end of the cold spell to enable several boats, with new commanders, to complete their training, or whether to detail these for operations at once. As the officers and crews had reached an advanced stage of training, it was decided to send the boats to the operational zone immediately; but to enable them to work up efficiency, they were sent to areas where enemy A/S forces were weak. Their operational orders stated: "Difficult situations are to be avoided until the commander considers his boat to be adequately efficient" (16).

This decision enabled a considerable number of boats to operate west and northwest of Spain in January and February, 1940. In view of previous experience no concentrated attack was planned, but pack operations against convoys were to be attempted at every opportunity. Except for special tasks, boats were not to leave their respective areas unless there appeared a good possibility of acting on an enemy sighting rep-,nt. As a result of Dönitz's personal contact

34

with his commanders and his participation in the discussions that followed every operation, long orders were unnecessary, for they knew at all times what was expected of them.

In general, the operations off the western end of the Channel and west and northwest of the Spanish coast were very successful. The sinkings averaged four to five ships, or about 25,000 tons[6] per boat per operation. The best results were achieved near the Faroes and in the North Channel; the area west of Finisterre was also promising. The operations presented no particular difficulties, yet the proportion of losses-four boats in eleven operations-was very high. Three losses occurred among the boats which were on their first operation; two boats had not even completed their training and working-up periods, because of the ice in the Baltic.

28. Action against Ark Royal, Renown and Exeter

The attempted attacks on Ark Royal, Renown and Exeter are worth mentioning. From a British radio message decrypted on 7th January by German Signals Intelligence, it was learned that at 0000 on 11th February Ark Royal would be in a definite position some 200 miles northwest of Madeira steering 015°, speed 22 knots; 180 miles behind her would be Renown and Exeter steaming at 16 knots. German Signals Intelligence inferred that these ships were proceeding to the Channel, which was confirmed by another radio intercept on 9th February. Though the chances of attacking them seemed slight, it was decided to make the attempt. U.26 and U.37, estimated to be in the Channel area, were ordered on 10th February to occupy certain positions in the Western Approaches. U.4S was in the same area, after having laid mines off Weymouth.

On 12th February an intercepted radio message to French patrol vessels stated that Ark Royal with four British destroyers would be in 45° N., 15° W., at 0900 on the same day. U.26, U.37 and U.4S were therefore ordered to assume position on the line Lizard Head-Les Sept Isles; U.4S north of 48° 40' N., U.26 south of 49° IS' N., and between them U.37. Ark Royal was expected to be steering an

---
6 Merchant ship tonnage is Gross Registered Tonnage (G.R.T.) unless otherwise stated.

easterly course early on 13th February: Renown and Exeter would probably appear in that vicinity on the 14th.

At noon on 12th February U.48 reported sighting a convoy 120 miles west of Land's End, which she pursued westwards until contact was lost in the evening. U.26, some 300 miles west of Land's End, was only making seven knots because of an easterly gale, while UAS, having moved west throughout the night, was now 340 miles west of Land's End. It was too late to send the boats to the planned positions, and they were ordered to remain in the Western Approaches until 14th February, when they were moved to new positions.

This brief undertaking with no result showed the difficulties of planning at short notice. The U-boats' speed of advance was always much influenced by the vagaries of weather and enemy defence.

29. Further Minelaying Operations
The winter weather aided minelaying, and U-boats' torpedoes were proving unreliable, so it was decided to use the first months of 1940 for further mining operations with both small boats and larger ones which also carried torpedoes.

Liverpool was mined early in January by U.30, apparently with effect, judging by reports of the temporary closing of the harbour and the declaration of mine-danger areas. While on her way to Liverpool, U.30 had attacked Barham with four torpedoes on 28th December, 1939, scoring one hit.[7]

Falmouth Roads were mined on 19th January by U.34, which also sank a ship south of Ireland, and sighted two battleships (probably *Rodney* and *Repulse*) near the North Channel. Loch Ewe was again mined by U.31 at the end of January, and mining of the Firth of *Clyde* was attempted by U.32 in January, and achieved by U.33 early in February. This last boat was later reported by German Radio Intelligence as destroyed by a British minesweeper.[8] But the British

---

7 On this date H.M.S. *Barham* was damged by torpedo when 50 miles off the Butt of Lewis.

8 U.33 was sunk by H.M.S. *Gleaner* in the *Clyde* on 12th February, 1940.

reported the *Clyde* to be dangerous owing to mines, so her task was accomplished.

Weymouth was mined at the beginning of February by U.4S, which later claimed to have torpedoed and sunk four ships, totalling 30,000 tons, in the Western Approaches. U.29 laid mines at Milford Haven on 2nd March, and later sank three ships, while U.28 mined Portsmouth, and later sank two ships. Liverpool was again mined early in March by U.32, who dropped her mines adjacent to those laid by U.30 in January. In all these operations-with the partial exception of the Firth of *Clyde*-the mines were laid as planned, and although there were no immediate indications of sinkings, it could be assumed from reports of the blocking of harbours and diversions of shipping that good results had been achieved (17).

30. Discussions on Extending Operations

In spite of restrictions imposed by the Prize Regulations, relatively good results had been obtained by the U-boats during the early months, while the enemy was still organising his convoys and his AIS forces. But sinkings were not sufficient to materially affect the war situation, and the German Naval Staff pressed for an extension of the area of operations into the Atlantic, thereby causing still more ships to sail in convoy, with more delays in shipping, and dispersing the British A/S forces. There were discussions on a proposed joint operation between a pocket battleship and U-boats, but nothing came of this. The attitude of F.O. U-boats was that direct results through sinking of enemy shipping were more valuable than strategic diversion or indirect pressure, and he wished to maintain the comparatively high rate of sinkings which a few U-boats had achieved in December, 1940, while operating round the coasts of Britain. He believed that his boats had in that month attained an average of 660 tons sunk per boat per day, though British post-war data showed the correct figure to be only 342 tons (18).

An operation for the mining of the harbour approaches to Halifax (Nova Scotia) was worked out in February. Originally a minelayer carrying 400 mines was to proceed there and operate in conjunction with a Type IX minelaying U-boat. Once again the operation was cancelled because of possible political repercussions in the United States.

A special department of the German Admiralty was occupied with arrangements abroad for the replenishment of U-boats. The plan, which envisaged the use of German merchant ships in or from neutral harbours, was first put to the test when U.25 entered Vigo to refuel in January, 1940. In December, 1939, F.O. U-boats contemplated using the anchorage on the Munnansk coast (known as *Basis Nord*) for replenishment of U-boats, as this place had been put at our disposal by the Russians. But it was never used for this purpose, and by April Germany had her own bases in Norway.

SURVEY OF THE ATLANTIC OPERATIONS OF THE FIRST SIX MONTHS

31. Defects and Losses

After the torpedo and minelaying operations between 1st and 10th March, 1940, there began a period of nearly three months, during which the war against merchant shipping was interrupted and the boats were employed on a purely naval task-the occupation of Norway.

Reviewing the first six months of war, it can be said that the Type VIIc boat (517 tons), designed for attacks on convoys, had proved very suitable for this task. She was easily handled, had good diving qualities, great endurance, was well armed, and, being small, was difficult to see at night. The Type IX was more 'conventional in design and rather difficult· to handle, but had longer range and carried more torpedoes.

Officers and men had received a thorough all-round training. They had confidence in their boats and performed their duties admirably. In independent actions they displayed dash and enthusiasm, and steadfastness in face of opposition. Although, owing to lack of forces, pack attacks on convoys had not so far achieved success, the few occasions on which the boats had operated in company had shown promise. There was still no solution to the problem of tactical control by a commander afloat, and no evidence of how far the German radio traffic helped the enemy A/S forces. F.O. U-boats took up this matter with the Naval Staff, for it was one of the main problems of controlled U-boat operations.

The Atlantic U-boats had operated in three "waves", with peak periods on 10th September with 21 boats, on 23rd November with 13, and on 7th February with 9. After the first full-scale operation in September, there was an average of 6·3 boats at sea daily between October, 1939, and February, 1940. This was somewhat below the figure anticipated by the U-boat Command, and was due to dockyard delays.

When the first wave returned for repairs, the naval dockyards had insufficient capacity to cope with constructional weaknesses that had revealed themselves only under war conditions. The engine bed plates of a number of boats had failed to withstand the strain of long passages. The engine exhaust valves (which closed *against* the water pressure) were found to be weak and badly designed. Returning boats had reported that when deeply submerged, these valves leaked to .such an extent that the subsequent pumping out betrayed the boat's position, owing to the noise.

Before the war, it had been recommended that the boats should be allowed to dive beyond the maximum limit of 50 metres, but this was turned down for reasons of safety. If deep diving had been practised, the defect in the exhaust valves would have been discovered, and rectified at once; some losses might then have been avoided and the additional strain on the dockyards reduced. The extraordinary amount of repair work lengthened the refits and caused an accumulation of boats in the yards; the situation was aggravated by a dearth of specialists and supervisors, and by faulty organisation. But these constructional weaknesses of the boats were small in relation to their otherwise good performance. In November, VA9, in taking evasive action, had dived to 170 metres without distortion of

39

the pressure hull. This, and her splendid resistance to depth charge attacks induced confidence in the other boats.

When the first losses occurred, the effectiveness of the enemy A/S measures and the question of appropriate countermeasures became the U-boat Command's main problem. Though the proportion of losses was high, it did not surpass expectations. Each loss was thoroughly investigated, and tactics were changed to counter and, if possible, outwit the enemy.

The British had scored an advantage by closing the English Channel. After U.40 and U.12 were mined, this short cut to the operational area was abandoned. As expected, the losses during the first six months were not covered by new construction. The numbers had sunk from 57 boats at the outbreak of war to 50 in March, 1940.

32. Torpedo Failures

Right from the beginning a number of attacks failed owing to defects in the magnetic pistol and the depth-keeping mechanism of the torpedo. Already in September many torpedoes were reported to have exploded at the safety limit (250 m. from the boat), these prematures being due to magnetic pistol failures. Besides rendering the attack abortive, a premature betrayed the U-boat's position. In some cases these near explosions caused slight damage to the firing boat.

As a readjustment of the magnetic fields of the pistol failed to remedy the defect, impact pistols were used from 2nd October onwards, and the more powerful effect of magnetic firing was lost. , Trials, which were at once started in the Baltic, revealed that the depth-keeping mechanism was not functioning properly and that torpedoes were running anything up to 1·75 metres too deep. This defect had apparently been ignored before the war on the grounds that a small increase of depth was not important when using a magnetic pistol. But a depth correction of minus two metres had now to be applied to torpedoes when using impact pistols. As a setting of less than four metres was impracticable in high seas, targets drawing less than four metres, such as destroyers, would escape being hit.

From 10th November magnetic pistols were again used. Though F.O. U-boats doubted the efficiency of the improved pistol, there was not much choice, since impact firing was also unreliable. But even these modified pistols produced prematures and explosions at the end of the run. The modifications necessitated changes in procedure for handling and setting torpedoes, which complicated the routine in the U-boats. There were so many reports of unexplained misses, that the magnetic pistol was again suspected. The specialists in the Torpedo Trials Department maintained that these were due to faulty aiming. This question gave rise to controversy between the U-boat Command and the torpedo specialists. Fresh trials in the Baltic proved the pistol to be at fault. Conferences and correspondence on further improvements now occupied more of U-boat Command's time than operational problems.

The failures also affected the personnel. Dönitz wrote on 21st January, 1940: "The inefficiency of the torpedo has had a serious effect on the morale of the U-boat Service... At least 25 per cent of the torpedoes fired were failures. Statistics up to 6th January, show that 40·9 per cent of misses were due to this cause. Confidence in the torpedo has been badly shaken... The object always is to fire torpedoes from the most advantageous position, but owing to misses and torpedo failures, these bold attacks have often involved risk of losing the boat. It is estimated that these failures have lost us at least 300,000 tons of shipping. I am certain, for instance, that the torpedo fired by U.47 (Prien) at the London class cruiser was a premature. It is bitterly disappointing for all concerned that, despite thorough peace-time training, the U-boats have not achieved the success they deserved, simply because of torpedo failures."

It was due to the personal efforts of Dönitz, who interviewed the crews after unsuccessful operations, that confidence was restored.

33. Secondary Objectives
F.O. U-boats invariably resisted any weakening of the main efforts

through detachment of his boats for special tasks, such as the landing of agents on foreign soil, and the escorting of raiders, replenishment ships and prizes. Throughout the war there were numerous requests for such secondary activities, which he was usually successful in resisting. For instance, at a discussion with the Naval Staff on 22nd January, 1940, he was asked to provide two U-boats to be stationed off Iceland. and two off the Norwegian coast in connection with the impending sortie of a raider. The comment in his diary was: "I cannot approve this request. My problem is to fight the bad weather and ice, to tackle excessive dockyard time, to cope with inefficient torpedoes, and not least to wage war on Britain. It is too much to expect me to provide four boats, merely for their psychological effect."

THE OCCUPATION OF NORWAY
MARCH -MAY, 1940

34. The Plan of Operations
At the beginning of March, 1940, few boats were at sea, for the North Sea boats had returned from the "Nordmark" operation, while the relatively high proportion of Atlantic boats that were active in the first half of February had returned to base. The U-boat Command now planned a further pack operation by eight boats in the Atlantic, and a renewed attack by smaller boats on the Scandinavian traffic in the North Sea. These plans did not materialise, for on 4th March the Naval Staff ordered all ships and U-boats to concentrate in German harbours in readiness for the attack on Norway.

On the following day F.O. U-boats attended a Naval Staff meeting in Berlin, to discuss preparations for the occupation of Norway and Denmark. The occupation was to be carried out by sudden, simultaneous landings in Narvik, Trondheim, Bergen, Egersund, Christiansand and Oslo. Troops were to be transported to Narvik, Trondheim, Bergen and Egersund by warships, and to Christiansand

and Oslo by warships and transports. Airborne troops were also to be used.

Reports that troops were standing by in the north of England, that British naval forces had returned to Scapa from the west, and other factors, seemed to indicate that the enemy also was preparing for military action against Norway on the plea of helping Finland-an eventuality which had to be borne in mind throughout the operation. After the German landings, it was possible that the enemy would react strongly by attacking the newly captured bases, or by interrupting the German sea communications to Norway.

Preparations for the German attack were to be completed by 10th March, though there was every likelihood of a postponement of the starting date. Originally the tasks allotted to the U-boats were beyond their numerical resources, and the Flag Officer had to decide on main operations only. Eventually the U-boats were given the following tasks: to cover the warships and assault troops after the landing; to counter, and if possible prevent, an enemy landing; to attack and drive off enemy naval forces operating against sea· communications between Norway and Germany.

Our occupying forces could best be covered by the, immediate closing of the appropriate fjords by means of U-boats, which would also prevent enemy counter-landings. But there were many points on the Norwegian coast, with its many fjords, at which enemy landings could be made, and few boats to cover them. It was therefore necessary to station groups of U-boats in the open sea within reach of the threatened areas, ready to pursue and cut off enemy forces as soon as the direction of their thrust had been ascertained. The more damage inflicted on the enemy forces as they approached, the greater the chance of successful German landings.

The disposition of U-boats was decided as follows:

Protection of the occupied harbours north of 63° N. (Narvik and Trondheim) by large boats, and of those south of that latitude (Bergen and Stavanger) by small boats.

Narvik: four boats in deep echelon.

Trondheim: two boats for guarding the inner approaches.

Bergen: protection by two boats in deep echelon for each of the two main entrances, and a fifth boat directly off the harbour.

Stavanger: two boats: one immediately outside the entrance, the other in the outer approaches, and to cover Haugesund.

Two attack groups, available for speedy dispatch to the Shedands - Norway area to attack ships bringing troops to Norway, consisting of six large boats northeast of the Shetlands and three small boats east of the Orkneys on the enemy's probable line of approach.

Four small boats east and west of the Pentland Firth, where enemy warships were expected to appear.

Two small boats off Stavanger and three west of Lindesnes. These were to be training boats, because of their small radius and inexperienced crews.

35. Admiral Saalwachter

Admiral Saalwachter, Naval Group Commander West, who was in charge of operations west of the Ryvingen-Hanstholm line, issued a directive on 8th March, defining the duties of the U-boats as follows:

- to lay mines outside the convoy and fuelling bases in the Orkneys and Shetlands and to attack all naval forces and shipping in this area;
- to intercept and attack enemy traffic in the Stadtlandet-North Shetlands area;
- to prevent the enemy penetrating into the occupied ports.

F.O. U-boats could not agree to the mining operation. In his view the boats on this task would probably arrive back in Norwegian waters too late to be of use in the main task of patrol and defence. All U-boats must be available for defence of the Norwegian area, and for attacks on enemy warships and transports. The sinking of ordinary shipping during this period must be abandoned, as being secondary to. the principal task.

This would be the first occasion in the war when German surface ships and U-boats would be operating in the same area, and special safeguards were arranged for their mutual safety. It was also vital that the U-boats' move to Norway and their waiting positions should not be discovered by the enemy. The undoubted efficiency of the enemy Radio Intelligence Service compelled complete radio silence in all areas outside the normal U-boat operational zones, except when making action or sighting reports.

Detailed Operational orders - "Hartmut" - were issued to all boats in a sealed envelope, not to be opened until ordered (19).

36. Preliminaries of the Assault

The size of the operational area and the peculiar formation of the Norwegian coast required the preparation of every available U-boat. All sailings were stopped, and boats already at sea were recalled. Dockyard periods were reduced and in some cases working up periods were curtailed. U-boat training ceased in the Baltic, and the training boats were quickly brought to operational readiness. By 10th March preparations had been completed and the boats lay ready in the harbours.

On 11th March the Naval Staff, fearing imminent British landings in Norway, ordered the Narvik and Trondheim U-boats and four large boats for Bergen and Stavanger to assume their positions. Eight boats put to sea, and two already in the Shetlands area were ordered to the Norwegian coast.

On 14th March the situation became more acute, when decrypted messages showed abnormal British submarine activity in the western approaches of the Skagerrak, north of the German danger area, and off Terschelling; altogether" fourteen submarines were identified. The Naval Staff assumed this activity to be connected with an operation against Norway, which was later cancelled because of the sudden conclusion of Russo-Finnish hostilities (20). At that time the German operation was not due until 20th March, and it was decided to despatch eight small U-boats to attack these submarines. But in order to maintain a sufficient number of large boats in the northern North Sea, the speed of the boats proceeding to Narvik and Trondheim was reduced and two of them were told to remain off Stadtlandet on the look-out for enemy activity.

After an apparently successful air attack on Scapa Flow on the night of 16th/17th March, the Naval Staff directed that at least four of the boats, then off the Norwegian coast, be moved to the north coast of Scotland. It was anticipated that damaged ships would be leaving Scapa Flow for repairs and that the British Fleet would eventually evacuate the anchorage owing to continuous German air raids.[9] To meet this eventuality these boats were disposed in deep echelon west of the Pentland Firth as far as the Minch, along the probable route of the British warships proceeding to less exposed bases. Two small boats (U.57, U.19) from the group operating against submarines in the North Sea were sent to the other side of Pentland Firth.

Although it appeared from one sighting report and from radio intercepts that the main British units had left Scapa, nothing was achieved. A systematic combing of the Shetlands-Faroes area in scouting formation also had no result. Contrary to Dönitz's intentions, the boats were left in the area until 26th March, when the Naval Staff allowed them to be withdrawn. All boats were recalled to Germany except three north of Scotland, one off Narvik and one off Trondheim. From 5th April only the two off the Norwegian ports remained in position. The returning boats were quickly replenished and attached to the operational groups.

The operations against enemy submarines in the Skagerrak lasted only a few days. The U-boats which were moved about in accordance with the latest radio intercepts, carried out a search patrol. Some sightings were made but the bad weather precluded action, and most of the boats were recalled.

The four boats remaining concentrated on the British submarine *Triad*, whose position had been accurately forecast by the Radio Intercept Service. On the strength of intelligence that the German

9 A German air raid on Scapa before dark on 16th March damaged *Norfolk* and *Iron Duke*, and shore targets in the vicinity were also attacked. Further raids on the night of 8th and 10th April caused no damage.

ship *Neuerfels* had taken refuge from British destroyers in Rosfjord near Lindesnes and a report from the German Naval Attaché in Oslo that 60 British warships had apparently been sighted off Egersund, these boats proceeded to the Norwegian coast off Lindesnes. They were later joined by U.21 and U.22 which had been making for the Pentland Firth. The Naval Attaché's information turned out to be a typically exaggerated agent's report. Only one escorted cruiser was sighted in the course of the day. While proceeding to Pentland Firth, U.21 grounded-probably due to bad navigation---off the island of Oddknuppen, southeast of Mandal, and was interned by the Norwegians. All boats had been ordered to avoid incidents off the Norwegian coast in order that operation "Hartmut" should not be compromised, but fortunately there were no complications.

37. Events on 9th and 10th April, 1940

In the meantime it had been decided that the German landings were to take place on the 9th April. The boats sailed, as planned, between 31st March and 6th April. On 6th April operational order "Hartmut" was opened. Most of the boats had reached the intermediate positions by the 8th. The British danger areas off the Norwegian coast had been declared on that day, and British forces could be expected in that vicinity. It therefore seemed necessary to bar the approaches to the landing ports as quickly as possible, and so some boats were ordered to take up their positions in the entrances to the Fjords.

On the morning of 9th April the U-boat Command could report all boats in their pre-arranged positions, with the exception of two, which arrived a day or two later (Plan 2). Between 0400 and 0500 on that day the German surface forces reported their arrival in Narvik, Trondheim and Bergen, and the boats were at once stationed off the entrances to the fjords, to prevent enemy penetration.

From radio intercepts on 8th April the German Command already knew that considerable enemy forces were at sea. This was confirmed by *Scharnhorst* and *Gneisenau* which sighted enemy warships at dawn some 60 miles west of West Fjord, and by U.56 northwest of Bergen, which sighted a battle squadron. Group V - in position northeast of the Shetlands to intercept ships thrusting northeast from the Scottish bases-was obviously no longer usefully situated, as the enemy was already to the north and east of them. The move of the Bergen U-boats into the harbour entrances left the area off the Norwegian southwest coast unoccupied, so Group V was ordered to proceed some 90 miles in a southwesterly direction to the middle of the ShetlandsNorway line.

Judging by the southwesterly course of the battleships sighted earlier, the enemy did not intend taking action against the German battleships to the north. He was more likely to occupy a key position in the south, ready to cut off the returning German forces. In the hope of preventing this maneuver, four boats (drawn from Group IX east of the Shetlands and Group VIII west of Lindesnes) were sent to intercept the ships as they proceeded south. The boats on both sides of the Pentland Firth were also moved to the east, by order of Naval Group Command West. This was contrary to the wishes of Dönitz, who wanted to leave them near the Firth, as further enemy movements in this area might provide opportunities for attack. From 9th April onwards many U-boats took up positions between the Shetlands and Norway.

Despite this strong concentration only one boat made contact with the enemy. On the evening of 9th April she intercepted the battle squadron that had been sighted in the morning, this time on a northerly course. During the night she sighted two heavy cruisers steering south. U-boats were sent to attack these vessels and also the enemy capital ships reported to have been damaged by German aircraft in the afternoon about 60 miles northwest of Bergen, but they did not make contact.

Reports received during the following day disclosed the difficult position of the German warships at Narvik. The U-boats had failed to keep the enemy out of West Fjord or to damage his forces. The reason for this was not then apparent. Confronted by enemy forces our Narvik destroyers were practically helpless, and being without fuel and supplies, assistance had to be sent. The Naval Staff ordered the immediate dispatch of four U-boats to Narvik and two to Trondheim. The boats of Group V northeast of the Shetlands, being the only ones within range, were detailed.

To the boats already in West Fjord fell the vital task of protecting the port of Narvik from further enemy attacks. The value of patrolling the outer fjords appeared doubtful, and they were ordered to positions further in, where they might effectively bar the narrows. The Narvik replenishment ships had not arrived and there seemed no prospect of conveying supplies by warship, because of the strong enemy forces operating off the coast. It was therefore decided to prepare U.26, 29 and 43-then in home ports-for supply and transport duty to Narvik (Section 43).

A reduction of U-boat numbers in the area between Norway and the Shetlands was now justified, for a British landing in southwest Norway no longer seemed imminent, since our land defences had been consolidated and the presence of our aircraft had further served to deter the enemy. Nevertheless, risks had to be avoided. Little could be expected from our surface forces, for they had suffered considerable losses and were due to return to Germany as quickly as possible. The task of the remaining U-boats was therefore to continue protection of the newly occupied areas, but not to seek targets in the open sea.

38. Torpedo Failures
The U-boats in West Fjord must have had opportunities to attack the British warships. There were no losses among our boats, yet they had failed to strike the enemy. The U-boat Command demanded an explanation by radio. There was no objection to transmitting, as the risk of being "D/F'd" could be accepted, and the enemy's knowledge of the presence of U-boats would have a deterrent effect on him. Replies came in throughout 11th April, and revealed an appalling situation: of twelve torpedoes fired at the enemy six to eight had been prematures. The only explanation seemed that the magnetic pistol did not function in latitudes north of 62° 30' N. It had been

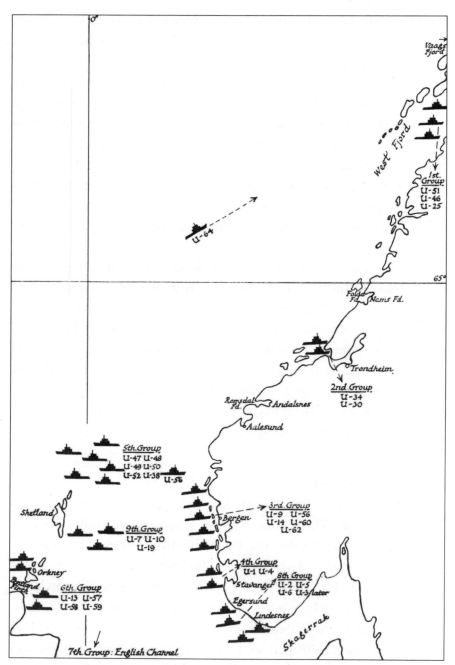

Plan 2. U-boat dispositions for operation "Hartmut", 9th April, 1940

suspected that in coastal operations the pistol might be influenced by the magnetism of the land. This suspicion had already been reported to the Torpedo Inspectorate in November, 1939, after U.38's operations off Kola and West Fjord, and now it seemed confirmed. The failure of the pistol had resulted in the complete ineffectiveness of these U-boat operations and menaced the boats themselves, for prematures allowed enemy destroyers to find them. We could always revert to impact firing, but there was still the faulty depth keeping of the torpedoes, already mentioned in Section 32. Any new orders to our boats would have to allow for continuing the attacks on all warships (including destroyers), but on the other hand the danger of exposure through prematures was serious (21).

Dönitz could not agree with the Torpedo Inspectorate's recommendation that, as depth keeping was faulty, magnetic pistols should be retained, and that other expedients, such as delayed salvo firing, should be adopted in order to prevent the sympathetic detonation of a salvo through one premature. He directed that in latitudes north of 62° 30' N., boats were always to have three torpedoes ready with impact and one with magnetic firing. Against targets of deep draught impact firing was to be used with a setting of two metres less than the target's draught. Against destroyers two torpedoes were always to be fired, one set to impact with a depth setting of three metres, and one set to magnetic with a depth setting of one metre less than the draught of the ship. But this was not the end of the story.

These failures had occurred at a time when everything depended on holding the Norwegian bases (particularly Narvik), and the consequences might have been even more serious. In the course of a few days the torpedo situation had become so critical that on 16th April Dönitz asked Grand Admiral Raeder by telephone for his direct intervention; for the situation was such that U-boat dispositions were no longer governed by operational necessity, but by the capacity of the torpedo to function in the area concerned (22).

39. Events North of 62° N.

The former Shetlands Group of U-boats which had started for Narvik on 10th April had several encounters with the enemy to the northwest of Trondheim. One boat had sighted two escorted ships steering northeast, and other reports from our naval forces showed that the enemy was moving further up the coast. As ordinary shipping did not frequent these waters, the ships were probably transports. On 12th April a decrypted British signal showed that two destroyers and a cruiser had sailed for Vaagsfjord. It was then concluded that a landing could be expected in that area.

On 12th/13th April the Radio Intercept Service, which proved most valuable throughout the Norwegian campaign, revealed the enemy's intention to land not only at Vaagsfjord but also at Namsos (Namsfjord-Foldafjord) and Andalsnes (Romsdalsfjord). Three boats of Group V (U,47, 48 and 49) were diverted by F.O. U-boats, one being dispatched to Romsdalsfjord and another to Namsfjord. The boat at Namsfjord was later reinforced by two small boats.

Meanwhile, the situation at Narvik had become critical, for on 13th April it was learned that one enemy battleship and nine destroyers had penetrated Ofot Fjord as far as the Narvik approaches. The U-boats had again been unable to stop the enemy and had failed to give warning of his approach. They were then ordered to Narvik to dislodge him. The Naval Staff, regarding the situation off Narvik as serious, issued the following directive:

"All large and medium U-boats are to be sent to the West Fjord-Vaagsfjord area. The large boats are not to leave Namsfjord until relieved by small boats. Two small boats are to be sent to the Romsdalsfjord area, three to Tronrlheim, four to Namsfjord and four to the Orkneys, after fuelling in Bergen or Stavanger. All small boats, including U.17, U.23 and U.24 which have been retained in Wilhelmshaven for *Fall Gelb*[10], are to proceed to Norway forthwith."

F.O. U-boats disagreed with sending all the large boats to the north,. on the grounds that they would probably arrive too late in

---

10 Cover name for the attack on France and the Low Countries.

Vaagsfjord-West Fjord, whereas in the Trondheim area (including Namsfjord and Romsdalsfjord) they would be in time to oppose the expected landings. Events proved him to be right. On the following day, when the British began to land in Namsos and Andalsnes, the boats bound for the Lofotens were recalled to Trondheim. They were reinforced by five boats from Bergen, where they had replenished from German supply ships. From 15th April onwards the operations were concentrated in the Narvik region with eight large boats, and off Trondheim with four medium and six small boats.

Reports showed that the boats in the north were operating under very difficult conditions. The calm weather, smooth sea and clear short nights favoured the enemy A/S forces. Owing to torpedo failures already mentioned, the U-boats were almost helpless. Although the fjords contained numerous creeks, the boats had few opportunities to recharge batteries. Accordingly on 15th April the boats in West Fjord withdrew to the entrance of the fjord, searching the bays en route. On the following day the boats in Vaagsfjord, Andfjord and Romsdalsfjord were also withdrawn to the entrances, and on 18th April the boats in Namsfjord were ordered to move out to the bay (Plan 3).

Since 11th April the boats had been moved from one position in the fjords to another. They found and attacked the enemy, particularly in Vaagsfjord. But again no results, owing to the torpedo failures. Prien, a most efficient commander, reported from Vaagsfjord on 15th April that" sitting shots" at large transports (20-30,000 tons) and cruisers at anchor had failed (23).

40. Impact Firing

It appeared that the reversion to impact firing had also been a mistake. Either the torpedo ran much deeper than was realised or the pistol failed to arm. Investigations in Germany disclosed that a considerable number of boats had been supplied with a new four-whiskered pistol, of which at least 10 per cent had misfired in recent days. This pistol had not been adequately tested, and so on 17th April it was decided to revert entirely to magnetic firing. Impact firing was

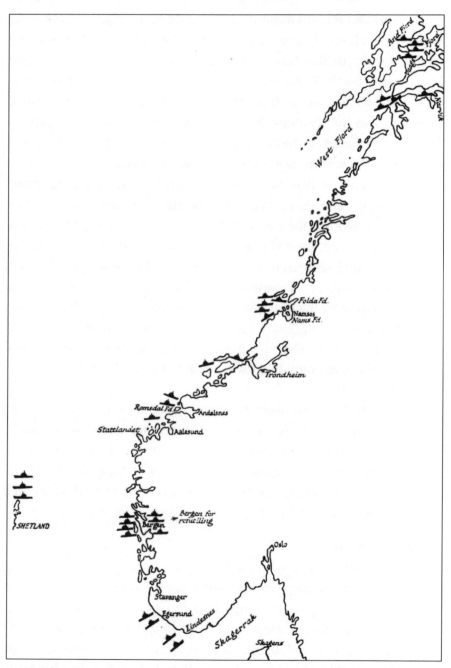

Plan 3. U-boat dispositions on 16th April, 1940 (The Norwegian operation)

to be used only in the very narrow fjords, because the latest findings of the Torpedo Inspectorate showed that in such areas prematures were likely to be caused by magnetic influence.

Even these measures failed, for on 19th April the position was as follows:

- **Magnetic Firing.** Of 22 torpedoes recently fired north of 62° 5' N., at least nine were prematures, which had also detonated other torpedoes of the same salvo (24).
- **Impact Firing.** Referring to the numerous failures which occurred between 12th and 15th April, the Torpedo Inspectorate reported that at trials the G7e torpedo had run up to 2·7 metres too deep. This meant that targets drawing less than five to six metres could no longer be torpedoed, since the shallowest setting for a torpedo fired from a submerged U-boat was three metres.

It was therefore impossible to use impact firing. The result was that" the Navy had no torpedoes that could be used north of 62° 5' N." (25). On 19th April all boats in Vaagsfjord, West Fjord and Romsdalsfjord-and on 20th April, those in Namsfjord-were ordered to a position north of the Shetlands, and so U-boat operations in the NorwegJan coastal area ceased. The boats now kept watch on the enemy supply route to Vaagsfjord and Tromsö. On 19th April Lt. Prien (U.47), who was the first to get there, encountered *Warspite* southwest of West Fjord. He attacked without success, firing two torpedoes, set to eight metres, at a range of 900 metres. His position was betrayed by one of his torpedoes which exploded at the end of its run, and he was attacked by depth charges from several destroyers. The following day, further south, Prien encountered a northbound convoy. Although holding a good position he did not attack, for he had lost all faith in his torpedoes, but continued shadowing until joined by three more boats (26). The strong escort prevented an attack. As they were now again entering the area of" zone 0," F.O. U-boats finally ordered the pursuit to be broken off, and the boats continued to the Shetlands.

The failure of the torpedoes fired at *Warspite* induced the belief that the enemy was fitted with degaussing gear. Prien's report and his personal record precluded the possibility of an error in control. It had been learned from reliable sources that many British merchant ships had been degaussed, and it could therefore be assumed that every known device would be applied to the protection of valuable warships. Our specialists-Professor Cornelius and Professor Gerlach considered it extremely improbable that degaussing equipment had been fitted in battleships, owing to the technical difficulties involved. But Dönitz was not convinced. To be on the safe side, orders were amended on 21st April to set torpedoes to five metres when attacking battleships. If the torpedo ran three metres deeper, a hit could still be expected with impact firing. However. such good opportunities for attack never occurred again.

41. Events South of 62° N.

After the departure of the large boats for Narvik, the boats of Groups VI and IX remained in the area between Shetlands and Norway. From 12th April they lay north and east of the Shetlands, where, in addition to their task of attacking northbound transports, they carried out an all-weather stationary patrol. After replenishing in Bergen, they were disposed east of Pentland Firth from 17th April, free to withdraw to the northeast in the event of enemy A/S measures becoming too strong. They remained here without incident until the end of their patrol period. The Bergen boats had remained on guard in the approaches till 14th April, without encountering the enemy. After replenishing, they were then sent to the Trondheim area, which seemed particularly threatened by enemy landings. They were relieved by U.17, 23 and 24 which had been held in Wilhelmshaven in readiness for *Fall Gelb*. These boats remained at Bergen until 25th April, after which date enemy operations in that area were no longer expected, and they also were transferred to the Orkneys.

The operation of the small training boats (U.I-6) in the Stavanger-Lindesnes region lasted only one week during which they were twice ordered to new positions within that area on the strength of

Radio Intelligence reports that the enemy intended to lay mines off Skudesnes. But no enemy surface forces were encountered, and the search was therefore directed against enemy submarines. In this hunt U.4 destroyed an enemy submarine[11], and U.I was torpedoed off Lindesnes by the British submarine *Porpoise*. On 17th April the Naval Staff ordered the immediate resumption of U-boat training, and the boats returned to base.

42. End of Norwegian Tasks

With the withdrawal of the boats from Narvik and Trondheim, the U-boats' two main tasks in the Norwegian operation-protection of the landing operations and defence against enemy landings-ended. The torpedo failures had been crippling, and, in view of the light nights and the excellent conditions for the enemy A/S location in the fjords, no further operations were to be attempted there. Only the boats in the Bergen approaches remained in position, protected by the Air Force, until 25th April. Those withdrawn from the coast which were fit for further operations were sent to the Orkneys and Shetlands area, where it was hoped the torpedoes would function.

On 24th April the disposition was as follows: Three small boats off Bergen, four small boats east of the Orkneys. Two small and five large boats between the Shetlands and the Minch. Operations were centred mainly in the latter area, because the British supply routes to Tromsö and Narvik were reported to lie here. Also, conditions-especially depth of water-were better there than to the east of the islands, where the boats had to contend with a constant and powerful A/S patrol which restricted their movements and kept them mostly submerged. Nothing was achieved east of the Shetlands, while to the west only one boat managed to sink three ships.

A directive from the Naval Staff on 27th April defined the further functions of the U-boats. They were to continue to occupy the Shetlands-Orkneys area, to take supplies to Narvik, and also to resume operations in the Atlantic with the strongest possible

---

11 H.M.S. *Thistle* failes to return from a patrol off Stavanger, where she was last heard of on 9th April.

forces. But the move of the large boats from the Shetlands area to the Atlantic was precluded by their lack of fuel, and the boats which had returned to base were not yet ready to resume operations. In Norway the enemy had not spared his depth charges, and long refits would be necessary. Moreover the crews required rest, for they were not unaffected by the strain of operations and by the failure of their torpedoes. This was particularly evident in the small boats of the Fifth U-boat Flotilla (U.56-61), which had all been on comparatively long operations, U.57 having spent 82 days at sea out of 111.

43. Transport of Supplies by U-Boat

As already mentioned, several U-boats had been ready since 10th April for supply transport duties to Narvik. Within a week the first three boats sailed, each carrying 40 to 50 tons of small arm and anti-aircraft ammunition as well as other military stores, but because of the difficult situation at Narvik, they were diverted to Trondheim to discharge their cargoes. On both outward and return passages there were several encounters with the enemy, particularly with destroyers patrolling the Trondheim approaches. At Frohavet a supply U-boat was attacked with depth charges while entering and again on leaving. On her return passage U.26 sank one ship of an enemy supply convoy.[12] The second wave (U A, U.32, U.IOI) also went to Trondheim. The cargo consisted of aircraft bombs, and 130 tons of aviation spirit carried in specially modified fuel tanks. The transport of aviation spirit was attended with danger, and almost proved fatal in one case when the fumes penetrated into the boat while submerged.

At the beginning of May seven boats in all were allocated for transport duties, but the Naval Staff, requiring them for operations, asked for their release. The Supreme Command of the Armed Forces allowed the release of three boats with small petrol carrying capacity. On 15th May a further request by the Supreme Command for more boats for the transport of petrol and bombs was rejected by the Naval

---

12 Store transport *Cedarbank*, a motor vessel of 5,159 tons, sunk on 21st April, 1940.

Staff, owing to the risk involved. As the *Luftwaffe* had meanwhile requisitioned adequate fuel supplies in Trondheim, it was decided to stop the transport of petrol, and to use one U-boat only for the carrying of bombs.

At the request of Army Group XXI in Norway, three boats were again fitted out for transport duties in support of the army's advance to Bodo and on to Narvik. At the end of May, when pressed by the Naval Staff, Army Group XXI relinquished them. After the British had withdrawn from Narvik on 10th June, these U-boat transports became redundant and all boats were again placed at the disposal of F.O. U-boats for Atlantic operations. A total of eight transport trips had been made

NORWAY IN RETROSPECT

44. The Vindication of the U-boat Command

U-boat operations in the Norwegian campaign had seriously failed. It was clear that, unaided, the boats could not accomplish the duties of protection and defence that had been set them. Yet in these navigationally restricted waters, frequented by the enemy, important successes should have been achieved. Why did the U-boats fail? The subsequent critical investigation by F.O. U-boats began with the U-boat Command itself, whose task had been to deploy the boats so that they could effectively strike at the several concentrations of enemy warships and transports. An analysis showed that four torpedo attacks had been made on a battleship (*Warspite*), fourteen to sixteen on cruisers, ten to twelve on destroyers, and more than ten on transports, apart from other minor attacks under less favourable conditions (27). The boats had therefore been in the correct positions, and the U-boat Command had not failed in its main task. True, it had not been difficult to form an accurate appreciation of the situation, for two conditions, rarely encountered at any one time, had existed:

timely intelligence of important enemy movements, derived from the Radio Intercept Service;

the availability of a considerable number of U-boats with which to exploit this intelligence (28).

45. The Vindication of the Boats

What of the U-boats? Had they shown skill, courage and tenacity, or were conditions too difficult for them? The most able U-boat commanders, Prien, Herbert; Schultze, Schiize and Liebe, had been in the vital zone in Vaagsfjord-West Fjord (29). The other Commanding Officers were mostly men of the "old guard" who had received a careful, all-round peace-time training from Dönitz himself, and were eager for battle. They had stuck grimly to their task in spite of very strong opposition, and had fought under the most difficult conditions (30). Prien, reporting on Vaagsfjord, stated that the enemy A/S forces were extraordinarily well trained, and as effective as off the enemy's main bases.

Unique opportunities of attacking important targets had been offered, and had been fully exploited. An idea of the results can be gained from this extract from Prien's report on his attack in Vaagsfjord and later on *Warspite*:

"15th April. In the afternoon, area patrolled and searched by enemy destroyers. From the odd courses of the destroyers, presume mines to be laid in several places. In the evening three very large transports (each 30,000 tons) and three smaller transports with two cruisers at anchor in the southern part of Bygden. Disembarkation of troops in fishing smacks in the direction of Lavangen-Gratangen. Transports and cruisers in the narrows at Bygden, some moored so close that they are only just clear of one another and present a continuous target.

2200 Boat prepares for first submerged attack. Intend to fire one torpedo at each of two cruisers and two large transports (one is a *Suffren* class cruiser), then to reload and attack again.

2242 Fired four torpedoes. Minimum range 750 metres, maximum 1,500 metres. Depth setting of torpedoes four and five metres. A wall of ships ahead. No hits. Enemy not even startled. Reloaded. Meter midnight ran in again on the surface. Very precise control data. Thorough check of all settings by C.O. and First Lieutenant. Fired four torpedoes, depth setting as in first attack. No hits. One gyro failure, torpedo exploded on a rock. Boat ran aground while disengaging. Got clear only to find ourselves near a patrol vessel. Detected. Depth charge attack. Commenced return passage because of damage to engines.

19th April. Sighted *Warspite* and two destroyers. Fired two torpedoes at the battleship from 900 metres. No hits. A torpedo exploding at the end of its run resulted in attacks on me by destroyers from all directions" (31).

The blame could therefore not be attributed to the boats or the conditions. Reporting to Commander-in-Chief, Navy, on 30th April, after a thorough investigation, Dönitz came to the following conclusions:

a. "The operational and tactical dispositions were correctly made; the A/S forces were powerful, and weather conditions very unfavourable with short nights and smooth sea.

b. Obviously the slow moving U-boat has less chance of attacking fast warship& than merchant ships, but prospects were not unfavourable considering the large volume of enemy traffic and the considerable number of U-boats employed.

c. The torpedo failures-all doubtful shots and misses apart-deprived the boats of certain success" (32).

46. What Might Have Been
When the boats returned, each unsuccessful attack was thoroughly analysed with the aid of the commanders' reports and firing records. It was not possible to determine from these documents whether a hit should always have been scored, but in the light of previous experience an approximate estimate could be made. Unfortunately these data are no longer available, but other documents have yielded the following information:

In the area north of 62° 30' N. hits should have been certain - in one of four attacks on a battleship; in seven of twelve attacks on cruisers; in seven of ten attacks on destroyers; and in five out of five attacks on transports (33).

That no hits were scored can be attributed to the failure of the torpedoes. It was impossible and indeed pointless to investigate which ships might have been sunk or damaged if the torpedoes had functioned. At the first torpedo hit the enemy would probably have altered his tactics and the situation would have changed. Commenting on Prien's report Dönitz wrote: "... The case of U.47 is a clear example of many attacks which have failed because of defective torpedoes, and have prevented the U-boats from contributing more effectively to the occupation of Norway. Had these failures not occurred, the role of the U-boats could have been far-reaching, since all other conditions were in their favour."

47. Crisis in the U-Boat Arm

The causes of the failures had been U-boat Command's main problem during the first eight months of the war. In the course of the Norwegian campaign this question became so critical that on 20th April Raeder appointed a special committee of investigation with officers of the U-boat Command and representatives of the Torpedo Inspectorate, under the chairmanship of RearAdmiral Kummetz, Inspector of Torpedoes (34).

The findings of the committee, together with the results of other enquiries, led to the courtmartialling of several members of the Torpedo Experimental Command and of some officials, who between 1936 and 1939 had been in charge of torpedo development. The following is an extract from Raeder's summing up:

"... The investigations have revealed insufficient preparation before issue of the torpedoes. The depth-keeping qualities of the G7a and G7e are inadequate for an operational weapon. The magnetic firing mechanism of the pistol is technically inefficient, and the impact firing mechanism does not function satisfactorily."

It was difficult to decide whether it was the peculiar magnetic influence in the north Norwegian coastal area, or the enemy degaussing equipment that caused the failure of the magnetic pistols. Prien's unsuccessful attack on *Warspite* suggested degaussing (35 to 38). The result of the investigations shocked the U-boat Command. Dönitz wrote on 15th May:- "The findings are more serious than I had expected. An official of the Torpedo Inspectorate informs me that the mechanism had been accepted in peace-time, after only two test runs, the results of which were not entirely satisfactory. Stich 'procedure can only be described as criminal...'" It had been expected that twenty years of experiment would produce a torpedo superior to that of the First World War. "A trackless torpedo with splashless discharge has been devised, but everything else is wrong. In all the history of war I doubt whether men have ever had to rely on such a useless weapon."

The U-boat Command was divided on the question of employing the boats again before the torpedo had been fundamentally improved. It was expected that electric torpedoes with satisfactory depth-keeping mechanism and improved contact pistol (incorporatnig electric contact) would soon be available (39)... "I cannot leave the boats idle without causing incalculable harm to the U-boat arm. As long as there is the smallest prospect of hits, operations must continue..." (War Diary of F.O. U-boats, 15th May, 1940.)

RESUMPTION OF ATLANTIC OPERATIONS
MAY AND JUNE, 1940

48. Successful Operations in the Atlantic

The sudden return of many boats for repairs after the Norwegian enterprise had led to congestion in the dockyards. For this reason only a few boats were ready for operations by the end of May, and it was not until June, 1940, that the war on shipping could be resumed in the Atlantic. For almost three months there had been no U-boats there, because of the Norway operation.

The U-boat Command was anxious to make a fresh start and to show results. The feeling of frustration engendered by the U-boats' failure in the Norwegian campaign had not yet been dispelled, and officers and men still had no confidence in the torpedo. It was hoped that in the Atlantic the number of magnetic pistol failures would be small.. But the dreary tale continued, for within six days of sailing the first boat, carrying the same unimproved .torpedoes, reported that of five fired, two had been premature and two had probably failed to detonate.

F .O. U-boats was now forced to revert to impact firing, and, to reduce the chances of failure of the whiskers on contact, commanders were instructed to use the broadest possible track angle.

Since no Atlantic U-boat reconnaissance had taken place for three months, it was hard to decide which areas offered the best prospects. In the absence of reliable information it seemed advisable to occupy the area northwest of Cape Finisterre, which had been most fruitful in February.

By the end of May it became obvious that the German campaign in France would be successful, and would affect the shipping situation in the Channel and the Atlantic. The main cross-Channel traffic between England and France, which ran between Dover and Calais, would at first be diverted westwards to Le Havre and Cherbourg. As more of the Channel coast became occupied, the traffic from the French Atlantic ports to England would gain in importance. At the same time, with the increasing danger of air attacks on British shipping in the Channel, a diversion of this traffic could be expected to the northern entrance of the Irish Sea, or even to Scotland. This forecast proved correct. Two boats were stationed in the western part of the Channel, but owing to fog and strong air patrols, they had no success. On the other hand the more distant area off the Channel, south of Ireland, and northwest of Cape Finisterre offered good prospects throughout June. Targets were also found between the North Channel and the Irish Sea, and in practically the whole area west of England. In three months the Britain-bound traffic had grown to almost pre-war volume.

At last technical improvements in the torpedo began to show

results. The modifications to the depth-keeping mechanism and the impact pistol were effective; torpedo failures decreased, and thanks to the favourable traffic situation, the boats achieved an unexpectedly high rate of sinkings, especially against convoys which were often weakly escorted-a sign that the enemy lacked the necessary forces, and that the heavy claims on his light craft off the Norwegian, Belgian and French coasts were now telling.

49. Resumption of Pack Operations

For the first time since October, 1939, there were enough boats at sea for pack operations, and in fact two convoys were attacked simultaneously. The information for these attacks was derived from the Radio Intelligence Service. Details of course and speed of convoy HX 48 were available. It was due to arrive at a point some 420 miles west of Lorient at 0630 on 17th June, there to be picked up by the home escort. To attack this convoy, a group of six boats under the tactical command of Prien was drawn up in a patrol line across the estimated line of approach of the convoy so as to intercept at midday on 16th June. If no contact were made that day, they were to close the rendezvous at 0630 on 17th June.

In addition, convoy WS 3[13] was known to have entered the Freetown area. This convoy consisted of the Queen Mary and two other large liners carrying 26,000 Australian and New Zealand troops, escorted by H.M.S. *Hood*, an aircraft carrier and several cruisers. Despite the lack of precise data, an attempt had to be made to find this valuable prize. With a speed of up to 17 knots, which made shadowing and subsequent attacks impossible, the convoy would reach the latitude of Cape Finisterre on about 13th June. As the U-boats had been extremely active in the previous few days, particularly west of Finisterre, it was expected that the convoy would keep to the westward of the usual convoy route, which followed the meridan of 12° W. It was therefore necessary to dispose the few available boats at wide intervals. Even if only one boat managed to attack, the attempt would be justified.

13 For designation of Allied convoys, see page Appendix I

Group Rösing, consisting of five boats under the tactical command of the Captain of the Seventh Flotilla, was drawn up in the area 13° 30' to 18° 45' W. and 45° 30' to 42° N.. Three of the boats were disposed in the south at 50-mile intervals across the probable line of advance, and the other two about 100 miles further north and somewhat to the, east, in anticipation that the convoy would alter to an easterly course when off Cape Finisterre. All boats were ordered to maintain radio silence and to attack only valuable ships. Preparations had been made for refuelling Group Rösing from German ships lying in Vigo and El Ferro!'

Neither of these two convoys was sighted. On 17th June the Radio Intercept Service reported that the rendezvous of HX 48 had been moved southwards, which placed the boats too far astern to gain contact. Both groups were disbanded, the boats being ordered to form east-west patrol lines at the entrances to the English and St. George's Channels, and against traffic from the French Atlantic coast to England. The subsequent results showed the effectiveness of these dispositions. Torpedoes were so quickly expended that only four boats made use of the refuelling facilities in Spain.

50. Other Operations

While the Atlantic boats which sailed in the second half of June operated in the Biscay area, the small boats of the Fifth Flotilla, which were ready after having completed their task in the North Sea (see Section 72), were disposed between the Minch and the North Channel, using Bergen or Trondheim for refuelling.

The first operation in the tropics, which was carried out by U A (*ex-Batiray*)[14], is worthy of note. This had originally been planned for November, 1939, when a U-boat was to operate with a supply ship. Now, in June, 1940, while outward bound, U A was ordered to attack the A.M.C.s of the Northern Patrol, whose positions and reference points were accurately available from Radio Intelligence. As a result the *Andania* (13,950 tons) was sunk.[15]

---

14 Built in Germany for Turkey.
15 Armed merchant cruiser *Andania* sunk by U-boat south-east of Iceland on 16th June,

As she proceeded south the U-boat hauled too far west and found little traffic. In the middle of July, after replenishing with fuel and torpedoes from the auxiliary cruiser *Ship 33*, as planned, she operated off Freetown, but had to return to base earlier than anticipated because of engine trouble. During her homeward passage our Radio Intercept Service learned that Force H was due at a certain rendezvous, and she was ordered to be in this position by 1950 on 16th August. U A obtained an accurate fix, remained in the position indicated for 24 hours and then continued her passage. Not until 20th August did our Radio Intelligence discover that Force H had passed this position two days later. U A's voyage had lasted twelve weeks, and she had sunk only seven ships, which was attributed to lack of skill in her commander. But the experience was of value since it established that service in the tropics presented no. unexpected personnel or material difficulties.

51. Capture of the Atlantic Bases

F.O. U-boats closely followed the events in France, whose defeat would involve:

The acquisition of bases on the French Channel and Biscay coasts, bringing a welcome relief to U-boats from the British patrol and minelaying activity in the North. Also the possibility of establishing a mine-free passage for U-boats through the Channel to the Atlantic bases, under the protection of German coastal defences.

A considerable shortening of the passage to the main British trade routes, with the possibility of employing Type II U-boats, which had a small radius of action.

Additional repair yards and berths, involving shorter refits and therefore more boats at sea.

Officers had been sent to France early in June, to select suitable bases for U-boats. On the day of the armistice with France, torpedoes, air-compressors, torpedo stores and personnel were sent by road from Wilhelmshaven to Paris and onwards for distribution among these bases. It was desirable at once to clear a U-boat route through the

---

1940.

Channel and off the proposed German bases in France. There were only sufficient minesweepers to clear the approaches to Lorient, and this was immediately put in hand.

After a tour of inspection of the Atlantic coast in July, Dönitz recommended to the Naval Staff that the bases should be developed in stages, as follows: (a) supply facilities for weapons, fuel and provisions; (b) facilities for short repairs; (c) the transfer of the U-boat Command to the west as soon as (a) and (b) were available for the Atlantic boats; (d) facilities for complete overhaul of U-boats.

The first stage was soon working, thanks to careful preparations in Germany and the speedy despatch of the necessary personnel to France. On 6th July, 1940, the first base, Lorient, was ready for use and on the following day U.30 entered to embark torpedoes. Although its facilities were limited, this base was able to maintain and supply the boats in the following weeks. Major repairs had still to be done in the German dockyards. It became evident within a few months that even one such base on the Atlantic coast greatly facilitated U-boat operations, and the development of the other Atlantic ports was hurried on.

THE NORTH SEA
FROM MOBILISATION TO NOVEMBER, 1939

U-boat operations in the area of the North Sea from the outbreak of war until the virtual end of this phase in July, 1940, are described in the following pages. These operations are marked by special features as regards type of U-boat and scope of activity. For this reason the operations are dealt with as a whole, which involves some overlapping with the chronology of events in other areas.

52. First Operations

As part of the precautionary measures before Germany attacked Poland, seven boats of the First Flotilla (250 tons) took up position in the southern North Sea for reconnaissance and protection against the west. They carried mines, which, in the event of war with the Western Powers, were to be laid off the French Channel ports and the south and southeast coast of England. With the easing of the tension in the Baltic, boats of the Third and Fifth Flotillas arrived in Wilhelmshaven between 23rd and 25th August, 1939, where they were under the command of S.O. U-boats . West (Lieut-Comdr. Ibbecken) at Group West H.Q. (Section 2). The situation in the west was now so tense that on 25th August Naval Group West established a further reconnaissance patrol of six boats on the Great Fisher Bank, and two boats of the First Flotilla were sent on reconnaissance off the Firths of Forth and Moray (east of $0°$). For this reason the number of boats in the southern North Sea was reduced to five and the mining of Dover and Calais had to be abandoned.

The boats sailed on 25th August and were in position by 27th August. These measures were relaxed two days later, probably for political reasons, when the Naval Staff withdrew three boats from the southern Group and three from the Great Fisher Bank for a rest period. The boats which remained at sea were to be relieved after a few days, but this did not happen, as the political situation deteriorated on 31st August and the positions had again to be fully occupied. The unexpected resumption of the precautionary measures brought a change in the dispositions; the minelaying planned for U.23 and U.21 of the southern Group was performed by two boats sent from Wilhelmshaven.

On 3rd September the following boats were in the North Sea:
- Five on a patrol line on the Great Fisher Bank (U.36, 12, 56, 59, 58);
- One on passage to the northern North Sea (U.20);
- Two off the east coast of Scotland (U.9, 19);
- Five in the southern North Sea (U. 15, 17, 13,23,21);
- Two on passage for minelaying operations (U.16, 24);

A few hours after the outbreak of war the boats in the south were ordered to lay mines regardless of the three-mile limit. The boat intended for Dunkirk was allotted a new waiting position and was later ordered to return to base, because there was to be no provocation of France. Within three days mines had been laid in the Downs, off Flamborough Head, Orfordness and Hartlepool. The other boats' spell at sea was uneventful. They remained in their reconnaissance positions as outposts for our defensive minelaying, until they were recalled or had to return for lack of fuel.

53. S.O. U-Boats West-Naval Group Command West

Dönitz, who on 31st August, 1939 had taken operational charge of the North Sea boats, regarded the war against shipping as the main objective of all U-boat operations, and the North Sea as of secondary importance, for in this restricted area there was no prospect of large-scale operations against shipping. Nevertheless, he immediately took steps to ensure that the U-boats were employed to the best advantage with a view to sinking both merchant ships and naval vessels. Since operations by surface forces had to be co-ordinated with those of U-boats, it was necessary to subordinate to Dönitz the Naval Group Commander, West, the Flag Officer responsible for the North Sea. This organisational change meant that the U-boat operations could not always be carried out as Dönitz desired. He considered that the. reconnaissance and patrol duties demanded of the U-boats did not accord with the war policy of a smaller naval power. The boats had not been built or trained for these duties, but for attacking the enemy. Other forces, and particularly the Air Force, were better suited for reconnaissance. In spite of many differences of opinion, however, co-operation between the two commands worked smoothly and to their mutual advantage.

It is difficult to present even an approximate picture of North Sea U-boat operations at that time. There are no contemporary surveys of the situation in the War Diary of S.O. U-boats West, but only a mass of odd notes for individual areas. Compared with the Atlantic, U-boat plans in the North Sea could be altered at short notice without affecting other operations; the North Sea boats reported back much more quickly than the Atlantic boats. They were employed as necessary for protection of home waters, reconnaissance of the enemy coastal area, and . co-operation with surface forces.

54. Problems of the North Sea

S.O. U-boats West had 18 boats available for North Sea operations, of which four were training boats of small operational value. Of these he could count on always having seven to eight at sea-a somewhat higher proportion than in the Atlantic. The larger Atlantic boats needed longer dockyard periods because of the greater complexity of their engines and diving installations. With the declaration of the British blockade the North Sea became a closed sea, as in 1914-18. Shipping off the east coast of England and from the Scandinavian and Baltic States to England was negligible in comparison with the incoming traffic from the west, and North Sea traffic was partially within range of the German air and surface forces.

For 250-ton U-boats it was almost impossible to conform to the Prize Regulations when operating off the east coast of England or in the North Sea itself. Even in a slight sea, a suspected ship could not be stopped since the only gun (a C30 machine gun mounted on the casing) could not be manned. Moreover, the enemy's aircraft would probably prevent the boats from carrying out such surface maneuvers. What were the possibilities of operating against naval forces-the main concern of the Naval Staff and of Group West? It could be anticipated that Britain, by sealing the North Sea, using light and heavy forces along the Shetlands-Norway line, would achieve an effective blockade. But there were opportunities for attack off the ports against heavy units and against traffic between the ports. For such operations the small North Sea boats seemed particularly suitable by reason of their size, their resistance to damage, and the difficulty of spotting them.

They could also be used for minelaying off the enemy coast. Germany held the secret of the magnetic mine, and it was essential to use this surprise before countermeasures were taken. The first mine laying operation by the southern group of North Sea boats having been accomplished quickly and smoothly, and the distances involved being small, it seemed possible for the same boats to carry out a whole series of such operations.

On this basis a list of tasks was compiled, which characterised U-boat operations in the North Sea in the first two months of the war:

- attacking naval forces off the British east coast bases;
- minelaying off the south, southeast and east coasts of England;
- attacking shipping in the Skagerrak and off the Norwegian coast.

Dönitz expected little result from the operations against naval forces, but he had to carry them out because the Naval Staff and Group West insisted. And, indeed, there was hardly an alternative course.

55. First Disposition against Naval Forces off the East Coast of Scotland

For attacking enemy warships there were only enough boats to occupy the Firths of Forth and Morav, and these would have to be concentrated in order to achieve the necessary depth of disposition. Even then it was doubtful if a sighting boat could report in time to allow the others to get into position, for the coastal waters were closely guarded. Besides these offensive tasks, the boats were to reconnoitre the east coast of Scotland as far as the Orkneys.

The expectations of the German Naval authorities were not realised, however, for practically no warships were sighted, and only one destroyer and one submarine were reported sunk.[16] Experience at sea confirmed the opinion gained from air reconnaissance and radio intelligence that the British heavy units were avoiding the North Sea, perhaps because of the U-boat danger, especially after the sinking of *Courageous*. At all events, it was evident that the enemy could only be brought into the North Sea by air attacks on his ships in their bases, or by striking at his Northern Patrol with our surface craft. This was a gloomy prospect, for the *Führer* had forbidden air raids and the German fleet was not then in a position to make sorties.

---

16 No British losses occurred at this time.

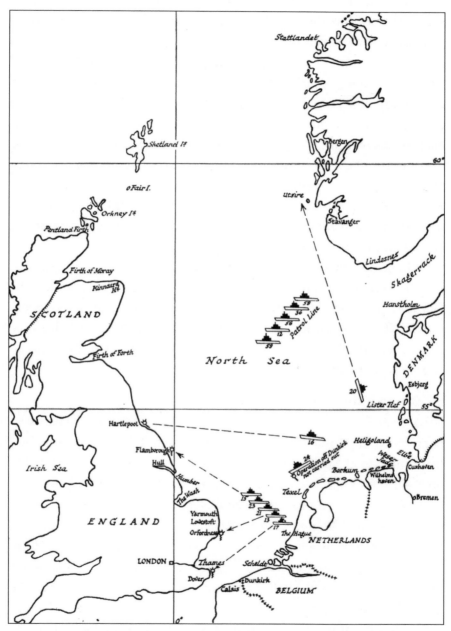

Plan 4. Disposition of North Sea U-boats at the outbreak of war

Between 10th and 20th September it was learned from the Radio Intercept Service that British forces including *Nelson* had been at sea to the north of Scotland and near the Hebrides. The next group of U-boats was therefore stationed west and east of the Orkneys with a focal point in the vicinity of Scapa. But they remained here only a few days, having to leave the area on 4th October on account of the impending attack on Scapa Flow by U.47 (Lieut. Prien). They were moved to an extended patrol line between Scotland and Norway, each boat covering a large area, but as might be expected they had no opportunities for attack. Moreover there was no possibility of stopping ships for search. For on 30th September, 1939, the Naval Staff, realising the danger to which U-boats would be exposed in the North Sea if they conformed to the existing Prize Regulations, cancelled this procedure for that area.

When, on 9th October, German reconnaissance aircraft sighted British forces advancing towards the Skagerrak to counter the German sortie to the north (*Gneisenau* and *Köln*), the boats were moved 50 miles northwards to intercept the returning British ships. The order arrived too late, for when the boats reached the area the enemy had already passed.

56. Scapa Flow - 13/14th October, 1939

An operation against this main British naval base by a U-boat had long been prepared. Soon after the outbreak of war, Dönitz had requested from the Naval Staff a sketch of Scapa Flow showing the probable obstructions. This, together with excellent aerial photographs taken by Luftflotte 2, and very accurate observations of the Orkneys area made between 13th and 29th September, by U.14, provided the data for an operation in which one boat was to penetrate through Holm Sound. After discussion with the Commander-in-Chief of the Navy, Dönitz asked Lieut. Prien to carry out the operation, a task which he accepted with enthusiasm.

The undertaking was fixed for the night of 13th/14th October, a new moon period in which slack water would occur during the hours of darkness. To avoid disturbing the local patrols, the Orkneys U-boats (see previous section) were withdrawn to the central North Sea. Two days before the operation air reconnaissance established the exact positions of an aircraft carrier and five heavy units in the Flow. This report was not picked up by Prien, however, as he was then lying bottomed off Scapa. German radio intercept reports indicated that the bulk of the ships had left on 13th October, so that Prien found only *Repulse* and *Royal Oak* in the Flow.

The result of the attack is well known. It is probable that *Repulse* was saved from destruction by torpedo failures.[17] While leaving through Holm Sound, U.47 encountered a very strong flood tide. This current and bright northern lights were the two factors which caused her most difficulty.

The British Admiralty's announcement of the loss of *Royal Oak* confirmed to us that the operation had been successful. At it was not known whether U.47 had managed to escape, U.1S was instructed on the following day to transmit a signal from the vicinity of Scapa which should lead the British to assume that Prien was already outside the Flow.

The success of the operation was due to good staff planning and particularly to the seamanship and determination of the commander.

57. Last Attempt against Naval Forces West of the Orkneys
After the successful attack on Scapa Flow it was to be expected that the British heavy units would more than ever avoid the North Sea. The only remaining chance of encountering them was presumably west of the Orkneys. A/S forces in this area were small and conditions seemed to favour the boats of the Fifth Flotilla, which were due to arrive in the second half of October. In addition to attacking warships, they were to operate against shipping in accordance with the Prize Regulations.

On 30th October, some 45 miles north of Cape Wrath, U.56 attacked *Nelson* at close range without success, probably due to a torpedo failure. There was now no further opportunity for attacks on

17 *Repulse* was not in Scapa Flow on the night of the attack.

shipping, for on 29th October the order forbidding surface approach and search of shipping in the North Sea was extended to include the area west of the Orkneys. Dönitz protested, but the Naval Staff maintained that the boats were exposed to excessive danger. Dönitz commented:

"… I cannot share this view. I consider that the decision as to whether a particular area is especially dangerous rests with the U-boat commander, and it is for him to take appropriate action" (40).

58. Minelaying off the English Coast

As precedence had been given to attacks on naval forces, minelaying had to be deferred for lack of boats. On 9th October the Naval Staff decided that minelaying was vitally important, particularly off the south coast of England. The longer nights provided suitable conditions and enough had been learned of the organisation and routes of British coastal traffic to enable boats to lay their small outfit of mines (9 to 12 TMB) accurately in the traffic lanes. It was planned to use both Atlantic and North Sea boats for minelaying off the west, south and east coast of Britain. The operations were carried out as follows:

Against naval bases: As a follow-up to the attack on Scapa Flow, with the object of damaging British naval forces and closing their North Sea bases: by U.21 off the entrance to Rosyth at the beginning of November; by U.23 off the entrance to Invergordon at the beginning of November.

Against enemy shipping: by U.19 off Inner Dowsing in the middle of October; by U.24 off Hartlepool at the end of October.

Two other minelaying operations were prepared for the Channel (Section 60). All these undertakings, which demanded the highest skill on the part of the commanders, were carried out as planned. Their effectiveness was first revealed by shipping warnings and diversions of traffic, and later confirmed by precise reports of ships sunk. But it was difficult to evaluate the total effect in comparison with results that might have been obtained by using the same boats on torpedo operations.

59. Action against Shipping off the Norwegian Coast

From observations by the boats in earlier operations and from air reconnaissance and agents' reports, it was evident that a considerable volume of important traffic, consisting of medium and small ships was running from the east to Britain. One route apparently passed westwards from Skagen (sometimes via Lister) well clear of the danger area, towards Kinnaird Head, or from the central North Sea southwards to the Firth of Forth. Another route appeared to be in the latitude of the Orkneys, running in an east-west direction.

An attempt had to be made to intercept this traffic, and, taking advantage of the extended contraband list of 18th September, 1939, to secure the cargoes for Germany. Accordingly two boats were sent to the southwest coast of Norway and later two more-old training boats were dispatched to the Skagerrak with the additional task of protecting German ore ships off the Norwegian coast and of escorting German trawlers returning from the north to Germany. Three returning Atlantic boats were also ordered to proceed through this area to intercept shipping. One of these, U.41, took two Finnish ships in prize.

The difficulty of finding and capturing ships was soon obvious. Their route to Britain passed through Danish and Swedish territorial waters as far as the Norwegian coast, thence northwards in Norwegian territorial waters via Vtsire and then out into the North Sea at night from various points in the inner leads. Vnder these conditions it was very difficult for single U-boats to locate the ships once they had broken out. This accounted for the poor results obtained by the boats working off the Norwegian coast, where only two ships were sunk, though many more had been stopped and searched. On 30th September the Naval Staff stopped operations against shipping in the North Sea because the risk involved in adhering to the Prize Regulations was too great.

During October there appeared to be an increase in the traffic from the east, the ships now sailing in convoy. Bergen was among the ports of departure. An attempt to intercept the convoys as they left Norwegian territorial waters failed, for two boats could not cover this extensive area.

60. U-Boat Activity in the English Channel

In the first two months of the war no area claimed the attention of the U-boat Command to the same extent as the Channel. The use of the Channel as a short cut to the main U-boat operational area southwest of Britain would considerably reduce the approach route:and hereby increase the effectiveness of the boats. In addition, the Channel obviously offered many valuable targets, for it was the main artery to London and the east coast ports, and for traffic between France and England.

It was clear that the enemy would do everything in his power to protect this area, as he had done in the First World War. Of the" first wave" of Atlantic boats U.31 passed through the Channel unhindered, while a second boat (U.35), finding it too dangerous, had given up the passage through the Dover Strait, but later she entered the Channel from the west and operated there successfully for more than a week.

During the emergency period before the outbreak of war the first reports had been received of British troop transports to France. As these reports continued in the first weeks of September, the Naval Staff decided to send U-boats to attack the transports, despite the grave risk to the boat. It was clearly impossible to attack any shipping while conforming to the Prize Regulations, but attack without warning was permitted on troopships and escorted vessels of any type. In the second half of September, two boats (U.12 and 15), with well-trained commanders, were dispatched to the Channel for this purpose. It was known from radio intelligence that both boats had entered the Dover-Calais area, but only one returned. Weather was bad and few patrols were met between Dover and Calais. The position of mines has been deduced from the existence of previously unknown buoys. No troopships were sighted, though numerous single vessels were encountered which however could not be attacked, so that the operation was fruitless.

As long as the limitations imposed by the Prize Regulations continued, it would be useless to send boats with torpedoes to this area, but minelaying offered good prospects, especially off the ports of troop embarkation and disembarkation. Acting on the Naval Staff's suggestion of 9th September, F.O. U-boats planned two operations for the mining of the south coast of England. first was carried out by U.16 which sailed on 17th October for Dungeness. Soon after she had sailed, it was learned that an Atlantic-bound boat (U.40) had been lost while passing through the Channel. It appeared therefore that the risk was great, and it was decided to await the report of the first minelaying boat before embarking on the second operation. The report did not arrive, however, for on 24th October U.16 signalled that she had been heavily damaged off Dover and would have to be scuttled.[18] The signal did not state the cause of the damage, but it was probably due to a mine, because in any other case there would have been insufficient time to transmit a report (41).

The situation was now as follows: U.31, U.15 and U.16 had passed westwards through the Dover-Calais area and U.12, U.40 and U.16 had been lost.[19]

In view of the high proportion of losses the second minelaying operation was cancelled, and the Channel was abandoned for a considerable time.

NOVEMBER AND DECEMBER, 1939

61. Transition to War on Shipping
In October the Prize Regulations underwent their first modification. From 2nd October all darkened ships in the whole area off the east coast of Britain (as far as approximately 3° E.) could be attacked at sight. From 17th October attacks without warning were allowed on all ships (except liners) definitely identified as enemy. These relaxations

18 U.16 sunk by H.M.S. Puffin and H.M.S. Cayton Wyke off Goodwin Sands on 24th October, 1939.
19 U.12 lost by mining in the Straits of Dover.

considerably enhanced the U-boats opportunities against shipping. Continuance of the unprofitable operations against naval forces was pointless, for prospects would deteriorate with the weather.

By the middle of November the transition to War on shipping was complete, and U-boat activity in the North Sea against warships became of secondary importance. Further U-boat operations against naval forces were not precluded; in fact they were often considered in the following months, especially in co-operation with the fleet. But except for the "Nordmark" operation in February, 1940, nothing of this nature took place.

At first operations were to be confined to the British coastal area where the Prize Regulations had been relaxed, and where targets were sure to be found. The first four boats were sent to the east coast, concentrating for navigational reasons on the Scottish coast, particularly in the region of Kinnaird Head. Considering the small striking power of the boats and the lack of experience of the crews the results were satisfactory.

During the following few months, operations were more and more confined to the Kinnaird Head area. Traffic approached this point from Scandinavia from directions varying from north to east. British coastal traffic converged from north and west and proceeded southwards in a continuous stream close to the Scottish coast. The defences were certainly strong, but not excessive in view of the amount of traffic.

62. Intensified Minelaying off the East Coast of Britain

It became known that the minefields laid off the east coast of Britain by German aircraft and surface craft had been very effective; particularly off the Thames and Humber. While there was' yet no indication of the results from those laid by U-boats, it was believed that they also had been satisfactory, for the U-boats had used magnetic mines and had laid their fields well. The U-boat operations against naval forces had been a failure. Whether the war on shipping, using torpedoes, would succeed could not yet be foreseen. So on 27th November, 1939, the Naval Staff, appreciating the general success of mine warfare, directed that the minelaying effort by U-boats should be increased.

A few days later Dönitz discussed with Raeder the future policy of U-boat minelaying. The conclusions were as follows (42):

a. "Minefields should be laid at as many vital points as possible in order to cause a general interruption and dislocation of shipping.

b. Places reached by narrow channels must be blocked by several fields, so that they will be unusable for a long period.

c. The inner areas must be mined before the outer approaches in order that subsequent minelaying will not be prejudiced.

d. The mines must be laid at a depth at which they will destroy. War experience has shown that the TMB mine, to be effective, should be used in a depth not exceeding 25 metres. In view of this the Mines Inspectorate was instructed early in November to devise a new U-boat ground mine with a much heavier charge. They have tackled this task energetically and two new TMC type mines with a charge of 1,000 kg. are now ready for testing…"

In the light of these considerations, the following North Sea minelaying operations were planned against naval bases:

- **Firth of Forth:** Two TMB minefields north and south of the mines laid by U.21 at the beginning of November, and three TMC minefields continuing to the east as far as May Island.
- **Moray Firth:** (Invergordon). Reinforcement of U.23's minefields by two TMB fields, and the laying of TMC fields further out. Minelaying against shipping (TMB): Cockle lightship (north exit of the Yarmouth Roads), Newcastle and Dundee.

Owing to lack of boats this programme occupied a considerable time. Delays occurred because certain fields could only be laid at new moon periods, and these difficult operations had to be carried out by highly competent officers. Minelaying activity reached its peak between the middle of November and Christmas, 1939, when there were ten minelaying compared with eleven torpedo operations. Close co-operation with the Operations Staff of Group West ensured synchronisation with the minelaying of the surface forces. The latter operated in shallow water areas, for which the U-boats were unsuited on account of the danger involved and because of their inability to lay mines while surfaced. Surface mine dropping gear had to be installed in the boat detailed for the operation off Cockle lightship, where shallow water precluded diving.

By Christmas, mines had been laid in the following postions:

Off Lowestoft:	(U.15)
Off Newarp Lightship:	(U.20)
Off Cockle Lightship:	(U.59)
Off Cross Sands:	(U.60)
Off Blyth:	(U.22)
South of Orfordness:	(U.19)
Off Lowestoft:	(U.58)
Off Newcastle:	(U.61)
Off Dundee:	(U.13)

Many of the operations demanded considerable skill on the part of the commander, particularly off the Cockle Lightship. U.61 failed to reinforce U.21's minefield in the Firth of Forth, as she had been unable to break through the inner patrol line to the gaps in the minefield off May Island. A further attempt by night to penetrate close to the coast from the North Lightship also failed because, as the light was extinguished, an accurate fix could not be obtained.

By Christmas, 1939, U-boat minelaying was declining, and only three' further minefields were laid, namely: off Cross Sand by U.S6 in January, off Invergordon by U.S7 in January, and off Cromarty by U.9 in February. The full programme proposed by F .0. U-boats on 30th November, 1939, was not completed because of other commitments such as the " Nordmark" operation and the Norwegian campaign.

63. British Submarine Operations in the North Sea

The first World War had shown the disadvantages of the North Sea as a base for naval operations. The broad expanse of shallow water off the German harbours inevitably tempted the enemy to undertake offensive minelaying operations. Loss of U-boats could not be avoided unless a constant check were kept to ensure that approach and departure routes were free of mines. Since this meant that we had always to use the same routes, the enemy soon learned of these, especially from Danish and Dutch fishermen, and was able to dispose his submarines accordingly.

During the emergency period in August, 1939, British submarines had been reported in the Heligoland Bight. Some of these reports were probably false. As fresh sightings were reported after the outbreak of war, it was decided, in view of the lack of AjS vessels, to send two training U-boats, then at Heligoland, to attack hostile submarines known to be lurking off Norderney and Horns Reef. In September a U-boat was stationed in the Heligoland Bight and another (U18) at the northern entrance to the Great Belt, but nothing was achieved, so they were withdrawn, for it was felt that employing the U-boats in this manner was playing into· the enemy's hands.

The first two attacks against U-boats were made north of Borkum on 8th and 11th September, and three days later a third occurred at the northern entrance to the Little Belt. The German commander reported that this latter attack had been made from Danish territorial waters. These and other attacks emphasised the threat to our approach routes, since we had insufficient ships and aircraft to patrol them continuously. As the U-boats failed to destroy or drive off these submarines, they were ordered on 11th September to keep submerged during daylight in the area between the Belt, the Sound entrances and the Skagerrak, and the order was later extended to cover all the North Sea routes. Further isolated attacks showed that the boats still ran a certain risk, particularly on light nights. The British submarines apparently had a good night periscope which enabled them to attack, while submerged, during twilight and light nights. It is possible that such attacks were helped by Asdic; that this was used in underwater attacks was later confirmed after the capture of the Seal.

An analysis of the intelligence gained up to December showed that the enemy was deploying a considerable number of submarines and giving particular attention to the southwest corner of the German danger area, the junction of the routes north of Borkum and the northern exit of Route II. The danger was emphasised by the torpedoing of the cruisers Nürnberg and Leipzig north of the German danger area and of the fleet escort F 9 in the Heligoland Bight on 14th December, 1939: "… Boats are still exposed to serious danger while entering or leaving their base…", to quote the War Diary. It was evident that increased A/S patrols had produced no improvement. Realising that in the long run the conduct of the war would be considerably hampered if enemy submarine activity were not checked, Dönitz gave the A/S service his full support and applied himself to devising countermeasures.

64.

A/S operations and the laying of A/S net barrages involved danger to our own boats unless adequate precautions were taken for their protection. It was up to F.O. U-boats to decide whether A/S operations could be undertaken in any particular area, and he therefore had to know the position of every U-boat. The positions of boats outward bound were easily estimated, but in the case of those homeward bound, this was only possible if each boat reported by W/T on leaving the operational area; and this risk had to be accepted.

Dönitz also discussed the laying of A/S nets in the Heligoland Bight. No deep mines could be laid in the three main German approach and departure routes, as the boats had to be able to submerge from enemy air attacks. Neither could the width of the channels be reduced, for it was difficult to keep to the middle-particularly in winter-even with the aid of navigational D/F. It was decided to lay deep mines on the likely routes and waiting positions of the British submarines, but only in the vicinity of our standing patrols, where the enemy had to proceed submerged (43).

The prevention of encounters with enemy submarines depended as much on passive measures as on our A/S forces. U-boats were warned of the positions of enemy submarines and diverted as necessary. The positions already known were promulgated in operational orders. Fresh intelligence was signalled to homeward bound boats and passed verbally to those about to sail. Homeward bound boats were not usually diverted, owing to the uncertainty of their D.R. navigation.

Though these measures reduced the enemy's opportunities, the attacks continued. The fact that only one U-boat was sunk (U.36 on 4th December by H.M.S/M. Salmon) can be attributed largely to the conspicuous tracks of the British torpedoes, which could be avoided if sufficient care were taken. In comparison with the small direct results achieved by enemy submarines, the indirect results were serious. The U-boats were compelled to proceed underwater by fixed routes at fixed times, .to make diversions, and to wait for escort. This lengthened their time on passage and reduced the period on operations.

65. The British Danger Area

As U-boat operations off the British coast became more effective, the enemy's A/S measures would no doubt be intensified. He would probably lay mines and A/S barrages off his own coast. Intelligence of such measures was vital for U-boat operations and for minelaying by our destroyers.

The first reports of enemy minelaying were received-mainly from neutral sources-soon after the outbreak of war. With the exception of a few reliable reports of the laying of minefields for local defence, there were none that warranted the restriction of our operations or the diversion of routes. Frequent reports at the beginning of December of mines off the Scottish coast seemed borne out by the observations of several commanders, who had failed to find any traffic in this area, with the exception of an east-west patrol off Montrose. The U-boats were not actually ordered to avoid this area, but were warned not to pass through it unless absolutely necessary, and then · only after careful reconnaissance. The announcement in December of the British danger area off the coast, from Peterhead to the Downs, did not alter the situation " as it seemed impossible suddenly to mine such a vast area" (44).

In order to discover details of the British routes through the danger area, the boats proceeding to the north coast of Scotland were directed to skirt its eastern edge. In addition, several boats were ordered to seek special routes for the German minelaying destroyers. An analysis of firsthand observations, together with radio intercept reports on the North Sea routes followed by British submarines, did not modify our belief that it was still possible to approach any point on the British coast. This opinion was strengthened by the fact that no German forces had yet suffered losses through mines in the North Sea. The first loss did not occur until April, 1940.

It is doubtful whether the enemy gained any great advantage by declaring the danger areas off the British Coast, for his aim, which was to deter the U-boats, was only partly achieved. The crowding of shipping into the narrow strip between the danger area and the coast may even have favoured the attacking U-boats (45).

DECEMBER, 1939 -MARCH, 1940

66. The Climax of Operations against Shipping

At Christmas 1939 there were no U-boats in the Atlantic or the:North Sea. This happened purely by chance. The intense cold of the winter did not begin to have an effect on the readiness of the boats until January.. As it was expected that all training would be stopped by the freezing of the Baltic, it was decided to send the boats of the Warnemiinde Training Flotilla and the Neustadt U-boat School to the North Sea. The minimum of boats necessary for harbour training was left in Neustadt. All operational boats (U.7, 9, 10, 14, 17 and 18) were sent to the North Sea through the Kiel Canal.

The attacks on merchant shipping which had commenced in the middle of November, 1939, were resumed after Christmas and were intensified from 6th January, when all ships in the British coastal area A between 56° and 61° N., and O° and 4°W., except American and friendly neutral vessels (Russian, Japanese, Italian and Spanish), were allowed to be attacked on sight. The attacks were to be made unobtrusively in order to preserve the illusion of mine hits. Area A was extended to 2° E. on 24th January, when a new Area C-off the east coast of England between Flamborough Head and Dover-was announced. On 9th February the intensified measures also came into force in the intervening zone, and thus applied to the whole of the British east coast.

Although the U-boats' tasks had been simplified by these orders, the operational areas were still selected on the merits of the attacking conditions they offered. Once again the area north of Kinnaird Head as far as the Orkneys and Shetlands was considered most suitable, but the southeast coast of England and the southern North Sea were also found to give good results in spite of navigational difficulties.

The small uncomplicated type of U-boat stood up well to enemy counter-attacks and the commanders were encouraged to approach close to the coast and penetrate into the bays. For instance U.23, in three operations penetrated into the bays of the Orkneys and Shetlands in search of warships and merchant ships (46).

That the results of these bold undertakings were small can only be attributed to the high percentage of torpedo failures. The rough weather caused more prematures and failures to detonate, which rendered at least 30 per cent of the torpedoes ineffective (47). As the boats' outfit of torpedoes was small, these failures were keenly felt, but had little effect on the morale of the crews.

67. Fleet Sortie-18th February, 1940 (Operation "Nordmark")

It had long been intended that German surface vessels, in association with a strong force of U-boats, should make a sortie into the northern

North Sea. In addition to the primary object of the operation the surface vessels were to lure the enemy from his bases and draw him through the U-boat positions. This could not be attempted, however, until sufficient U-boats could be disposed on the enemy's probable approach route.

An operation of this type was planned for the end of January, 1940, using at least eight medium and small boats. But the freezing up of the dockyards delayed the medium boats, so that additional small boats had to be detailed and other boats kept back in order to have the required number by the end of the month. The intense cold further delayed both U-boats and surface forces and the date was changed to 14th February. The following disposition was ordered:

three boats to comb the area between the Shetlands and Norway, where the British forces would be expected;

- two in Fair Island Passage;
- three off Pentland Firth;
- three as tactical reserve near the north coast of Scotland.

In view of the low speed and small radius of action of the Type II boats, their date of departure had to be accurately calculated. There was a further postponement till 17th February which placed the boats at a disadvantage from the point of view of fuel, as they had sailed on 10th and 11th February. However, eleven boats were able to participate. During their outward passage two reported technical defects. They were therefore allocated to areas north of Kinnaird Head for attacks on shipping. In order that the boats' positions should not be betrayed and the plan compromised, they were instructed to confine attacks to valuable targets.

68. The Altmark Incident

On the afternoon of 16th February it was reported that the homeward-bound supply ship Altmark was being pursued in Norwegian territorial waters off Egeroy and had taken refuge in Jossing Fjord. Three boats were at once ordered to proceed at maximum speed to the fjord.

Towards evening it was learned from German Signals Intelligence that a British force west of the Hebrides, consisting of *Warspite*, *Hood* and some destroyers had received an urgent order from C.-in-C., Home Fleet. It was assumed from the position of this squadron that it would proceed via Fair Island Passage to support the British forces off Jossing Fjord. A few hours later a further radio intercept indicated that the British ships were proceeding to the Pentland Firth, whereupon the orders to reinforce the Fair Island group of U-boats were cancelled and all boats told to concentrate in and east of Pentland Firth. At least six boats lay on the enemy's track. During the night, however, it was reported that the British force which had pursued the Altmark was on its way back to Britain and that the battleships would return to the *Clyde*. Hence the U-boats were re-disposed to conform to the original" Nordmark "plan. Thick fog precluded air reconnaissance prior to the operation, and as Altmark no longer needed assistance, the sailing of the German surface forces was again postponed till 18th February.

69. Failure against British Warships

On the night of 17th/18th February a homeward-bound convoy on a southerly course was sighted some 20 miles east of Ronaldshay (north-east tip of the Orkneys). An escorting destroyer (Daring) was sunk. The U-boats were forbidden to attack the convoy as the German fleet sortie was still pending. More British light forces were sighted, seeming to indicate the start of large-scale enemy operations.

About 1700 a U-boat reported an outward-bound convoy on a northerly course SO miles east of Pentland Firth. This seemed a favourable target for the German Fleet. Instead of attacking, the boats were ordered to shadow the convoy so as to lead the German Fleet to the attack on 19th February. But contact was lost and not regained. The last sighting of the convoy on a westerly course indicated that it had put in to Kirkwall, and the boats resumed their former positions.

Dönitz regarded the luring of British forces into the North Sea across the U-boat positions as being the main object of the German fleet sortie. This seemed a more promising plan than the chance meeting of the German heavy forces with one of the rare British convoys. But the lure did not work, for up to the evening of 19th February the enemy had apparently been unaware that the German ships were at sea. As the German fleet was due to commence its return passage on the morning of 20th February, Dönitz asked whether it could be kept a further 24 hours in the area west of the Shetlands. This was left to the discretion of the Commander-in-Chief afloat, who decided to commence the return passage according to plan, and the ships entered the Jade at noon the following day.

The joint operation having failed, it was decided to try to intercept the convoy which had put in to Kirkwall, and was due to sail for Bergen on 20th February. According to German Signals Intelligence reports of 19th February, this convoy was to be protected by a remote escort of cruisers and by *Warspite*, *Hood* and *Rodney*. The U-boats waited in vain east and northeast of Kirkwall from the evening of 19th till 21st February, when they were ordered to new positions north of Kinnaird Head, but soon had to return to base to refuel. In the War Diary of F.O. U-boats for 20th February the whole operation is regarded as a failure, involving lost opportunities for U-boats to sink valuable enemy shipping.

"… An operation of this type cannot be repeated unless the Commander-in-Chief of our Fleet makes a determined effort to achieve a meeting with the enemy and to draw him into the U-boat ambush. A favourable situation might have developed if *Hood* and *Warspite* which had been ordered to the Pentland Firth, had gone further into the North Sea in support of the forces pursuing Aitmark. If in fleet operations the task of drawing out enemy naval forces receives insufficient consideration or is regarded as a secondary objective, the employment of U-boats cannot be justified, since it involves a reduction in enemy sinkings at the rate of approximately 60,000 tons a month…"

After consultation, F.O. U-boats and the Naval Group, Commander West-who was responsible for surface ship operations in the North Sea-agreed that U-boats should not participate in the next fleet sortie.

70. The Southern North Sea

The two operations carried out in February at Cross Sand (U.59) and North Hinder (U.lO) had been so successful that it was decided to occupy these areas again. The first three boats available after the" Nordmark" operation, which were allocated to these areas, achieved most satisfactory results. Further plans, including those for a pack operation against convoys off the Norwegian coast, were not carried out, because the normal conduct of operations was interrupted at the beginning of March by 'preparations for the capture of Norway, which have already been described.

APRIL - JULY, 1940

71. After the Capture of Norway

After the Norwegian campaign all North Sea U-boats returned to Kiel for repairs and rest. Most of the boats were then sent to the Baltic for training duties with schools and flotillas, for a large number of boats was required for training the crews for the boats of the 1939 war building programme. The new boats would be commissioned in increasing numbers from 1941 onwards. Only eight boats were now left for North Sea operations, seven of them being of the latest 290-ton type-ll (U.56-62). But they were not clear of the dockyard until 15th May and did not participate in the invasion of France and the Low Countries. Ever since November, 1940, when the attack was first muted, at least three boats had been standing by to take up positions off Rotterdam and Antwerp. When on 13th April the Narvik situation became critical, these three boats (U.17, 23 and 24) were sent to Norway.

But now, with the attack in the West, it became necessary to draw on two training boats from the Baltic, which were sent to the Dutch coast, where-again because of torpedo. failures-they only succeeded in sinking two ships . The boats of the next wave were also only moderately successful, for the area was closely patrolled, and navigation was difficult because of sandbanks and minefields. As the situation developed, they were sent successively to the Scheldt estuary, the West Hinder-North Goodwin area and as far as Cross Sand. No attempt was made to attack the heavy traffic between Calais and Dover, for the unpleasant experiences of October, 1939, had not been forgotten, and indeed the conditions had become even more dangerous through additional minefields. Moreover, it was considered that the likelihood of torpedo failures did. not warrant the risk of employing U-boats in that region. Because of its limited operational area and difficult conditions for attack, the southern North Sea was soon abandoned and the boats were sent to the west of the Orkneys and to the Moray Firth. Here, in a persistent attack, the auxiliary warship *Astronomer*[20], which was well escorted, was sunk, the U-boat responsible being pursued for 43 hours before making her escape.

72. End of the North Sea Operations

The occupation of Norway, Holland and Belgium had completely altered the situation in the North Sea. Up to March, 1940, attacks had been made off Scotland against Britain-bound shipping from the east, and in the southern North Sea against ships from Holland and Belgium. British trade with these countries had now ceased. With the occupation of the French Channel coast, shipping to London and the English east coast ports had come within range of the German Air Force and light naval forces. It was expected therefore that the enemy would restrict his Channel shipping to a minimum, but as he had to supply the east coast ports and make use of their loading facilities, the traffic to the east coast would be diverted round the north of Scotland.

The situation can be summarised as follows:-There was no enemy traffic outside the danger areas in the North Sea or in the southern North Sea. It was only to be found close under the British coast. Henceforward, targets could be expected in the following areas:

---

20 S.S. *Astronomer* (8,400 tons) carrying boom defence gear for Scapa, was torpedoed and sunk on 2nd June, 1940, in 58° 04' N., 2° 12' W.

west and east of the Orkneys ;

north and south of Kinnaird head;

off the southeast coast of England.

It seemed inexpedient to station boats permanently in these areas, for once the FrenchAtlantic ports became available, U-boats could proceed thence to the western approaches and the west coast of England, where many more valuable ships would be found.

Experience in recent months-particularly that of U.SS in May-had shown that the enemy A/S defences east of the Orkneys and off the north coast of Scotland had improved. In view of this, and the short, light nights, these areas were abandoned, and as a temporary measure the boats were sent to areas outside the North Sea, from the _Minch to North Channel, whence they could return to Bergen and Trondheim for refuelling. The first North Sea boat to enter Lorient was U.SS on 27th July.

"… As the North Sea has lost its importance and the few small U-boats are now operating in the Atlantic, the War Diary of S.O. U-boats West is temporarily closed this 31st day of July, 1940…"

In fact this marked the end of U-boat operations in the North Sea, for in the following years there Was no question of a resumption of operations. The British A/S defences had so improved that our boats were kept away from the coast. Moreover, every U-boat that could not be used in the Atlantic was required in the Baltic for training the new crews. Not until the end of 1944 was a last attempt made to operate off the east coast, using the new small electric U-boat (Type XXIII), fitted with Schnorchel.

RESTRICTIONS IN ATTACK

73.

It is not intended in this history to go deeply into questions of international law. The following pages deal only with the progressive alterations in orders to U-boats, from" operations in accordance with the Prize Regulations" to " unrestricted U-boat warfare within the operational area."

THE FIRST PHASE

74. First Operations in accordance with the Prize Regulations

The initial orders to the boats of the "first wave" instructed them "to wage war against merchant shipping in accordance with the revised issue of the Prize Regulations until such time as the danger areas are declared." The conditions were those of the London protocol, whereby merchant ships could be sunk only after being stopped and searched and after steps had been taken to ensure the safety of the crews. Anticipating that such procedure would often prove impossible, particularly near the enemy coast, the following clause was added to the order; "As long as war against merchant shipping is governed by the Prize Regulations, attacks are to be aimed at ships which, by the protocol, may be sunk without warning. These are;

troopships, i.e. vessels which are observed to be carrying troops or war material, or which may be identified in other ways;

vessels escorted by enemy warships or aircraft;

vessels taking part in enemy actions or acting in direct support of enemy operations, for example by passing intelligence. Participation in operations is presumed if a merchant ship prepares to resist or takes any action calculated to jeopardise the U-boat.

The observance of the Prize Regulations was only obligatory if the enemy ships were unarmed. The stopping of an armed merchant ship would involve an engagement in which the U-boat would be exposed to the greater danger, for one small hit in the pressure hull would rob her of her ability to dive and transform her into a slow surface craft of negligible fighting capacity.

The arming of enemy merchant ships would almost certainly compel us to abandon the Prize Regulations. Hence the U-boats were ordered to " operate against shipping in accordance with the Prize

Regulations until the announcement of the danger area." On 3rd September, 1939, a radio message timed 1256 ordered; "Commence hostilities against Britain forthwith" and this was followed by a second message at 1400: "U-boat warfare against shipping is at present to be carried out in accordance with international rules."

There is no doubt that from the outbreak of war the U-boats endeavoured to carry out their orders to the letter and took precautions to ensure the safety of enemy crews.

The situation at sea was more unfavourable to us than had been expected, for apart from the Prize Regulations additional restrictions were imposed because of our reserved political attitude towards France, and also because of the unfortunate Athenia incident.

75. Relations with France affect Operations

The German Government, intending to leave the responsibility for initiating hostilities to the Western Powers (48) and trying to avoid involving France-despite her nominal declaration of war - ordered that no hostile action was to be taken against that country.

3rd September, 1939, radio message 1752:

"France considers herself at war with Germany as from 1700. Defensive action only is to be taken when encountering French warships or shipping."

6th September, Radio message:

"Situation regarding France still unclarified. Defensive action only is to be taken when encountering French forces or shipping. Ships identified as French are not to be stopped. Avoid incidents with France at all costs."

By this order French ships were better treated than neutrals, which according to the Prize Regulations could be stopped, searched and, if found to be carrying contraband, captured or sunk. Thus the U-boat commander had to attempt to find out if a ship were French before stopping her. This was extremely difficult at night, and in the vicinity of the enemy coast often impossible, so that U-boat operations were greatly handicapped.

The order forbidding attacks on French warships or convoys had another disadvantage; the U-boats ran a great risk in approaching warships or ships in convoy whose nationality was unidentifiable from a distance. If, before the moment of firing, the target was identified as French, the attack had to be abandoned; _but if the U-boat had closed the target, she was liable to be detected and pursued. Moreover it was certain that the French forces had no order to spare U-boats. To obtain the torpedo control data for attacks on warships the periscope could be raised for a few seconds only. Any additional observation would endanger the boat. The necessity for establishing the nationality of the target before firing entailed a serious risk.

The Naval Staff was quite aware of the embarrassment caused by this attitude towards France. Reports from Radio Intelligence of mixed convoys in the Atlantic and the Channel, escorted by French and British warships, further confused the situation. As long as it was necessary to avoid incidents with France, the Naval Staff could hardly give general permission to attack convoys.

It was evident from radio intercepts and Attachés' reports that troops were being transported to France in mixed convoys. In order that these transports might be attacked and that operations against Britain-bound convoys might proceed without restriction, the Naval Staff requested the Supreme Command of the Armed Forces to remove the restrictions applying to French ships, or at least .to permit attacks on all convoys found north of Brest; for the normal supply traffic to France would not be involved, as this ran to the southern ports. The *Führer* decided on 10th September, 1939, that" Convoys north of Brest may be attacked if escorted by French or by French and British forces."

By the middle of September it was apparent from the behaviour of the French forces on the western frontier of Germany that the French government intended to intensify operations against Germany. If we could not keep France out of the war, the prohibition of attacks on French ships merely gave the enemy a strategic advantage. But the prohibition continued, for on 21st September the Naval Staff again

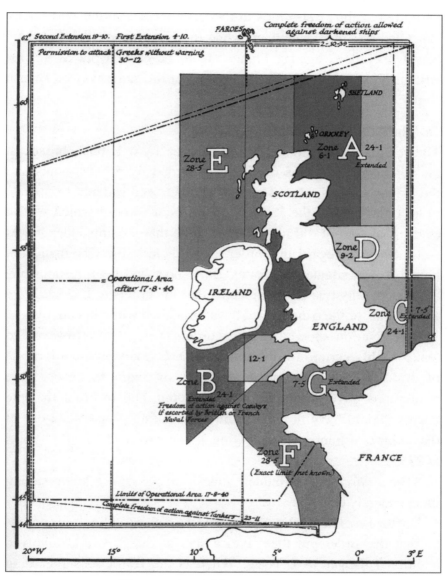

The extensions of the operational area

97

ordered S.O. U-boats to take every precaution to avoid attacking French ships (49). S.O. U-boats replied that he could not accept the responsibility for enforcing this decree while operations were permitted against troopships in the Channel. The order was finally cancelled on 24th September, when the Government decided that" Naval operations against France are to be carried out as against Britain. French ships are to be treated in the same way as British ships."

76. The Athenia Incident

The report of the sinking of the Athenia by a U-boat, broadcast on 4th September, was originally regarded by S.O. U-boats and the Naval Staff as false. The U-boats had been ordered to operate in accordance with the Prize Regulations, a copy of which was in every boat, and .it did not seem possible that a commander would consciously disregard this order. Nevertheless, the Command felt bound to investigate the matter. Ifa U-boat had been responsible, there were only two possibilities:-Either the orders to U-boats were ambiguous, or the Athenia had been torpedoed while in convoy.

Investigation showed that the orders were clear. However, to make doubly certain for the future, S.O. U-boats on the afternoon of 4th September reminded all boats by radio to observe the regulations governing attacks on shipping, and in order that the enemy should have no opportunity of making propaganda out of the sinking of liners, the following signal was made to all U-boats at 2353:

"The *Führer* has forbidden attacks on passenger liners sailing independently or in convoy."

But the Prize Regulations permitted the sinking of liners in convoy, so that this order put them into a special category, and involved additional danger to U-boats. Whereas the restrictions regarding French ships were raised by the end of September, those affecting liners generally were gradually removed and finally cancelled in the summer of 1940.

When U.30 returned on 30th September, 1939, her commander,

Lieutenant Lemp, reported having sunk the Athenia in error. He was convinced that she had been an auxiliary cruiser until he heard the B.B.C. announcement. He was sent to Berlin where he was instructed to keep the incident strictly secret. He had acted in good faith, and as there was no question of negligence, no disciplinary action was taken (50).

77. British Measures and German Reaction

At the outbreak of war the Naval Staff discussed the possibilities of intensifying U-boat warfare, but before any plans could be put into practice the events in the Atlantic precipitated action. It was soon evident that the enemy had incorporated his shipping into the framework of his AIS organisation. His ships had been instructed to report the sighting of U-boats. They were being armed, and at night they proceeded without lights.

In the early weeks the first indications of the effect of operations came from the SSS reports of British ships. Helpful as these were to the Command for checking U-boat activity, they were most dangerous from the boats' point of view. Commanders reported that almost every British ship used her radio either on sighting or on being stopped, and that within a given time British aircraft or naval forces always appeared on the scene. The SSS call, coupled with a position report, could therefore be regarded as the transmission of operational intelligence.

To counter this danger Dönitz, on 21st September, suggested to the Naval Staff that all merchant ships using radio on being stopped should be sunk without warning. While British vessels could be sunk without search, neutrals using radio on being stopped should come into the same category, for they were committing a hostile act in passing intelligence to the British AIS forces. Raeder referred the matter to the *Führer* on 23rd September, who ordered the following on 24th September:

"… All merchant ships making use of radio on being stopped are to be either sunk or taken in prize. Efforts are to be made to save the crews."

On 21st September F.O. U-boats also requested permission to attack all darkened ships on sight. Such ships were frequently observed in coastal waters, and their suspicious behaviour suggested patrol duties. Although the *Führer* gave his approval the Naval Staff did not authorise the measure until two weeks later, by which time there was no longer any doubt as to the general arming of enemy merchant ships.

2nd October, 1939:

"… Darkened ships encountered off the British and French coasts can be assumed to be either warships or auxiliaries. Complete freedom of attack against these vessels is permitted between 44° N. and 62° N., and 7° W. and 3° E."

78.

According to German reports the first U-boat to be attacked by a British ship (S.S. Manaar) was U.38 on 6th September, 1939.[21] Two weeks later the British Ministry of Information published a report of a ship firing at a U-boat and driving her off. On 26th September the First Lord of the Admiralty announced the general fitting-out of British ships with anti-submarine weapons. On 1st October the Admiralty informed merchant ships that "the U-boats were pursuing new tactics, and the British ships should adjust their procedure accordingly." There was an additional clause: "Merchant ships are instructed to ram U-boats"-which was an unmistakable call for offensive action.

The increasing danger to the boats in attacks on shipping in coastal waters had caused the German Naval Staff to issue the following order on 30th September:

"… Observance of Prize Regulations in the North Sea and Baltic is to cease. Enemy convoys, troopships and any ships which take action endangering U-boats may now be attacked."

As the continued observance of the Prize Regulations would have

---

21 The British account shows the German claim to be exaggerated. S.S. *Manaar* fired one round only from her 12-pdr. gun, after the U-boat had opened fire. She was subsequently sunk by torpedo.

resulted in serious U-boat losses, the *Führer* on 4th October approved measures designed to counter the arming of British merchant ships:

"... U-boats are permitted to attack, without warning, enemy merchant ships which are observed to be armed, or which are listed by the Naval Staff as being armed. The area in which darkened ships may be attacked is extended to 15° W."

An intensification of operations against armed merchant ships was now possible, but the U-boats still ran a considerable risk on surfacing if the ships' guns were camouflaged.

To counter this danger, which would increase when all enemy shipping was armed, further steps were taken a fortnight later.

17th October, 1939:

"... As enemy ships may be expected to offer resistance or resort to ramming, U-boats are permitted to attack without warning all ships identified as hostile"

and on 19th October:

"... The area in which darkened ships may be attacked is extended to 20° W."

As neutrals were still subject to the Prize Regulations procedure, and because of the strong air patrols Dönitz issued the following order on 19th October:

"... Ships are not to be boarded for examination. They may be stopped by gunfire, and their papers examined, but must be sunk only with torpedoes. U-boats are not to engage in gun actions with merchant ships."

79. The Treatment of Neutrals

The following is an extract from the Naval Staff War Diary of 3rd September, 1939: "The current international law governing the conduct of naval warfare is included in the battle orders for the German Navy. The orders enjoin *the strict observance of all rules of neutrality issued by the individual countries and observance of the general agreements of international law. Operations against shipping are to be governed by the revised edition of the Prize Regulations.*"

The U-boats had strict orders-which were in force throughout the war and to which attention was repeatedly called-to treat neutrals with consideration. If, nevertheless, neutral ships were occasionally sunk in circumstances contrary to the Prize Regulations, this was not due to malice or carelessness but to the conditions prevailing in the operational areas, as for instance at the sinking of the Danish ships *Vendia* and *Gun* (51). A U-boat commander naturally regards every ship he stops with suspicion, and closely studies her every movement in order not to be taken by surprise. Considering the U-boats' light gun armament and surface vulnerability, extreme caution was necessary.

80.

On 28th September, 1939, neutrals were requested by Germany to warn their ships not to arouse suspicion through alterations of course, use of radio, zig-zagging, darkening ship, or refusing to stop when ordered. To the U-boat commanders this injunction was of vital importance for it would help them to distinguish between neutral and enemy. In order to have a check on the behaviour of neutral ships, and to assess the political implications of any incidents which might occur, U-boats were ordered from 6th October to report any cases of incorrect procedure on the part of neutrals.

All neutrals were treated without discrimination, although it was ordered on 28th September, 1939, that Italian, Spanish, Japanese and Russian vessels were only to be stopped to discover the type and destination of their cargoes, and were not to be taken in prize or sunk. It was explained further that "Political action was being taken to ensure that ships of these countries will not carry contraband."

On the following day a modification was added whereby these vessels were not to be stopped if their nationality could be readily identified. This order was issued to reduce the danger involved in unnecessarily stopping ships.

Even with later changes in U-boat procedure, when all ships in certain areas could be attacked without warning, the above-mentioned neutrals and U.S. ships were permitted to pass unmolested through zones A and B.

THE SECOND PHASE

81. Procedure in respect of Liners

The special ruling on liners, decreed by the *Führer* after the Athenia incident, remained in force for some weeks. To guard against future errors the Naval Staff defined liners as:

"… Ships which the U-boat commander presumes to have accommodation for more than 120 passengers. Details are contained in the' Merchant Ship Recognition Manual.' Main features for recognition are the number of boats carried (four or more on each side) the number of portholes, and the length and number of promenade decks…"

From 17th October all enemy ships could be sunk without warning, except that all liners, even if armed or sailing in convoy, remained immune. But when it was learned beyond doubt that the enemy was using them extensively as transports, permission was given on 27th October to attack liners sailing in convoy.

The enemy subsequently armed his liners heavily, equipping them with depth-charges, and employed them as auxiliary cruisers to protect convoys and for trooping. A list, giving the names and armament of those known to be employed as escorts or auxiliary cruisers, was issued to U-boats. Then on 17th November:

"… attacks without warning may be made on all liners clearly identifiable as hostile, whose armament is visible or is already known to exist."

In practice, however, only those could be attacked whose armament was visible, for once sighted, there was no time to refer to published lists, and once the target had passed through the periscope crosswires, U-boats had no margin of speed to haul ahead again for an attack.

The independent unarmed liner long remained immune from attack, but on 23rd February, 1940, there was a slight modification to this complex series of orders: "Immediate freedom of attack is permitted against liners showing no neutral markings, and against those darkened (except for navigation lights), provided they are within the area in which other darkened ships may already be attacked."

Full freedom of attack against all liners, armed or unarmed, followed in successive areas until finally, on 17th August, 1940, the whole area around Britain was included. But by this time there were probably no longer any unarmed liners.

82. Contraband Regulations

The regulations regarding unconditional and conditional contraband were contained in the German Prize Regulations. The boats were also provided with a mechanical" Prize Indicator," -a sliding disc giving the procedure to be adopted and the articles of the Prize Regulations that applied in each case. The "extended" contraband list-published by the German government on 12th September, 1939, in answer to the British proclamation of 3rd September-facilitated the U-boat commanders' task in certain respects.

The boats were instructed to disregard the regulations in one special circumstance. On 16th October, 1939, it was agreed with the Danish government that in return for the delivery of a quantity of Danish produce to Germany, we should allow consignments of provisions to be shipped to Britain in exchange for fodder for the Danish cattle industry.[22] The names of the Danish ships engaged on this service were published and the ships, bearing a Maltese Cross, were allowed to proceed unmolested.

To counter the export ban imposed on Germany by Britain on 27th November, the following order was issued on the 29th:

"Unconditional contraband carried in neutral ships about to pass through the English Channel is to be regarded as bound for an enemy destination, as these ships are obliged to call at English control ports."

22 This agreement remained in force until the occupation of Denmark in April, 1940.

83. Intensified Measures

During the first three months of war contraband regulations had been so tightened up that the moment had now arrived to adopt the ultimate form of operations, by permitting attacks without warning against all shipping found in certain specified areas. The first step in this direction was taken on 24th November, 1939, when a note was sent to neutral maritime powers warning them against using the waters around the British Isles and off the French coast, where special precautions for the safety of neutrals could no longer be undertaken. They were advised to use specified routes, outside the so-called "U.S.A. zone", and to institute legislative measures similar to those of the U.S.A.

First, however, the Naval Staff with Hitler's approval issued two special orders directed at tankers, and at Greek ships:

On 23rd November, 1939

"... all tankers, other than American, Russian, Japanese, Italian and Spanish may be attacked in the American safety zone West of 2° E. When attacking neutral tankers, U-boats are to remain unobserved and to use electric torpedoes, in order that the illusion of internal explosion may be created..."

The cargoes o'f tankers were of particular importance to the enemy's war effort, and could therefore be classed as absolute contraband. By creating the illusion of internal explosion, it was hoped to avoid political repercussions. On 30th December the order was given that:

"... Since the Greeks have sold and chartered numerous ships to England, Greek ships are to be regarded as hostile within the area 20° W. to 2° E. and 44° N. to 62° N. U-boats must try to remain unobserved while attacking..."

There were slight differences in the boundaries of the areas laid down for attacks on darkened ships, tankers, and Greek ships respectively, and to simplify the task of the U-boat commanders, the following order was issued on 9th February, 1940:

"... Darkened vessels, Greek ships and tankers may be attacked in the U.S.A. zone, with a common limit at 2° E..."

U-boats frequently reported having encountered armed fishing vessels and trawlers steaming with wrongly placed lights. It seemed that the enemy hoped by this means to lure the U-boats in to attack. Careful neutrals set their lights correctly and illuminated their nationality markings. Ships with insufficient lighting were therefore regarded with suspicion and measures were taken against them on 17th February, 1940:

"... All ships in the U.S.A. zone, which do not exhibit illuminated nationality markings are to be regarded as hostile..."

84. Extension of the Unrestricted Area

Six weeks after neutrals had been warned of the German danger area-which had given them sufficient time to act on the German proposals-the U-boats were first allowed to attack at sight in the area off the north coast of Scotland. The North Sea U-boats were then mainly concentrated here for attacks on shipping proceeding towards Kinnaird Head.

The progressive removal of restrictions is shown by the following measures:

6th January, 1940 (ZONE A)

"... all ships in the North Sea between 51° and 56° N. and 4° W. and 0° may be attacked without warning. Endeavour is to be made to remain unobserved during attacks in order that the enemy may suspect mines."

For political reasons an exemption was ordered on 11th January for bona fide American ships and friendly neutrals (Japanese, Spanish, Italian and Russian) and on 2nd February the Danish " Maltese Cross" ships, which seem to have been forgotten, were added to the exemption.

Within a month three further announcements were made:

12th January 1940 (ZONE B)

"... All ships excepting friendly neutrals, in and to the west of the Bristol Channel may be attacked without warning."

24th January (ZONE C)

"... The area off the southeast coast from Flamborough Head

to Dover, and eastwards a little beyond the British danger area is unrestricted."

(EXTENSION OF A AND B)

"Area A is extended to 2° E., Area B southwards and southwest to 10° 30' W. and to include the whole of the Irish Sea. Irish territorial waters extend for 10 miles."

9th February, 1940 (ZONE D)

"… Area between zones A and C is now unrestricted."

The outbreak of war with Holland and Belgium changed the situation in the southern North Sea as follows:

10th May, 1940

"… Area C is extended eastwards to the Dutch coast at Texel, and southwards and westwards to include the whole of the Channel."

85. Intensify Action

To intensify action against Britain and France, U-boats were permitted on 24th May to operate unrestrictedly in the area west of Scotland (Zone E) and the area off the French Atlantic coast (Zone F).

This last measure completed the ring round Britain. Within a strip of some 60 to 100 miles around Britain and off the French Atlantic coast all ships, apart from the exceptions already given, were attacked without warning. Outside this area operations against neutral ships were still conducted in accordance with the Prize Regulations. Ships taken over by Britain after the occupation of Norway, Belgium and Holland were considered as enemy vessels, but attacks on sight were only permitted if these ships were armed. The rules of neutrality were applied to United States' and Danish ships and other friendly neutrals.

After the defeat of France, German naval operations were directed exclusively against Britain. It was found that the declared area west of Britain was not wide enough for effective interruption of the contraband trade by neutral ships, for enemy air patrol made it impossible to operate in conformity with the Prize Regulations. As a result of the reciprocal tightening up of the contraband regulations, there was no longer any legal trade between Britain and the neutrals. But Germany considered that the arrival of neutral vessels in British control ports and the adoption of the Navycert system aided the enemy war effort. It was necessary therefore to intensify countermeasures to the utmost, and on 17th August, 1940, all the waters around Britain became the "operational area" and total blockade was declared. The danger area was bounded by a line joining the following points:- From the French Atlantic coast at 47° 30' N. 2° 40' W.-45° N. 5° W.-45° N. 20° W.-58° N. 20° W.-62° N. 3° E., south to the Belgian coast and then along the Belgian and French coast to the point of departure.

In this area U-boats were now permitted to attack, without warning, all vessels including liners, with the sole exception of a few specified ships belonging to the Irish Free State.

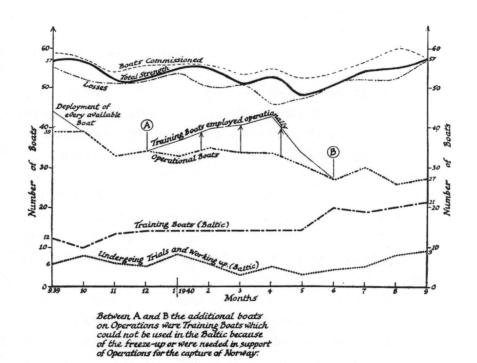

Between A and B the additional boats on Operations were Training Boats which could not be used in the Baltic because of the freeze-up or were needed in support of Operations for the capture of Norway.

U-boat strength during the first year of the war.

OPERATIONS BETWEEN ICELAND AND IRELAND (1940 AND 1941)

THE NORTH CHANNEL

86. Review of the First Year of War

Before proceeding to a description of further operations, we may pause to review the achievements of the U-boats during the first year of warfare. When war broke out 57 U-boats were available. In the course of one year 28 had been lost, and 28 new boats had been commissioned.

Although the total remained the same, their operational potential was greatly impaired, for of these 57 boats only 27 were now ready for operations, compared with 39 when war-began. By the summer of 1940 a larger proportion of new boats was undergoing trials, including working-up practices, while at the conclusion of the Norwegian campaign it had been necessary to allocate additional boats for training the new crews. These crews would be needed in increasing numbers from the beginning of 1941, in order to man the boats of the war construction programme.

Some training boats had been used in operations in September, 1939, and from January to May, 1940. Including these, the average number on operations during the first year of the war was 33, 14 of which were normally at sea in the Atlantic and North Sea. Since about half of an operational period was taken up by the outward and homeward passages, there were usually not more than seven to eight boats in the operational zone at any given time. 46' per cent. of all boats taking part in operations had been lost.

Against these losses the boats had achieved the following successes in the first 12 months of war:

Warships (source, British Admiralty):

Battleship	*Royal Oak*
Aircraft Carrier	*Courageous*
Destroyers	*Daring*
	Exmouth
	Whirlwind
Submarines	*Spearfish*
	Tarpon (possibly due to mines)
Auxiliary Cruisers	*Ardania*
	Carinthia
	Scotstown
	Transylvania
	Dunvegan Castle

Merchant Ships (Allied and neutral):

- According to U-boat reports-an aggregate of 440 ships, totalling 2,330,000 tons.
- According to the German Naval Intelligence Division-435 ships, totalling 1,915,000 tons.
- According to British Admiralty figures (not available during the war)-353 ships, totalling 1,513,390 tons. (52)

Without examining in detail the discrepancies in these sets of figures, it is evident that the U-boat reports included a large number of ships which were never sunk. Misled at night and sometimes dazzled by torpedo " prematures " exploding near the targets, the commanders often believed that they had sunk a ship if after the first attack they could not find her again. This error will be readily understood by anyone with experience of conditions in a U-boat conning tower during night attacks, especially in stormy weather. Furthermore, the German sinking figures include the known mine successes of the U-boats, which are not included in the British figures.[23]

---

23 British figures give 625,978 tons of Allied shipping lost through mines of all kinds in

87. Advantages of the Atlantic Bases

The arrival of the first U-boat at Lorient in July, 1940, marked the beginning of a new phase, in which the performance of individual boats was to reach its zenith.

After the hard struggle of the first few months of the war and the disappointing results in the Norwegian campaign, the generally favourable conditions in the Atlantic in June and July, 1940, came as a surprise to the U-boat Command. The appearance of many independently routed ships and weakly escorted convoys seemed to indicate that in spite of his vastly superior resources, the enemy too needed a fairly long time to bring his depleted and overworked light forces up to the standard that prevailed before the operations off the Norwegian and French/Belgian coasts. On the other hand, the British might be holding back some light forces against a possible invasion of the British Isles. The U-boat Command was only too ready to employ as many boats as possible to exploit these favourable conditions, but prospects regarding numbers were bad.

As mentioned in Section 86, the number of operational boats had dropped from 39 to 27 during the first year of the war. This decline was continuing, while the war construction programme could not have any appreciable effect until the beginning of 1941. Would it not therefore have been better to turn again to the U-boats of the training flotillas to increase the numbers? Dönitz would not consider such action. He was convinced that the war on British shipping could only be decisive by using large numbers of U-boats as quickly as possible, and he decided that immediate operational requirements must be subordinated to training the crews.

The losses continued in the next few months until on 1st February, 1941, there were only 21 boats left-the lowest number during the whole war. The monthly average sinkings per boat was nevertheless much higher between July and December, 1940, than in the first ten months of the war, which can be attributed-apart from the above-mentioned favourable conditions-to the effect of the new base at

---

the first year of the war. The proportion of losses due to mines laid by U-boats is not known.

Lorient and the later establishment of further bases on the French Atlantic coast. The use of these new bases, where repair facilities were quickly made available, relieved the situation in the German dockyards. The periods under repair were shortened, and thus there were more boats at sea. The average number of operational boats available from September, 1939, to July, 1940, was about 33; the average number at sea was about 14, or approximately 42 per cent. of the available boats. From August, 1940, to July, 1941, the average number available was about 30, of which about 16 or approximately 53 per cent. were at sea. Thus in the latter period the proportion of boats at sea was approximately 11 per cent. higher. The fact that our bases were nearer to the enemy meant a considerable reduction in the outward and homeward passages, hence a greater percentage of boats in the operational area.

The actual gain cannot be accurately stated. The passage from Lorient to the North Channel is some 450 miles shorter than from Wilhelmshaven or Kiel. However, the saving of time was much greater than the saving of mileage, since in the North Sea, Skagerrak and Kattegat there were large areas which, because of the danger of submarines and mines, could only be crossed at night, with escort. Obviously this had often contributed to the lengthening of the passage. At least a week was saved on each sortie, and the number of boats in the operational area was thus raised by 25 per cent. and more per month.

The further bases established on the Atlantic coast during 1940 and the favourable conditions in the operational area led to a considerable increase in U-boat successes, despite the drop in the number of boats available.

88. Operations oft the West Coast of Britain

As the Naval authorities had expected, German possession of the French Channel coast caused the enemy to divert his shipping from the English Channel to North Channel almost immediately. In June, 1940, and the following months, most of the U-boats had operated at the western entrance to the English Channel. By the end of July, however, it was apparent that the diversion of the convoy traffic had been completed, so almost all the boats were sent to the North Channel. Some Type II (small) boats did occasionally appear singly at the north entrance to the Minch and between the Shetlands and the Pentland Firth. Their task was merely to ascertain the traffic situation in this area, so that action could be taken in the event of further diversion of traffic to the north. Boats proceeding to and from the north had to cross the approaches to the English Channel and St. George's Channel, where they could sufficiently observe the shipping.

There were at times surprisingly high sinking figures in successive short operations near the North Channel. The U-boats pursued homeward-bound ships close in to the coast and attacked convoys whose escorts could not cope even with single U-boat attacks. Particularly successful were the operations of Type IIc boats-the improved 250-ton coastal boats. Equipped with six torpedoes, they were stationed on the main traffic routes in the North Channel, at the north entrance to the Minch and just west of Pentland Firth. Their diving ability, maneuverability and splendid resistance to depth charges and bombs encouraged the commanders to persistent bold operations in the vicinity of the coast. Lt. Liith and Lt. Wohlfahrt, the commanders of U.137 and U.138, distinguished themselves particularly in this area.

The boats were disposed singly just west of North Channel, some of them within sight of the coast. At first, with few boats at sea, they had no definite attack areas, but at the beginning of August as the number increased they were formed into a north-south patrol line, with the object of intercepting the general east-west traffic. Although the enemy's naval patrols' were still weak, his air force presented difficulties. On the strength of the reports from commanders, Denitz was obliged to order a new east-west patrol line on 20th August, at the same time indicating certain points on which the U-boats should concentrate. This allowed them to withdraw from the coastal area, where the air patrol was too dangerous. The angle of the boats' operational area to the traffic route was indeed less favourable, but on the other hand convoys had also been reported proceeding in a southeasterly direction to the North Channel, which provided a small angle of interception.

Despite their proximity to the enemy coast, the boats reported all convoys which could be reached by other boats, and all sinkings, provided the enemy already knew the position of the attack. The U-boat Command strove to discover without delay every diversion of enemy traffic in order to instigate countermeasures. When two days passed without any sighting reports from the boats, F.O. U-boats decided to order a new disposition, which would allow the boats more freedom to patrol a larger area. From 27th August, 1940, he disposed the boats in a north west south east patrol line close in to the Irish and Scottish coasts between the latitude of central Ireland and the north end of the Minch.

This form of disposition was maintained until 24th September. From 15th to 24th September many convoys, including HX 72, were sighted and successfully attacked (53). Their positions indicated that enemy traffic was running approximately in the latitude of Rockall Bank. Accordingly the boats were redisposed to make the most of the opportunities provided by this apparently limited dispersion. Whereas they had up to now been stationed largely in a north south direction, the U-boats were now disposed in deep echelon in an east-west direction. Two boats, one of which was reporting the weather, lay far to the west on the 23° west meridian; five to six medium and large boats (having adequate speed for long-range operations) were disposed between 9° and 12° West. Two small boats, whose low surface speed was inadequate for operations involving distance, were stationed off the North Channel. This disposition offered only slight chances of finding the enemy; if ships should be intercepted, the prospects of a successful concentration for attack were very favourable, but if not found, the U-boats were more than ever in doubt as to the next move. The boats did not intercept a convoy at either end of the line and the disposition was cancelled after a few days.

In the last ten days of September only two reports were received of homeward bound convoys: a returning U-boat sighted a convoy in latitude 51° North on a northwesterly course, and a decrypted radio message from a British aircraft reported a convoy off Porcupine Bank steering northeast. Vp to that time it had been understood that homeward bound traffic generally ran north of 58° North, but now it seemed that the enemy was using a wider dispersion. With only five boats it was difficult to reconnoitre a large region, so they were closed in to search in a southwesterly direction. On 2nd October the boats left the North Channel in scouting formation, 60 miles apart, for a search to the southwest. They turned about on 6th October and took up a new line west of Rockall Bank, where on 9th October they intercepted a homeward bound convoy: but in the heavy sea with bad visibility contact was soon lost. A patrol line, formed on the following day ahead of the convoy's track, was likewise unsuccessful. On 11th October the boats were given new attack positions west and north of Rockall Bank. The choice of this area proved right, for various convoys were found, and between 17th and 20th October several boats made extremely successful attacks, in which they expended most of their torpedoes, and had to return. Now only four boats remained in the area west of Britain. They lay just west of the North Channel on an east-west patrol line. Of these, U.32 completed the destruction of *Empress of Britain*, which had been set on -fire by an aircraft on 27th/28th October. Ensuing British A/S operations claimed both this boat and U.31.[24]

89. Convoy Battles

The few pack attacks on convoys in the first year of the war had shown the possibilities of this type of operation. The commanders therefore received a standing order to report all convoys against which other boats might be able to concentrate.

With so few boats, it was seldom possible to concentrate them as a result of sighting reports, unless the convoys were outward hound.

---

24 U.32, sunk on 30th October, 1940, by H.M.S. *Harvester* and H.M.S. *Highlander*. U.31, sunk on 2nd November, 1940, by H.M.S *Antelope*.

With inward-bound convoys before the nearest U-boats arrived, most of the targets had disappeared into the North Channel, which was heavily patrolled. There was no purpose in going out to the open Atlantic to operate on homeward bound convoys, since prospects of finding them were slight. But when data were provided for finding a convoy further west, use was made of them. Such occasions were naturally few. We still had no air reconnaissance of our own and it was seldom that Radio Intelligence could deduce the exact position of a convoy.

In June, 1940, attempts to attack HX 48 and US 3 from positions decrypted by the Radio Intelligence Service had failed. A further operation was also a failure; three boats attempted to find an HX convoy, which, according to radio intercepts, was to join the home escort forces in 57° N. 17° W. on 15th or 16th August. The Radio Intelligence Service later learned that this rendezvous had been altered by 50 miles to the north; the boats had therefore to chase the convoy, and in the high sea with poor visibility only one boat found it, sinking one ship.

The Radio Intercept Service was again very prompt in reporting to the U-boat Command, four days before the event, the rendezvous of SC 2 with its home escort at 57° N. 19° 50' W. for 6th September, 1940. Three U-boats were drawn up, one at the rendezvous position, one further to the northeast and a third to the southeast. The northeasterly boat intercepted the convoy on 6th September, but once again the weather upset calculations. In wind up to force 8, the four boats approaching one after the other managed to sink only five ships, three of which were sunk by Prien. Despite the storm aircraft appeared, unpleasantly complicating the situation for the U-boats.

This excellent help from Radio Intelligence was to last several months. Although the boats were still unaided by air reconnaissance, they took part in three convoy actions before the end of October. In each case there was time to bring up more boats, as the homeward convoys had by chance been located far to the west.

Operation Against HX 72 (54)

In attacking the convoy SC 2 on 10th September, U.47 (Prien) had expended all torpedoes but one. His boat was therefore detailed for meteorological duties sending in reports twice every 24 hours from west of 23° West, which were urgently needed for German air raids on Britain. Although the British DjF service could presumably plot the position of this U-boat twice daily, convoy HX 72 did not avoid Prien on 20th September.

Route instructions for a British convoy-picked up at this time by the German Intercept Service-seemed to tally with this convoy, for the course was the same as that reported by Prien. On this assumption five boats (U.99, 65, 48, 46 and 43) were directed to take up certain positions through which the convoy would pass at daybreak on the following day. This order was soon cancelled, when during the night the convoy altered course to the southeast, presumably because the radio traffic of the shadower had been intercepted. Operating directly on the shadower's reports, U.48 came up and fired all her torpedoes, while Prien, having no torpedoes, continued to shadow for the oncoming boats. In that one night, all boats expended their torpedoes, so that no further efforts were made on the morning of 22nd September to regain contact. On their return the boats reported a total of twelve ships sunk and three damaged. The British Admiralty figures show eleven ships sunk and one damaged.

Dönitz concluded his War Diary for 22nd September, 1940, as follows:

"Five boats, which lay up to 380 miles away at the time of the first sighting, were able to attack this homeward-bound convoy as a result of the accurate shadowing reports: 13 ships sunk.[25] This success was due to:

- early interception far to the west of the weakly escorted convoy;
- correct tactical procedure of the boats in shadowing and operating over wide areas;

25 Author's note: based on the boats' radio reports.

- favourable weather.

"Results were prejudiced by the fact that Prien had already expended his torpedoes and that some of the others had few left.

"The action of the past two days has shown the soundness of details, worked out before the war, concerning attacks on convoys and the use of radio when in contact with the enemy."

Operation Against Convoy SC 7

On the night of 16th/17th October VA8, in her attack area northwest of Rockall Bank, made contact with a homeward-bound convoy. Five more boats lying east and north · of Rockall were sent to operate against it. U.48 attacked on the same night, but lost contact after being pursued with depth-charges. The other boats were ordered to search along the general line of advance of the convoy (120°), towards the North Channel.

On the evening of 17th October another boat (U.38) reported having sighted the convoy on the previous night, but to the north of the assumed line of advance. The boats were now uncertain as to the situation, so they were ordered to form a patrol line just east of Rockall Bank by the morning of 18th October. The convoy would have to pass this way during the hours of daylight. No contact was made by noon: this might be explained by U.38's report, according to which the convoy would by-pass the patrol line to the north. The U-boat Command immediately sent an amended disposition-" Proceed north to operate against the last position reported": however the boats did not need to execute the order, as the convoy now ran into the patrol line. The ensuing night brought the enemy his worst losses of the whole campaign, for according to British Admiralty figures no less than twenty ships fell victim to the U-boat torpedoes.

A partial description of the action is to be found in an extract from the War Diary of Lt. Kretschmer, the commander of U.99, which gives an idea of the general conditions:

"18th October:

0200 On receipt of the urgent radio message 'To U.100, U.28,

U.l23, U.l01, U.99 and U.46. Be in position in patrol line from naval grid square 2745 to naval grid square 0125 AM by 0800...' I proceed to my position at maximum speed, although I cannot arrive until 1100. I therefore report by short signal to F.O. U-boats: 'Owing to position, cannot comply with dispositional order. My position is naval grid square 41 AM...' (Note: Some 100 miles southwest of the new patrol line position.)

0903 Sight a U-boat conning-tower, bearing 060°. Shortly afterwards a medium boat appears on the horizon, proceeding in a northwesterly direction. It must be VA6, the boat on the left flank of the patrol line.

1128 In position. Proceed up and down across the patrol line. Medium U-boat in sight, bearing north. It must be U.101, which is proceeding up and down along the patrol line.

Radio message received at 1208: '... To F.O. U-boats from U.38: Convoy in 1539 AM at 0200 (Note: some 100 miles northwest of the patrol line) course 110°, no contact...' That means that the convoy will pass the patrol line to the north. At 1530 the patrol line is cancelled by radio from F.O. U-boats: '... U.100, U.l23, U.101, U.46: Operate on U.38's report. Convoy probably in 2580 at 1400.'

(Note: Some 30 miles north of the north end of the patrol line.)

F.O. U-boats cannot suppose U.99 to be in the patrol line. I proceed in an east-northeasterly direction.

1745 Wind: southeast, force 3; sea 3; moderate cloud. U.lOl, which is two or three miles north, signals by searchlight: 'Enemy sighted to port.'

1749 A warship is sighted, bearing 030°, steering east. Soon afterwards, smoke to left of her. Finally the convoy. While hauling ahead to attack, we sight a steamship in the southeast, apparently on a westerly course.

1928 Submerge for attack.

1950 Surface, as the ship is making off slowly to the east. Haul further ahead: at 2000 pass within a few hundred metres of a U-boat on the surface, apparently U.101 again.

2024 Another U-boat has torpedoed the ship. Shortly afterwards, exchange recognition signals with U.123. Convoy again in sight. I am ahead of it, so allow my boat to drop back, avoiding the leading destroyer. The destroyers are constantly firing starshells. From outside, I attack the right flank of the first formation.

2202 Weather: visibility moderate, bright moonlight. Fire bow torpedo by director. Miss.

2206 Fire stern torpedo by director. At 700 metres, hit forward of amidships. Vessel of some 6,500 tons sinks within 20 seconds. I now proceed head on into the convoy. All ships are zig-zagging independently.

2230 Fire bow torpedo by director. Miss because of error in calculation of gyro-angle. I therefore decide to fire the rest of the torpedoes without the director, especially as the installation has still not been accepted and adjusted by the Torpedo Testing Department. Boat is soon sighted by a ship which fires a white star and turns towards us at full speed, continuing even after we alter course. I have to make off with engines all out. Eventually the ship turns off, fires one of her guns and again takes her place in the convoy. I now attack the right flank of the last formation but one.

2330 Fire bow torpedo at a large freighter. As the ship turns towards us, the torpedo passes ahead of her and hits an even larger ship after a run of 1,740 metres. This ship of some 7,000 tons is hit abreast the foremast, and the bow quickly sinks below the surface, as two holds are apparently flooded.

2355 Fire a bow torpedo at a large freighter of some 6,000 tons, at a range of 750 metres. Hit abreast foremast. Immediately after the torpedo explosion, there is another explosion with a high column of flame from the bow to the bridge. The smoke rises some 200 metres. Bow apparently shattered. Ship continues to burn with a green flame."

"19th October:

0015 Three destroyers approach the ship and search the area in line abreast. I make off at full speed to the southwest and again make contact with the convoy. Torpedoes from the other boats are constantly heard exploding. The destroyers do not know how to help and occupy themselves by constantly firing starshells, which are of little effect in the bright moonlight. I now start to attack the convoy from astern.

0138 Fire bow torpedoes at large heavily-laden freighter of about 6,000 tons, range 945 metres. Hit abreast foremast. The explosion sinks the ship.

0155 Fire bow torpedo at the next large vessel of some 7,000 tons. Range 975 metres. Hit abreast foremast. Ship sinks within 40 seconds.

0240 Miss through aiming error, with torpedo fired at one of the largest vessels of the convoy, a ship of the Glenapp class 9,500 tons.

0255 Again miss the same target from a range of about 800 metres. No explanation, as the fire control data were absolutely correct. Presume it to be a gyro failure, as we hear an explosion on the other side of the convoy some seven minutes later.

0302 Third attempt at the same target from a range of 720 metres. Hit forward of the bridge. Bow sinks rapidly level with the water.

0356 Fire at and miss a rather small, unladen ship, which had lost contact with the convoy. We had fired just as the steamer turned towards us.

0358 Turn off and fire a stern torpedo from a range of 690 metres. Hit aft of amidships. Ship drops astern, somewhat lower in the water. As torpedoes have been expended, I wait to see if she will sink further before I settle her by gunfire.

0504 Ship is sunk by another vessel by gunfire. I suppose it to be a British destroyer, but it later transpires that it was U.123. Some of her shells land very close, so that I have to leave the area quickly. The ship was Clintonia, 3,106 tons .

0530 I commence return passage to Lorient."

Operation Against Convoy HX 79

It was impossible to take further action against SC 7, for it entered the North Channel on 19th October. Some of the U-boats had to return as their torpedoes had been expended; the others proceeded westwards at full speed to meet a homeward-bound convoy (HX 79), sighted by Prien on his outward passage while 200 miles west of Rockall Bank. Prien maintained contact, and enabled all the other boats to close and attack the convoy by night. According to British Admiralty figures, twelve ships were sunk.

Although there was sufficient fuel for the operation to be prolonged, it had to be abandoned on 20th October as all boats were then out of torpedoes. Only four boats remained in the operational area; two of them were employed as weather boats further west and were thus of small operational value.

Dönitz's views on these operations can be seen from his War Diary of 20th October:

a. "The operations justify the principles on which U-boat tactics and training have been developed since 1935, i.e. that U-boats in packs should attack the convoys. Operations in pack formation were made possible by the development of radio communications since the First World War.

b. The execution of such attacks is possible only if the commanders and crews have been thoroughly trained in these tactics. This shows the need for comprehensive training in wide . sea areas, which would be impossible if we did not keep the Baltic free of enemy forces.

c. Such operations can only be carried out if there are sufficient boats in the operational area. Vp to now this has happened only occasionally.

d. There will be more of these operations as numbers increase, and there is more likelihood of intercepting convoys with the additional reconnaissance.

e. Moreover with more U-boats, the British shipping routes will not be left unoccupied after such attacks, as was the case today, when nearly all the boats had to return for torpedoes.

f. Successes as achieved in the above-mentioned operations cannot always be expected. Fog, bad weather and other conditions may, from time to time, reduce the prospects to nil."

The capacity of the individual commanders will always govern the results.

90. Estimation of Enemy Shipping Losses

According to the Armed Forces High Command communiques of 19th and 20th October, 26 ships of SC 7 and 17 of HX 79 were sunk. These figures were based on the collective reports made by F.O. U-boats after receipt of the radio messages from the individual boats. The differences between these figures and those later made available by the British Admiralty are considerable. The commanders avoided sending long radio messages, because of the danger of bearings being taken. From their short reports it was often impossible to determine exactly how many ships had been sunk from a certain convoy, e.g. HX 79. The following is an illustration of this point: A commander had sunk two ships shortly before the convoy action and had not informed F.O. U-boats. In the convoy battle he sank four more ships and at the end of the action sent a short signal: "Have sunk six ships." Obviously F.O. U-boats assumed that all six had belonged to the convoy.

		Contemporary Radio Reports From U-boats	German Supreme Command Communiqué	U-boat Commanders' Reports On Return	British Admiralty Figures (Post-War)
SC 7	Sunk	30	26	25	20
	Damaged	-	-	3	1
HX 79	Sunk	17	17	15	12
	Damaged	-	-	1	1

The differences amount to five ships in the case of SC 7 and three ships in the case of HX 79, and are understandable in view of the difficulties of observation during night convoy battles, when it was often impossible to keep a torpedoed ship in sight until she sank. On the whole U-boat commanders underrated the capacity for survival of torpedoed ships, or overrated the destructive capacity of their torpedoes. The efficiency of the British salvage organisation was not realised.

At Dönitz's headquarters the sinkings were examined on the commanders return, and efforts were made to clear up cases of confusion. Dönitz while reminding his commanders not to overestimate sinkings, used to say:-" We (the U-boat arm) want to be a reliable firm" (55).

91. Enemy A/S Measures still Ineffective

U-boat commanders in later years often referred to the earlier period, from July to October, 1940, as the" happy time," for this described their feeling of invincibility during these months. At only one other time-when operations were started off the American coast at the beginning of 1942-did the men of the U-boat arm feel entirely equal to the enemy's defences. Nevertheless the U-boat Command did not relax in their efforts to gather all possible details of the enemy's A/S vessels, equipment and methods.

At the time it was difficult for the Germans to see why enemy escorts and A/S forces had such little effect. It seemed that they were met less often than before and during the Norwegian campaign. With weak A/S forces, the enemy would find it difficult to pursue a U-boat until forced to surface because of the exhaustion of her batteries and air capacity (56). After a year of war it was apparent that direct hits by depth charges were very few, whereas the greater danger lay in protracted pursuit by the enemy, for after a certain length of time the boat had to surface. Small leaks and other damage resulted from near misses, which upset the buoyancy and trim of the boats, necessitating additional maneuvering and causing premature exhaustion of the batteries.

Whereas the duration of the chase was limited by the small number of A/S vessels, the endurance of the' U-boats had been improved since the outbreak of war. The crews had gained much experience and were ready for any situation.

But more serious was the threat from the aircraft which, from August onwards, patrolled the operational area. Near the land small shore-based aircraft were employed, while further out Sunderland flying boats, though nearly always first sighted by the boats, were very troublesome with their wide range of action, and heavier load of bombs, and were tenacious in pursuit. They prevented the medium and large boats from remaining in the North Channel, but could not stop occasional penetration in pursuit of a convoy.

92. Enemy Submarine and Minelaying Operations

In August, 1940, the only U-boat losses were the result of British minelaying and submarine operations. At the beginning of the month, believing Route Blue to be no longer safe, F.O. U-boats had ordered a new outward route for three boats about to leave Wilhelmshaven (Plan 5). British submarines kept appearing to the north of this channel, either attacking German ships (including U.62, torpedo boat Luchs and transports) or being intercepted by our surface and air patrols. The earlier route appeared less dangerous, since two probing reconnaissance sweeps had been made in July without incident. However, of the first three boats again to use this route, U.2S struck a mine on 3rd August, while on the following day an A/S vessel and a motor minesweeper, searching for her, were sunk in the same minefield. As a result, the next boats were again diverted to Route Blue and Dönitz demanded that all boats should in future have an anti-mine escort when entering or leaving North Sea bases. When these escorts were instituted, the threat from the air became so great that all boats based on Kiel were ordered to proceed through the Baltic exits. From the middle of August these U-boats were attached to the daily convoys of steamships proceeding from Kiel to Seelands Rev.

The North Sea boats continued to use Routes Blue or Green under anti-mine escort until the middle of September. Then, with the intensification of mining in the North Sea, came the order that all U-boats sailing to and from Germany were to proceed via the Baltic. This procedure remained in force until the end of the war, except when ice conditions prevented using the Baltic, or when there seemed temporarily even more danger of mines in the Baltic entrances than in the Heligoland Bight.

Occasional radio intercept and agents' reports on minefields in the area between Iceland, the Faroes and Scotland were at first disregarded. In general the boats' courses lay in deep waters, and they were not troubled by occasional mine warnings. But on 7th August the boats were ordered henceforth to avoid the waters on both sides of Fair Island. According to radio intelligence the area contained stationary hydrophone and radar location sets.

The enemy made every attempt to destroy Lorient after it fell into our hands, for this base was unpleasantly near England. His first success was the sinking of the homeward-bound U.Sl off Lorient on 19th August, by H.M. Submarine *Cachalot*. As this U-boat had last reported on 18th August, it was certain that she was lost in the coastal waters, probably due to mines.[26] Corroboration was provided when, for the first time on 22nd August, enemy aircraft were observed laying mines off Lorient, after which the entrance had to be closed. While the area was being swept, it was found that the mines had delayed action devices necessitating special caution. A few days later mines were found southwest of Penmarch at depths of over 100 metres.· Further minefields were discovered at the end of September.

The minefields had been laid by the enemy submarines which, starting in mid-September, increasingly used their torpedoes against incoming and outgoing U-boats. The bridge watches in the U-boats probably failed to observe all the attacks, but those that were spotted sufficed to show that the danger was not to be underestimated. By the end of October the following attacks had been observed: on 20th

---

26 H.M.S. *Cachalot* laid 50 mines south of Penmarch on 19th August, 1940, and another 50 in the same area on 23rd September, 1940. On 20th August at 0116 she made a surface attack on, and torpedoed U.51. H.M.S. *Porpoise* liad 48 mines off Les Sables on 13th September, 1940.

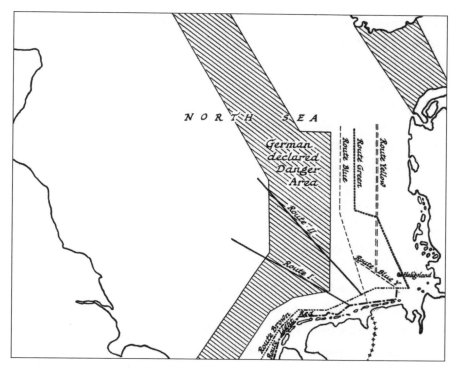

Plan 5. Outward and return routes used by U-boats throughout the war.

September, on leaving Lorient, U.58 was attacked with torpedoes by a *Clyde* class submarine. On the same day the catapult ship *Ostmark* was torpedoed off Belle Isle. On the following day, while entering Lorient, U.138 was attacked with four torpedoes. On the 15th October, on leaving Lorient, U.65 was attacked with torpedoes, and on the 18th, while entering Lorient, VA3 sighted a submerged enemy submarine.

As long as our forces were inadequate for continuous patrol, sweeping and submarine hunting, the only course was to adopt passive countermeasures. Experience in the North Sea had shown that the best way was to provide close anti-mine escort for boats while in shallow waters, allowing them to enter deeper water only after dark. Within a few weeks the following procedure was introduced, which lasted with but small alterations until 1944 (57).

Outward bound boats were escorted while in the harbour by anti-mine escort with" influence sweeps" as far as the entrance (Les

127

Trois Pierres). There, if necessary, vessels with heavier antiaircraft armament and submarine chasers joined the escort. Some three miles west of IIe de Groix the escort ceased. The boats then carried out test diving and, if it were daylight, continued submerged. Care had to be taken always to have some 30 metres below the keel so as to avoid ground-mines. If dark, they proceeded on the surface and passed through the submarine danger area at high speed on zig-zag courses. When a few miles west of the 100-metre line, the boats proceeded normally.

As long as our own escort forces were inadequate, outward bound boats had orders to report by short signal when they had passed the particularly dangerous area, but not until they had reached 10° West. Had this not been done, we could not have known whether any outward bound boats had fallen victim to a new minefield, and it was always vital to know where U-boats were lost. Errors as to the causes and positions of U-boat losses could lead to dangerous mistakes in evaluating the enemy's A/S organisation, and hence to faulty operational measures. It was for this reason, too, that the "passing report" was continued, despite the objection that it furnished information to the enemy.

Our active countermeasures against the enemy's submarine operations, including our flanking minefields, seemed entirely successful, for no more attacks were reported after the end of October. The danger was of course still there; it had only been temporarily averted.

On 30th September U.31 reported that while attacking a convoy at night she had herself been attacked with torpedoes by a British submarine forming part of the escort. Submarines had more than once been observed accompanying convoys. The German viewpoint was that these were intended for protection against German surface raiders.

Occasionally British submarines were sighted west of Ireland. In two or more cases they had carried out attacks. However, the German commanders considered the chances of being torpedoed in the open sea to be very remote. The lenses of the German periscopes were considered better than those of the British, whose submarines could be recognised from a much greater distance owing to the height and breadth of their conning-towers. It was almost impossible for British submarines to approach without being observed, and if they did manage to attack, the best protection was a good look-out against any approaching torpedoes, especially near our bases.

93. Plans for Operation "Sealion"

The U-boat arm was not affected by the preparations instigated by the German Supreme Command in midsummer 1940 for Operation" Sealion." For all other branches of the Navy the intended landing constituted a ,type of operation requiring special preparations. For the U-boats it meant only a change from attacks on shipping to attacks on naval forces, and a change of location from the North Channel to the English Channel.

As at the outbreak of war and in the Norwegian campaign, it was planned to employ all available operational and training boats, except new boats under trials and those working up. Training boats in the Baltic would have to be equipped for active service and brought to North Sea ports. Accordingly Dönitz requested a fortnight's warning from the Naval Staff for" Sealion." This allowed ample time to assemble them in their new operational areas.

According to estimates on 6th August, 1940, if no further losses were incurred in the next few weeks, the contingent of U-boats would consist of 7 large boats (Type IX), 12 medium boats (Type VII) and 20 small boats (Type II): a total of 39.

Supplies of fuel and torpedoes were to be provided at the following bases:

In the west: Lorient.
  Alternatives: St. Nazaire and Brest.
In the Channel: Cherbourg.
  Alternative: Le Havre.
In the southern North Sea: Rotterdam.
  Alternative: Den Helder and Flushing (58).

It was intended to concentrate the U-boats in the operational area off the English south coast, with another formation at each end of the Channel. Any spare U-boats were to be drawn up in the Orkneys area and south of the Firth of Forth to attack ships which might be attracted by our feint maneuvers in the northern North Sea.

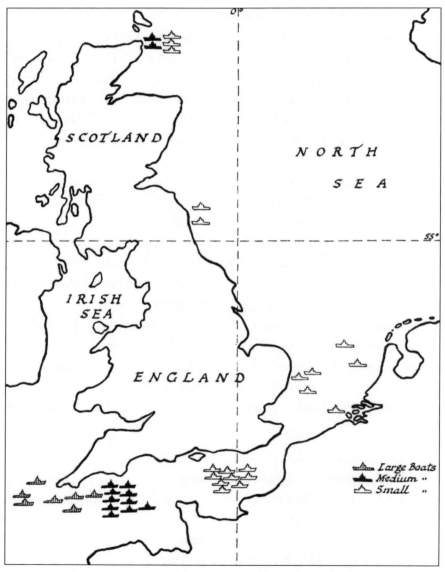

Plan 6. Basic U-boat disposition for operation "Sealion"

The basic disposition of all the U-boats taking part is shown in Plan 6. A more detailed disposition was not needed, since events would cause the boats' positions to be frequently altered. Gaps would have to be left in any minefield which might be laid between the Channel Islands and Start Point, so that the boats could be brought from the western end to the middle of the Channel if required.

U-boat operations against merchant shipping in the North Channel would have to go on as long as possible, and so would the training of home-based U-boats. Raeder promised, during his visit to the Paris Headquarters of F.O., U-boats on 5th September, 1940, that he would be personally responsible for ordering the commencement of the preparations by the U-boat arm.

Dönitz himself believed neither in the success of an invasion in 1940, nor in an early conclusion to the war. To a prospective U-boat commander undergoing training in midsummer 1940, who was afraid that he would not see active service-for many of his superior officers thought the war would soon be over Dönitz said: "Don't worry. The war will go on for many months. Don't forget that we are fighting the most powerful navy in the world."

NOVEMBER 1940 - JANUARY 1941
INCREASING DIFFICULTIES IN INTERCEPTION

94. The Problem of Interception

F.O. U-boats could best judge the performance and progress of the service on the basis of the average tonnage sunk by each boat on each sea day. Over-estimation of sinkings made wartime estimates higher than those taken from British Admiralty figures. However, the figures available during the war did give a clear picture of the fluctuations. It can be seen that November, 1940 to January, 1941, was still a very successful period, though there was a decrease in performance. This decline was undoubtedly caused by the enemy's countermeasures, in particular those of his A/S forces. U-boat losses were still small and the commanders remained unperturbed, but the indirect effect was increasingly apparent.

During September and October the boats had gradually been moved further west. Only here could they manoeuvre adequately to attain attacking positions. For near the North Channel the constant patrols had restricted the boats' freedom of movement, and they had to lie in wait for the chance approach of shipping, which brought poor results. Only the small boats remained near the land, while the large boats made occasional thrusts into the North Channel in pursuit of ships, but now generally avoided the coastal area. In October, 1940, operations were still concentrated between 10° and 15° West, moving west of 15° from November onwards. There, in the open Atlantic, the main problem was to *locate* the convoys.

This change in disposition was bound to lead to fewer encounters with the enemy, and hence to a reduction in the effectiveness of individual boats. But the actual drop in sinkings after October was relatively greater than the reduction in contacts with the enemy, and this is attributable to two further factors, namely, fewer convoy battles as a result of 'fewer U-boats, and the prevalent stormy weather (59).

95. Fewer U-boats-Fewer Battles

British Admiralty figures show that in October, 1940-for individual boats the most successful period of the campaign-the average tonnage sunk each day by each U-boat was 920. That high figure resulted mainly from the actions against SC 7 and HX 79. The December average was 697 tons, including the ships of HX 90. In November, 1940 and January, 1941, respectively the boats sank an average of 430 tons and 507 tons; in neither month did they succeed in intercepting a convoy sufficiently far west to allow any large number of U-boats to reach it before it entered the North Channel. Thus the number of convoy battles clearly governed the extent of sinkings. Interception of convoys depended on reconnaissance. Successful convoy battles were more likely when the convoy was located in ample time, so that given favourable weather, even if all the boats were not lying on the general convoy route, more could be brought up before it disappeared in the North Channel or before contact was lost in the west.[27]

From November, 1940 to January, 1941 very few boats were in the operational area-less in fact than at any other period of the war. West of the North Channel only four to six boats operated. The aim was always to have a certain depth of disposition across the general route of shipping, and the formations were often moved to more suitable positions as a result of fresh information. In spite of this we succeeded in intercepting only one convoy, on 1st December.

96. Effect of Weather

Operations were further prejudiced by the weather. If contact were made in bad weather, the heavy sea caused many more misses and torpedo failures due to bad depth-keeping. At times torpedoes could not be fired. Even experienced crews found it impossible by day to keep their boats at periscope depth. At night the commanders sometimes saw their targets pass close by, while their boats plunged in the heavy seas without being able to aim with any prospect of success.

Reactions varied widely at Command Headquarters when terse short signals were repeatedly received, reporting no operations because of weather. During very bad weather the U-boat Command alone had the power to order the boats to calmer areas, which was often done. When ordered to move rapidly to another position, boats often had to proceed blindly and this constituted a danger, since the best protection was to see. the enemy first. If boats were transferred, several days might be lost in the process, by which time the former area might enjoy more favourable weather than the new region. Despite the efforts of the German Meteorological Service, accurate forecasts could never be made for the Atlantic and no reports from the United States or the Western Atlantic were available. In general, weather conditions were therefore not a good basis for tactical changes in the dispositions. F.O. U-boats reviewed the problem as follows in the War Diary of 13th December:

---

27 There was also a steady drain on shipping due to attacks on independently routed ships and on ships dispersed from convoys.

"After continuous reflection as to the advisability of transferring operations to the calmer areas further south, I am convinced that in spite of the bad weather in the north, the traffic situation will allow more ships to be sunk there in a given period than in the south. Since the sinking of enemy shipping is the decisive factor, I shall continue to concentrate on the north."

97. Further Operations

The operations against SC 7 and HX 79 in October, 1940, resulted in a shortage of U-boats in the northern battle area at the beginning of November. At this time Lt. Kretschmer, the outstanding commander of U.99, while en route for the North Channel, sank three British ships, including the armed merchant cruisers Laurentic and Patroc/ us. His success was facilitated by the indifferent handling of the two cruisers (59a). The following is an extract from U.99's War Diary:

"3rd November, 1940:30 miles northwest of Porcupine Bank. Wind north, force 3; sea 3; visibility good.

1530 Smoke, bearing 310°; later, coal-burning freighter steering a zig-zag course approximating 060°. While hauling ahead, we sight smoke from a ship, bearing 285°, which is on roughly the same course.

2140 Fired torpedo at first ship, range 1,200 metres. Hit abreast the mainmast. Ship settles by the stern. She is the British S.S. Casanare, 5,376 tons. I at once make for the second ship, which is no longer in sight as darkness has fallen. We must reach her before she observes the torpedoed vessel, which is now showing lights as the crew abandon ship.

2202 Unfortunately she is also using radio. Second ship again sighted, bearing 240°, also a third bearing 300°. The second turns about and makes off at high speed on a steady course. We attack the third. On approaching, we see that she is a liner with two funnels and a foremast. The mainmast is shortened. Probably an armed merchant cruiser. Some portholes are not darkened in the bow. She is definitely a warship. She is not at full speed.

2250 Torpedo fired from 1,500 metres. Hit under the after funnel. Among other plain language messages, the ship radios: "Torpedoed engine-room, all fires out." She cannot manreuvre, but settles only slightly. The deck lights are on: some red stars are fired from the bridge; boats are lowered'. She is the 18,724-ton British liner Laurentic, probably being used as an armed merchant cruiser. The second ship is sighted again nearby.

2328 Unexplained miss on Laurentic, which is stopped.

2337 Finishing shot from 580 metres. Hit under the forward funnel. No particular effect.

2340 Laurentic fires accurate stars hells continuously. I make off at top speed to the vicinity of the second ship, which has stopped to pick up the crew of a lifeboat."

"4th November, 1940:

0002 Fire at stopped ·vessel, range 1,200 metres. Hit forward of the bridge. Ship radios name and position in plain language and lowers the boats. She is the British liner Patroc/us of 11,314 tons, now probably an armed merchant cruiser.

0022 Second torpedo fired at Patroclus, range 1,200 metres. Hit aft. No particular effect. Ship has cargo of barrels. Some empty barrels drift loose.

0044 Third torpedo fired at Patroclus, range 950 metres. Hit under the bridge. More barrels are set adrift. The ship which has been settling on even keel now lists to starboard. I decide to finish her off with gunfire.

0058 Fire four rounds of 8.8 cm. from 100 metres. Score two hits, one of which explodes some ready-use ammunition on the superstructure deck. I then have to turn about and make off, because Patroclus is replying with accurate time-fuse shells.

0118 Fourth torpedo fired at Patroclus. Hit under the foremast. No particular effect except that more barrels go adrift. The crew are slow to reload the torpedoes, so I use the interval to approach Casanare, passing Laurentic which is still afloat, high in the water.

0215 While we interrogate the crew of one of five lifeboats where

Casanare sank, an illuminated Sunderland is suddenly sighted, circling us at a distance of some 500 metres.

0239 Submerge.

0400 After reloading, we surface again at 0404. En route for the armed merchant cruisers, we sight an escort vessel. The two ships must have sunk before she arrived.

0453 Second finishing shot fired at Laurentic, range 1,400 metres. Hit aft. Ship sinks by the stern in a few minutes and her depth charges explode.

0516 Fifth torpedo fired at Patroclus. Hit in forward hold. More barrels are set adrift, otherwise no particular effect.

0525 Sixth torpedo fired at Patroclus. Hit amidships in the engine-room. Ship disintegrates abaft the foremast. The after part heels over and sinks quickly. The forward part sinks slowly. I make off at high speed, as the escort vessel appears on the scene and illuminates the area with a searchlight, then fires starshells from 0605 until 0900.

1118 Submerge because of approaching aircraft, bearing 110°, which drops one bomb very inaccurately. Surface again at 1403..."

The other boats had remained in an east-west patrol line near the North Channel. With this disposition, F.O. U-boats obtained few details of the enemy situation. Since convoys and other vessels were navigationally restricted in this area, where the approach routes converge in the North Channel, the observers could draw no conclusions as to the general course followed in the open sea.

After a few days, F.O. U-boats, anxious about the lack of information, ordered a new disposition. On 9th November he stationed two small boats in the North Channel and two large and two medium boats to the northwest and southwest, roughly in 16° West. Should they manage to obtain any information, they could be formed into a pack to attack the convoy. But no news came in, and F.O. U-boats, eager for even the smallest clue, ordered all boats that were west of 15° West to transmit a daily report on any shipping sighted. This order included Italian U-boats (Section 99). So far the British had not shown any particular reaction to U-boat radio transmissions. But this new order would probably help them more than us. In his Diary for 15th November, 1940, Dönitz writes:

"... Whereas the danger of betrayal of the boats' positions is only slight, these reports will furnish information which will allow me to dispose the boats effectively and to concentrate them in certain areas..."

From this it appears that Dönitz was attempting to justify his action, although he obviously regarded it with some misgivings, for within a few days the order was cancelled.

The available information indicated that in the second half of November the enemy was using the area to the northwest of the North Channel for his homeward convoys. U-boat reconnaissance was accordingly concentrated in that area, and encounters with the enemy were more frequent than later on in the war, although they did not lead to a single convoy battle. A typical day was 24th November, when no less than four convoys (three homeward- and one outward-bound) were sighted by German and Italian U-boats, but the weather prevented a concentration of boats for attack. Conditions remained unfavourable until 1st December, when U.101, lying 450 miles southwest of North Channel, came upon a homeward-bound convoy, HX 90. As usual, at the end of the ensuing action most of the boats had to return as they had no torpedoes left, so that numbers in the operational area were greatly reduced, with little chance of finding a further convoy reported by the Radio Intercept Service. It was learned from radio intelligence on 3rd December that convoys had been diverted around the area in which HX 90 was attacked. One was to proceed much further north, while the other, SC 13, was to haul 70-120 miles to the south. The four remaining U-boats in the operational area (later reduced to three) were drawn up on the latter route, but in the strong westerly gale failed to intercept the convoy.

Detailed dispositions up to 16th January, 1941, need not be described, for no set operations and no choice of area were possible with the few boats at our disposal. These were transferred to the vicinity of Rockall Bank to follow up any clues on the enemy's shipping. Whether in east-west or north-south patrol line or in actual attacking positions, the boats were always contiguous. A certain east-west depth was always maintained against the general convoy route.

As there was never more than one such formation in the battle area, it was more important than ever to ensure that the enemy had no knowledge of the boats' presence. Early in January messages from British D/F stations-giving bearings of U-boat positions-were decrypted, showing that the enemy was now more successful in taking bearings on our radio messages and short signals than at the beginning of the war. Transmissions from our concentrated formation might result in the enemy's avoidance of the area; boats were therefore ordered to use radio only if essential to the development of a convoy battle or if the enemy already knew of their position. The meteorological U-boat had to be stationed where avoidance of her area by the enemy would not spoil the other boats' chances. However, all the U-boat Command's attempts to achieve concentration against convoys remained unsuccessful; in no case did more than one boat manage to attack the convoy sighted.

98. The Convoy Battle with HX 90

This successful action on 1st December, 1940, involved the loss of ten ships and damage to another, though at the time the U-boats claimed sinking fourteen ships and damaging three. The following extract from Dönitz's Diary for 1st December, 1940, deals with the preliminaries of the action and reveals the difficulties due to inadequate reconnaissance:

"At 1800 U.101 makes contact with a homeward-bound convoy in position 54° North 21° West. All the U-boats are favourably situated for an engagement: U.101, the most westerly boat, is nearest, while all the others are within range, some of them able to come up during the first night. The others can all get into position by the following night at the latest, if only contact is maintained. To that end, U.101 is ordered not to attack until the arrival of the remainder. She shadows the convoy until the following morning, when she reports: 'Out of torpedoes. Diesel engine breakdown.' As some boats are bound to be in the vicinity by now, U.101 is ordered to continue shadowing until they make contact.

"To obtain a general survey of the situation, Command orders all boats to report whether in position to attack. Two boats report in the affirmative, while it is presumed that U.95 is also near, as she has requested homing signals. U.99 arrives and at 0940 reports sinking an armed merchant cruiser which the Radio Intercept Service first gave as Caledonia, later correcting this to For/err. But contact is lost for the rest of the day. The convoy appears to be protected by strong A/S escort forces. There are two ways in which contact could be regained:

"(a) By the boats themselves, in which case it would be necessary to have a rough idea of their present positions. Only three boats have answered the request for a position report. U.94 is still some way off, U.47 south and U.43 northwest, astern of the convoy.

"(b) By the few available aircraft, namely one FW 200 from I./ KG. 40, Bordeaux, and two BV 138 from Gruppe 406, Brest.

"But no contact is made and the situation remains uncertain throughout the day. The current operation clearly shows the disadvantages of small numbers in such cases. It is essential to concentrate in order to achieve a major success, but there are not even enough boats to be certain of maintaining contact. Lack of speed and limited visual range make the boats' task even more difficult. Aircraft could succeed where' the U-boats fail. Even a few reports would be of the greatest importance. The three aircraft are dispatched in agreement with I./KG. 40, although with such a small number there is little hope of success. In fact, they do not make contact.

"Finally at 1644, U.94 sights the convoy. All boats, including U.101 which has no torpedoes, are directed towards it. It is vital that contact be maintained until darkness.

"While making for the convoy, U.43 makes contact with several outward-bound ships some 60 miles north, in pursuit of which she is drawn far to the west, but she manages to sink two of these, aggregating 20,000 tons.

"At 2340, U.94 reports: 'Convoy destroyed'..."

99. Italian U-boats in the Atlantic

A short resume of Italian U-boat operations in the Atlantic is necessary, for these boats occupied much of the U-boat Command's time. On 24th July, 1940, the Italian Navy requested permission to bring a number of boats from the Mediterranean to the Atlantic. They wanted them to operate under German control from a base in Western France, for which the Italians would be responsible. As every contribution to the task of disrupting Britain's sea communications was welcome, the suggestion was accepted. In August the Italian Naval Command dispatched three boats to the Azores area.[28] Meanwhile a base was prepared for them at Bordeaux. It was ready on 23rd August and was entered from 4th to 10th September by the three Italian boats from the Azores area.

In conference with the Italian Rear-Admiral Apron in Paris on 20th August and in Bordeaux on 30th September, Dönitz had explained the situation regarding the base and the boats' first operations. The first step was the appointment to both staffs of an experienced U-boat commander as liaison officer, and the establishment of a direct teleprinter line between the two Headquarters'. The Italian U-boats were at first under the control of Supermarina in Rome, and when Bordeaux was ready, were subordinated to the Italian S.O. U-boats, who himself came operationally and tactically under the German F.O. U-boats.

The first conclusion from the conferences with Apron and the Italian commanders was that they were badly lacking in operational experience. Dönitz therefore entirely approved Supermarina's first disposition in the Azores area and west of Spain, for in those areas, where the enemy patrol forces were small, the Italian commanders could gain some experience of Atlantic conditions, which they would

---

28 The Italian Admiralty had already sent three of their U-boats to the Canaries and Madeira area in June and July, 1940. These returned to the Mediterranean.

certainly require later for the northern area. At a conference on 5th November, the following measures were instigated with a view to increasing enemy sinkings:

Whenever possible, Italian commanders were to be sent to Gdynia for short courses and to take part in the tactical training.

Italian commanders were, if possible, to train for long-range operations in German U-boats.

Small-scale tactical exercises in the south of the Bay of Biscay by the Bordeaux-based boats, to be directed by the German Liaison Officer, Commander Rösing. The slight risk of enemy interference had to be accepted.

The following rules were laid down for co-operation:

The general operational command, co-ordination of operations, allocation of operational areas and decisions on the form of co-operation remain the responsibility of F.O. U-boats.

Within this necessary and unified command, the Italian S.O. U-boats will have a large measure of independence and responsibility. The Italian U-boats will in fact be controlled by Italians.

The Italians must learn and adopt German tactics and procedure. Experience has shown this to be essential, if success is to be achieved and indeed if co-operation is to be possible.

This last condition was a delicate matter; in view of the Italian sensibility to all questions of national pride, great tact had to be used. Dönitz himself said: "In view of their character, the best plan seems to be to allow them to find out their own shortcomings and gradually gain from our experience..." This attitude avoided any friction. The first impression was confirmed that the Italians were eager to co-operate under the leadership of F.O. U-boats (60).

100. Failure of Co-operation with Italian Boats

The first three boats left Bordeaux again for their new operational area on 10th October.[29] There were six of them west of the North Channel by 1st November-a greater number than the Germans

---

29 The first British sighting of any Italian U-boat outside the Mediterranean was by a submarine in the Bay of Biscay at the end of October, 1940.

had there. Their area lay south of 58° North between 15° and 20° West, beyond the reach of enemy air patrols and coastal A/S forces. Although Dönitz did not expect many sinkings, he hoped that the Italian U-boats would serve to extend his reconnaissance. Apart from attacking convoys, they were to shadow them for the German boats. As enemy reports had to be passed rapidly, arrangements had been made to ensure that any radio message would be received by F.O. U-boats within an hour. Out of consideration for the Italian character, Dönitz had decided against drafting German radio operators to the Italian boats.

There was no objection to the Germans and Italians operating simultaneously in the same area. The German U-boats carried silhouettes of the Italian U-boats and German commanders were currently informed of the types to be expected in their area, so that they should not mistake them for British submarines. This was hardly likely in view of the striking differences in the respective silhouettes. All Italian boats in the Atlantic, and later, in the southern operational areas, were furnished with German recognition signals.

During the first period of Italian operations in the Atlantic up to 5th December, 1940, Dönitz attempted to co-ordinate the dispositions of the Germans and Italians with a view to the widest reconnaissance and the deepest east-west dispositions.[30] There is no need to examine in detail the various alterations in the Italian positions within their battle areas. They did not give the expected support. Although they sighted many convoys, it was never possible to bring up the German boats, because the sighting reports either came in too late or were corrupt, or again, contact was lost at once. When at the beginning of December the use of two Italian boats merely to report the weather failed to produce results, Dönitz abandoned the attempt at joint operations. His opinion of the Italians can be seen in the following extract from his War Diary of 4th December:

"As no weather reports have come in from the Italians, I feel

---

30 By November, 1940, the Italians had sent 26 of their U-boats to the Atlantic. In May, 1941, the number was reduced to ten, and two were sent to the Baltic for training.

compelled to detail a German boat for the task. This most recent attempt at modest co-operation has failed...

"... Unfortunately this is not the only disappointment. I did not expect the Italians immediately to sink many ships in a strange area, with sea and weather conditions outside their experience-they are not sufficiently well-trained. But I did at least hope that they would contribute to better reconnaissance of the operational area. During the whole period I have not received a single useful sighting report from them. Several belated, almost incomprehensible messages or inaccurate reports are all I have received. They failed to shadow even for short periods.

"While the German U-boats have sunk more than 260,000 tons in one area, the Italian sinkings there amounted to 12,800 tons (8,000 of which is doubtful) and one destroyer.[31] I am not at all certain that their presence in the German U-boats' area, their inability to remain undetected, their use of radio and their clumsy attacks do not prejudice more than they help our operations.

" The main reasons for their failure are:

a. They cannot attack unobtrusively or remain undetected.
b. They do not understand the technique of hauling ahead of a slow target.
c. They have no idea of surface attacks by night.
d. They do not understand how to shadow and report.

"My plan for their instruction in the essentials of operational procedure was rejected by the Italian Naval Staff in Rome. My attempts to make use of them off the North Channel failed. Actually their support is quite useless-a lamentable fact in relation to the total war effort. In my opinion the basic cause of their failure lies in the Italians themselves. They are not hard or tough enough for this type of warfare. Their thoughts are too slow and orthodox, when they should be adapting themselves to changing conditions. They are inadequately disciplined and cannot remain calm in the face of the enemy. I am compelled to dispose the German U-boats for operations

---

31 There is no confirmation of this in British records.

without considering the Italians. We can only hope that in the course of time they will gain experience."

The Italians were not made aware of this decision. They were still sent to areas adjoining those of the German U-boats; they were informed of the most recent reports and enemy sightings and were disposed so as to supplement the German boats. But they no longer figured in Dönitz's calculations. Rear-Admiral Parona, Italian S.O. U-boats, undoubtedly did everything in his power to accustom his boats to Atlantic conditions and to train them to the necessary pitch. From 1941 to 1943, individual commanders achieved useful results but the overall effect of the Italian boats remained slight.

AIR RECONNAISSANCE FOR U-BOATS

101. The Problem of Air Reconnaissance

Since Dönitz's efforts to locate convoys with U-boats alone remained unrewarded, it may be wondered why no air reconnaissance was provided. Had there been no pre-war preparations for aircraft to support U-boat operations? In peace the Navy had certainly envisaged air co-operation; they regarded aircraft as vital for U-boat operations. Joint manreuvres with reconnaissance aircraft and U-boats had shown co-operation to be possible. These exercises had been carried out in the North Sea and the Baltic, areas which aircraft could reach from Germany, but air support was also planned for the Atlantic. In the winter war game of 1938/39, in which officers of the Naval Air Command participated, a daily reconnaissance had been made around Britain and Ireland; the outward course of the aircraft was over the North Sea and the Shetlands, the return route over France.

Suitable types of aircraft were expected to be ready within the near future. At the outbreak of war, however, such types were not available and it was impossible to aid the U-boat operations west of England. In 1939, discussions on Atlantic reconnaissance took place between F.O. U-boats and the officer appointed to the command of the future long-range reconnaissance unit, I. / JKG. 40.[32] The air experts believed that aircraft would be able to fly over France to the main U-boat operational area west of the Channel and back. But there was no air support, as I. / JKG. 40 was not ready for operations until the summer of 1940. When the conquest of France gave us air bases on the Atlantic, the problem of support for Atlantic operations was again raised by the Naval Staff. On 8th June, 1940, the U-boat Staff Officer in the Naval Staff Operations Division wrote:

"… With the newly acquired operational bases in northwest France the possibility arises of air reconnaissance of the enemy convoy routes and disposition in the area south and southwest of Ireland and perhaps even in the remoter areas to the west and north. The task of the aircraft will be to intercept enemy convoys and other valuable ships, shadow them and, even if contact should be lost, regain it on the following morning…"

On 18th June, 1940, the Naval Staff issued the first directives for support of the U-boats by the Naval Air Force. Dönitz was asked to propose plans for direct co-operation between his Headquarters and those of the Naval Air Commander. In the same month the *Luftwaffe* Operations Staff were approached to discover the intentions of their Commander-in-Chief regarding air warfare at sea and air support for the Atlantic operations (61).

At first the only available aircraft were those of the Naval Air Force, namely Coastal Reconnaissance Gruppe 406 under Naval Group West and Coastal Reconnaissance Gruppe 506 under Naval Group North. The following entries on air co-operation appear in the War Diary of F.O. U-boats:

"… 26th July, 1940 - Conference with Naval Air Commander… West At present only four Do 18.. From 29th July some Do 17 and three Do 26 will be available and later some He 115.

14th August - From today KG. 40 (Fourth Fliegerkorps) will operate on reconnaissance in our operational area off the North Channel.

---

32 1st *Gruppe* of the 40th Bomber *Geschwader* (full strength about 30 aircraft).

1st October - The *Luftwaffe*, which should reconnoitre to the northeast and southwest of the operational area, i.e. around Rockall Bank, has, despite all my endeavours, reported no forces available for this task.

15th November - I approach Naval Groups North and West with a request for reconnaissance northwest of Scotland and west of Ireland.

16th November - Both groups agree to the suggested reconnaissance and order it to be carried out today... The reconnaissance planned in the area near the North Channel can only be partly carried out in the northwest because one aircraft crashed.

9th December - Air reconnaissance by Gruppe 406 (mostly type BV 138) must be provisionally postponed for two months owing to mechanical defects in the aircraft.

14th December - A loose form of co-operation has been achieved with the following units:

    a. Coastal Reconnaissance Gruppe 406, Brest, which is under the tactical control of Naval Group West; their long-range BV 138 will not be employed for some two months.

    b. KG.40, Bordeaux. They are independent, and co-operation is due only to personal contact. Type FW 200. At present there is usually only one aircraft available daily.

    c. Luftflotte 5. They require previous notice for reconnaissance in a specified area. To date, only one flight made. Several requests were recently refused owing to lack of aircraft."

Five months had passed since the capture of the Atlantic bases, but no progress had been made. In fact air reconnaissance was negligible; usually one aircraft, and never more than three, were available daily for operations, and F.O. U-boats was not able to direct these to suit his requirements.

102. F.O. U-Boats demands Air Reconnaissance Forces

By the late Autumn of 1940 the problem of locating targets had become urgent, and Dönitz again sent the Naval Staff a list of his requirements for air reconnaissance. His war diary for 14th December, 1940, stated:

146

"The war has shown that the lise of U-boat packs against convoys is right and can be very effective. However, in every case contact with a convoy was achieved only by chance. Should no convoy approach them, the boats might be at sea for days without result. They waste their time in the operational area, unable to make the most of their striking power,"

and later:

"The power to dispose the aircraft for reconnaissance must lie with the Command for which they are working. Further co-operation once a convoy is sighted, such as shadowing and the sending of homing signals by aircraft at daybreak, must be directed by the Command in charge of the convoy action. This will not interfere with tactical control by the flight commander. In other words, F.O. U-boats must determine the reconnaissance area and the number of aircraft required; he must be able to direct all forces in order to ensure an effective, unified operation..."

103. 1./KG.40 Bordeaux subordinated to F.O. U-boats

A conference on further operational plans was held in Berlin. On 2nd January, 1941, Dönitz at the suggestion of the Commander-in-Chief, Navy, approached General JodI, Chief of the Operational Staff in the Supreme Command, stating his requirements, including the necessity for operational subordination of the air reconnaissance units. He wanted a minimum of twelve very long-range aircraft to be available always for daily simultaneous reconnaissance of the operational area. The outcome of this discussion was a decision by the *Führer* whereby from 7th January l.jKG.40 was to be allocated and subordinated to F.O. U-boats for tactical reconnaissance. This was the only long-range unit (of FW 200) capable of penetrating as far as 20° West.

The *Führer*'s decision was made while Goring was away on a hunting trip, and was contrary to his wishes. On 7th February Goring had a discussion with Dönitz in France, at which he attempted to persuade the latter to agree to a cancellation of the *Führer*'s order. But Dönitz was adamant, for he saw no other way of solving the problem. Goring conducted the discussion in an unprofessional manner, making it clear that little support could be expected from him. Though he appeared to realise the necessity for supporting naval operations, he saw in the subordination of I.jKG.40 to F.O. U-boats the beginnings of a naval air force, and his objections to this outweighed all other considerations (62).

TRANSITION TO PACK TACTICS

104. Location the Main Problem
Before the war Dönitz had developed the tactics of controlled pack operations to counter the convoy system, which in the First World War had beaten the U-boat. Pack operations were made possible by developments in radio telegraphy. Its use on many exercises had justified the principle of controlling the dispositions through commands on shore or afloat. As a result of these exercises and the winter war games of 1937/38 and 1938/39, Dönitz had estimated that in the event of war with Britain 300 operational U-boats would be needed to produce decisive results. He repeated this statement in his memorandum to the Commander-in-Chief, Navy, during the emergency in August, 1939, believing that emphasis on the completely inadequate numbers at that time might lead to immediate action. The main problem was to find the convoys and to concentrate for attacks. This required large numbers of U-boats.

105. Developments against Convoys
There was a vast discrepancy between the required 300 boats and the 35 available when war came. The only course was to attempt to use these few to the best advantage and, when the enemy introduced the convoy system, to apply the principles formulated in peace-time. Convoys were already reported in the first weeks of September. Believing that in the Atlantic there would soon be no independently-routed vessels, we had in October and November, 1940, begun to attack convoys by means of controlled operations.

The attempts had failed due to shortage of boats. But independently-routed vessels could still be found and U-boats could operate close to the coast, while convoy escorts were not yet strong enough to ward off the attacks of single boats. It therefore seemed best to dispose the U-boats singly between Britain and Gibraltar. They could be directed from Germany to the weak spots in enemy traffic and defences, thus forming local concentrations. In this way limited control was possible. It was never doubted that the U-boat campaign would eventually develop into strictly controlled operations against convoys. The transition occurred gradually between September, 1940, and the spring of 1941, at first because the German Command desired this, and later because enemy measures left no alternative. Great Britain's sea and air defences were strengthened against the threat of German invasion; the boats were driven from the coast and single targets became less frequent as the convoy system developed. The ocean was empty. How was the. enemy to be found? The only course was to build up the system of controlled operations against convoys and gradually to adopt " pack" tactics.

During the winter of 1940/41 there had been too few boats to form even one pack and all were concentrated in a limited area with loosely connected attack areas. Not until the spring of 1941, when more boats were available, were operations characterised by the group disposition, with several attacking groups drawn up simultaneously in various busy areas, each boat having a precise function within its group. This' procedure reached its zenith in 1942.

106. The Control of Pack Operations

In large-scale naval operations with surface ships, the Commander-in-Chief afloat and the officers commanding the squadrons know to a greater or lesser extent the positions and movements of all the forces. This was generally not the case in U-boat operations. They extended over long periods in unexplored areas where enemy patrols were an uncertain factor. The task of the U-boat Command was to bring as many boats as possible up to the enemy and there their task ended. Each boat had then to act on its own initiative. The decisions and control measures in convoy operations were often based on insufficient knowledge of the general situation and on inaccurate, sometimes contradictory, reports.

107. Forms and Areas of Dispositions

Each phase of the war produced problems involving the form of disposition and the location of U-boats. Broad disposition across the enemy routes gave the best chances of interception. Boats could be separated by much more than their visual range, since convoys occupy a very large area. But to reach the convoy, the boats had to lie relatively close together on its mean line of advance and the disposition had to have a certain" depth." From September, 1940, until spring 1941, with usually only five to seven boats in the operational area, it was necessary to achieve either breadth . or depth. Prospects were

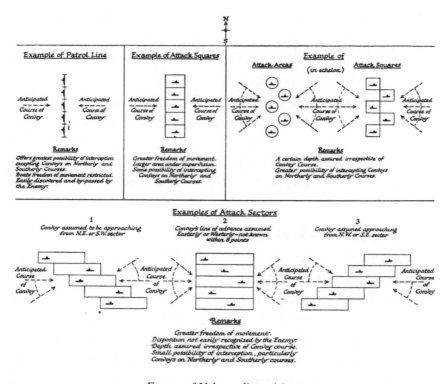

Forms of U-boat dispositions

150

poor unless exact details of convoys had been obtained from Radio Intelligence, and this seldom occurred. Therefore broad dispositions had to be given preference, but this meant that for successful convoy attack, there had to be sufficient warning to allow the most distant boats of the broad formation to close. If, for example, an east-bound convoy were reported at dawn 150 miles west of the North Channel, it would take 24 hours to reach the North Channel and this would scarcely allow the other U-boats to concentrate in daylight, when air patrols kept them submerged. Thus the operational area must be at a sufficient distance from the English coast.

108. Shadowing and Regaining Contact

The shadower's task was to remain by the convoy, while the other boats set course to intercept the target, some of them from distances up to 300 or 400 miles. Whenever possible the shadower had to make hourly shadowing reports.

Shadowing entailed constant opening and closing, submerging, surfacing and pursuing-a task calling for the highest skill, tenacity and nerve on the part of the commander. His task was vital to subsequent operations, perhaps even to the success or failure of a whole period, and for him the actual attack was a secondary consideration. If the convoy escort were strong, the Headquarters had to forbid the commander to attack as long as only he was within range of the enemy. If, as in 1940, the escort forces were weak, a single boat was able to maintain contact over a long period. For instance, U.93 shadowed an outward-bound convoy for five days in October, 1940, although nothing came of it, as the other boats were engaged in attacking SC 7 and HX 72'. U.93 attacked alone, but was unsuccessful due to the hesitant conduct of the overwrought commander.

Within a few hours the enemy would probably deduce the presence of a shadower from the nature, frequency and bearings of his radio messages, even if the boat had not already been sighted or located by radar. Every effort was made to shake off this unwanted observer, to force him to submerge, or to prevent his attacks.

Therefore it might be better that the sighting U-boat, after making her first report, should refrain from running comments by radio, or severely curtail them. After much discussion in the Communications Section and among the staff of F.O. U-boats, it was finally decided that shadowing reports must be continuous in order to concentrate the other boats.

There was all the difference between the evaluation of the shadowing reports in the U-boats and in the plotting room of F.O. U-boats. The Staff Officer at Headquarters could often forecast the convoy's probable diversionary course, detect the shadower's mistakes in dead reckoning, and sometimes warn the boats of enemy countermeasures, as revealed by Radio Intelligence.

If contact were lost and not likely to be regained with the existing disposition, the boats were directed to carry out special search operations. At first these were simple, entailing only a systematic search for the lost convoy, or the formation of a patrol line ahead of the probable diversionary course of the enemy. The patrol line was also used, if there were danger of missing the convoy at night. This was done for HX 72, sighted by Prien on 18th October, 1940. The other boats were drawn up in a patrol line in the area which the convoy was expected to reach on the following morning.

In the Headquarters plotting room calculations were made on the basis of the estimated visibility, the positions, search courses, and speeds of the boats. In practice changes in the weather and other conditions in the Atlantic often caused the boats to be badly out of position. In such cases long wave homing signals-which contained the estimated true bearing and distance of the shadower from the centre of the convoy-allowed other boats to set an accurate course for interception.

The request for homing signals came either from other boats-if they had not found the convoy by dead reckoning-or from Headquarters. Although communications orders stipulated frequent changes in the wave-length of homing signals, it was obvious that the convoy escorts would also take bearings on the shadower. The risk had to be taken as these signals were the only means of checking the navigation of the boats.

109. Permission to Attack

In pre-war exercises in controlled U-boat operations every opportunity to attack by day or night had to be exploited. Submerged and surface attacks were regarded as equally valuable. The first year of the war saw a change in this respect, for experience showed that it was much better to attack on the surface at night, using a high speed to assume a good attacking position and-then to evade pursuit.

In cases where the same boats would be able to attack a convoy on two successive nights, the U-boat Command forbade them to attack in daylight. The U-boats, streaming towards the target by day, no longer spent themselves in submerged day attacks followed by the inevitable pursuit; they maintained contact just within visual range and when darkness fell, formed up on all sides. The greater their number the more difficult it was for the convoy to shake them off. When U-boats had less than 24 hours remaining to reach their night attack positions, attacks were in no way restricted.

The radio message "Attack when darkness falls " indicated that Command had completed arrangements for the concentration of boats. After this, Headquarters observed the development of the situation and intervened only if contact should be lost.

110. Independence of U-Boats in Attack

The commanders strove to attain a suitable firing position. If the escort were close to the convoy the attack could be made from outside it, from, say, 1,000-3,000 metres. Usually it was necessary to find a gap in the escort line, through which the U-boat must penetrate. Many commanders purposely drove into the midst of the convoy, for once among the ships they were protected from the escorts and were often able to expend all their torpedoes. A strong escort, as usually found on the second night of a convoy operation, would often keep the boats far from the ships, compel them to submerge or chase them far ahead or astern. It was therefore vital to continue shadowing reports throughout the night. Should this be forgotten in the heat of battle or only incompletely accomplished, Command Headquarters intervened by making a particular boat responsible for shadowing. Every night attack was made on the surface. German boats never employed the tactics of approaching the enemy half-submerged, with tanks already flooded. This method, not unknown in other navies, was considered ill-advised.

At dawn the boats had to withdraw promptly from the immediate vicinity of the convoy. If they left it too late they were forced underwater by the escorts and pursued and held off for a long time. Under such conditions it was difficult to maintain unbroken contact. For this reason Headquarters were not perturbed if shadowing reports ceased for a few hours after daybreak.

JANUARY - APRIL, 1941
AIR RECONNAISSANCE

111. Reconnaissance by 1./KG.40

On 7th January, 1941, I./KG.40 was placed under the operational control of F.O. U-boats, who commented:-"… This order marks a decisive advance in U-boat warfare. It is only the first step in this direction and in view of the few aircraft available and the various technical difficulties still to be solved, the immediate effect will not be great. However, I intend to gain the best possible results from the co-operation…" (63).

But these tentative hopes were not to be realized. In two of the earliest reconnaissance flights on 16th and 28th January attempts were made to lead the boats to sighted convoys, but they were fruitless, for in both cases the air reconnaissance failed to regain contact with the convoy on the second day.

The first successful contact by aircraft of I./KG.40 with British shipping was due to a U-boat. U.37, while on her way to Freetown, had on 8th February sighted a homeward-bound Gibraltar convoy

(HG) off Cape St. Vincent. No FW 200 had so far appeared in this area, and a surprise bomber attack promised success. The boat was ordered to shadow the convoy, with a view to homing the aircraft on to it. On the 9th February U.37 attacked the convoy (HG 53) about 160 miles west-southwest of Cape St. Vincent, sinking two ships. She" homed" six FW 200, which attacked in the afternoon, sinking another five ships. She continued to shadow and sank a further ship on 10th February. At this time Hipper was in the vicinity of the Azores and received permission to attack the convoy, acting on further homing signals from U.3? But she only succeeded in sinking a straggler, the British s.s. Iceland, on 11th February. That evening Hipper gave up the search for HG 53, and proceeded south to intercept SL (S) 64 on the strength of German Radio Intelligence. Her attack on this convoy early on 12th February resulted in the loss of seven out of nineteen ships. These operations showed the possibilities of a combined attack by aircraft, U-boats and surface ships-the first example in naval history.

In the battle area northwest of the North Channel no change was made in the U-boat dispositions and method of attack. The aircraft available from I.jKG.40 were still too few to allow the U-boats to abandon their own reconnaissance. Usually only two aircraft operated each day. Whenever a special area was to be reconnoitered by four or five aircraft, or when a special bomber operation was planned, this necessarily depleted the air reconnaissance both before and after the air operations.

Thus air reconnaissance was still only an occasional aid, and F.O. U-boats still had to place his boats " where he thought best". This" hit or miss" policy was even less satisfactory than before, for in January,. 1941, the British began to spread the convoy routes over a wider area, and to send the convoys further north. Naturally it took us some weeks to collect the data from which this change was established. Until 10th February the U-boats operated west of North Channel as far as 20° West, when they began to follow up the convoy diversions to the north. The battle area stretched in stages as far as the coast of Iceland. The longest north-south extension occurred on 27th February and again on 2nd March, when seven boats were stretched between Iceland and Rockall Bank. But the northward movement of the U-boats was not conducive to co-operation with KG.40, whose aircraft, being based at Bordeaux, could only reach the southeast corner of the area. For reasons which they did not state to F.O. U-boats, the *Luftwaffe* found it impossible to transfer KG.40 to Stavanger airport. From the middle of February the usual procedure was for the FW 200 to take off from Bordeaux, reconnoitre the area northwest of North Channel and then land in Stavanger, returning on a reciprocal route on the following day. This procedure-though often cancelled because of the Norwegian weather-led to a number of convoy sightings and to several large-scale operations.

112. Support from the Air

On 19th February an aircraft en route for Stavanger sighted a westbound convoy, OB 2f37, 80 miles northwest of Cape Wrath. All the boats, which were then in a bunch south of Iceland, were directed to proceed southeast at maximum speed to form a patrol line ahead of the reported convoy course. On the second day the convoy was picked up by two aircraft. Their reports were so inexact that searching on that day remained without result. Further patrol lines by the boats on the next day also failed to find the convoy and the operation was abandoned on the evening of 21st February.

Two days later an aircraft returning from Stavanger sighted another westbound convoy, OB 288, 40 miles southeast of Lousy Bank. Approaching the position given by the aircraft, U.73 was able to make temporary contact a few hours later. The aircraft which took off on the following morning had insufficient range to find the convoy, but the U-boat report of the previous day was sufficiently accurate for the boats to find it again east of their patrol line. Four boats attacked and destroyed the convoy during the night, reporting nine ships sunk, which is corroborated by the British Admiralty. In this operation, as in the simultaneous operation against OB 2f39, torpedo failures prevented even greater results. The latter convoy was sighted by U.552 (Lt. Topp). With two more boats, also on their first operation, Topp pursued the enemy for three days, but was himself unable to obtain results owing to the heavy sea and torpedo failures. Two ships were reported sunk and one damaged. British Admiralty records give three ships sunk and one damaged.

It was by chance that OB 290, the next Atlantic convoy to leave the North Channel, was also attacked between 25th and 27th February. The sighting was not made by aircraft, but by Lt. Prien who was proceeding north. Two returning boats without torpedoes were ordered also to maintain contact until the arrival of U.99 (Kretschmer). Prien's shadowing reports enabled six FW 200 to carry out an effective bomber attack-another instance of U-boats leading aircraft to the target. Prien reported sinking altogether 22,000 tons. British Admiralty records give three ships totalling 15,600 tons sunk, two damaged and nine sunk by FW 200.

An extensive but unsuccessful operation began on 2nd March, when an aircraft proceeding to Stavanger sighted OB 292 just west of the North Channel. All available boats were assembled in patrol line by 3rd March, while three FW 200 searched in vain for the convoy. The three aircraft reconnoitred the area southwest of North Channel more fully than the northwestern sector, so it was assumed that the convoy had been diverted to the north, and the boats were ordered to proceed slowly northwards. On the third day of the operation an aircraft returning from Stavanger found a convoy of the same composition 150 miles north of the position reported on the first day. Presumably the weather had forced it to heave to. The boats were drawn up in a new patrol line. At dawn on 5th March they proceeded eastwards to meet the convoy, but were unsuccessful. It had passed out of the range of our aircraft, and as there was no way of finding out which direction it had taken, the operation was abandoned that evening.

113. Air Support Inadequate

After this unsuccessful operation, F.O. U-boats decided that for the time being no more U-boats should be sent against convoys reported by aircraft. The aircraft had hardly sufficient range to direct the U-boats to outward-bound convoys. They were able to maintain contact for one or two hours (as far as 10° West) on the day of sighting, but on the second and most important day the westbound convoys would be beyond their range. In the case of convoys on northwesterly and southwesterly courses, air contact could be made only if the ships happened to be on the direct route of the aircraft, and even then there was not enough fuel for searching, shadowing, or sending homing signals. The aircraft could not even remain long enough over the convoy to deduce its mean line of advance. No air reconnaissance could be provided for attacks on homeward bound convoys as the aircraft could not reach the northern area. Aircraft reports on convoy positions were often badly in error. A comparison of convoy positions reported by aircraft, U-boats and the Radio Intercept Service showed that the aircraft reports were sometimes as much as 70 miles in error. This was the reason for the failure of the actions against OB 287 and OB 292 (64).

Too few aircraft had been available for all these operations. Daily reconnaissance by two aircraft-relying only on visual location-could not be effective. F.O. U-boats estimated that once the British knew of the aircraft/U-boat co-operation, their convoys would always be diverted on sighting an air shadower (65). With a view to keeping the air shadowers unobserved, they were ordered on 3rd March not to bomb the convoys. F.O. U-boats took this step reluctantly, being aware of the tonic effect of successful air attacks on aircrews engaged in long and wearying reconnaissance. But the large Kondors found unobserved shadowing impossible, and on 31st March general freedom of bomber attack on all targets was restored (66).

114. Steps to strengthen Air Support
The situation could only be improved by the allocation of more aircraft, which, according to the Commander-in-Chief of the *Luftwaffe*, would be forthcoming. Aircraft of longer range were in process of development and construction (67). The FW 200 must serve until these were available. During the following months

additional fuel tanks were installed in the FW 200 to improve their range.

On 3rd May F.O. U-boats issued the following orders to improve the methods of determining position:

"… Aircraft will take off on the same route at intervals of one to two hours. Convoys are the objective of reconnaissance. They should be reported as quickly as possible by homing signals giving position, course and speed. Composition of the convoy should be reported later. Contact should be maintained as long as fuel permits. All subsequent aircraft will fly towards the convoy reported by the first aircraft, and will make independent, complete reconnaissance reports as already detailed. The first aircraft's report will be checked with the others. Each aircraft must report its own navigational data, uninfluenced by any report of the preceding aircraft…" (68).

To check the aircraft position reports, the H/F-D/F shore stations were ordered to take bearings on the aircraft radio transmitters. Until this new procedure had been tried out, F.O. U-boats was reluctant to allow the U-boats to act on convoy reports from aircraft. The boats now moved further west, and the intended procedure could not be tested in the following months, nor were there any more combined operations west of North Channel. However, at the direction of F.O. U-boats, KG.40's daily reconnaissance was continued in the area west of Ireland and northwest of North Channel. All information regarding enemy traffic, even if negative, was useful in deciding the boats' operational areas.

115. More Torpedo Failures

As mentioned in Section 112, torpedo failures occurred during the attacks on OB 288 and OB 289 in February, 1941. The experience of U.552 provides a typical example. In her attack on OB 289 on the 23rd, she fired three single torpedoes at ranges of 300 to 600 metres, one at 3,000 and a salvo of three at 1,500 metres, all of which failed to detonate. Though subsequent investigation did not reveal the cause of the failures, it was found that with one exception the boats concerned had embarked torpedoes in German bases during the very

159

severe winter. The Command believed that the failures might be due to deterioration of the engine lubricant caused by the intense cold, but the experts could not confirm this.

116. Temporary Transfer to the West

The convoys OB 287, OB 288, OB 289 and OB 293 had been sighted in the north of the operational area, and OB 292 had also deviated northwards. From previous experience F.O. U-boats could assume that the British would keep using this area for some time, so from 10th March the U-boats were moved up to the south of Iceland. Five days later they intercepted a homeward bound convoy, HX 112, from which two ships were reported sunk and six to eight damaged. British records give five ships sunk and two damaged. Mter this operation all was quiet in the northern area. Single vessels were occasionally sighted, but the number of encounters was insufficient. Convoys had been reported west of Rockall Bank by aircraft and returning U-boats. It seemed that the enemy had again altered his tracks, thus confirming the belief that rigid convoy routes had been abandoned. F.O. U-boats commented:

"... Possibly the enemy traffic has been diverted to the south. From past experience sudden and complete alterations in the shipping routes are unlikely. Despite heavy losses, the British have always gone back to using the same areas..." (69).

There was another reason for moving the boats. During the operations against OB 293 and HX 112, four U-boats had been lost, while another was missing. Among them were the boats of the three aces, Prien, Ketschmer and Schepke, all old and experienced campaigners. No reasons could be given for their loss, but as they had all been in the area south of Iceland, it seemed prudent to evacuate it. The group of U-boats was therefore sent to the southwest. The first move was made on 26th March, and another on 30th March, extending for the first time beyond 25° West. In this new area the boats found and attacked SC 26, and thirteen ships were reported sunk and one damaged. British records show ten ships sunk.

The boats remained in this area until the middle of April.

Meanwhile a number of commanders had returned from the area south of Iceland. Their verbal reports did not confirm the impression from signals and aircraft reports that here the enemy patrol and escort forces had been particularly strong. It was confirmed that the enemy had no new methods or new A/S weapons, and therefore the loss of so many U-boats in March could only be considered as normal. The reason for evacuating the area south of Iceland seemed no longer valid, and on 17th April the boats commenced to return eastwards, where there was more likelihood of interception. They proceeded southwest of Iceland and were then disposed south and southeast of that island as far as Outer Bailey Bank. Both formations stretched into the area southwest of Rockall Bank, while for the operation against HX 121 a patrol line was formed 50 miles east of St. Kilda. While fear of new British A/S methods and devices had been allayed, the last three weeks had proved that there was no longer any point in limiting the western movement to 20° West.

- C H A P T E R   3 -

THE ATLANTIC AND THE MEDITERRANEAN (MAY-DECEMBER, 1941)

SEARCH IN THE NORTH ATLANTIC

117. U-boat Strength up to the Summer of 1941

The reasons for the U-boats' ultimate failure are many. Here it suffices to mention only one aspect, which became apparent during the summer of 1941. From the outbreak of war F.O. U-boats had done everything in his power to obtain enough boats for a successful campaign against Britain. The German Admiralty had never ceased to advocate a vigorous construction programme, though there were some differences of opinion among the Naval Staff as to the proportion of effort allocated to U-boats.[33]

Losses early in the war led to a decrease in strength which was not made good by new construction until May, 1940. At this time the small Type II boats were the most numerous. The increase in numbers continued steadily: from 1st May, 1940 to 1st May, 1941, the numbers rose from 49 to 124, and then very rapidly to 236 by 1st December, 1941.

The number of operational boats however did not begin to rise until February, 1941, because from May, 1940, more boats were needed for training or undergoing trials. On 1st February, 1941,

---

33 The reader may wonder why in September, 1939, Germany did not at once give priority to the construction of the 300 U-boats then considered essential for decisive results against Great Britain. The answer to this question may reside in Hitler's illusion - which persisted after the fall of France, perhaps even up to the attack on Russia - that with Germany supreme in Europe, Britain would be compelled to sue for peace. The directive to the author of this work did not include considerations of this nature. A detailed account of Germany's U-boat building policy from 1922 until 1945 will be found in Appendix I at the end of this volume.

the proportion of operational boats to the total number was 1: 4·3. This unsatisfactory proportion was unavoidable in the interests of training. The proportion on 1st August, 1941, of one operational boat for every 2·6 completed was to continue until the end of the year. It was not until after nearly two years of war-in July, 1941-that the actual number of operational boats increased beyond their initial figure.

118. Increase is Too Late

From February, 1941, the boats in the Atlantic began to increase, slowly at first, but sharply from May onwards, until the big increase in August. At first sinkings increased correspondingly. While 125,000 tons were believed sunk in January, the figure for May was 325,000 tons. But from July, 1941, sinkings decreased sharply, descending to the level of the first six months of war, and this in spite of our possessing three to four times as many boats as in January, 1941.

The fact is that the increase in numbers did not come until the enemy's strengthened AI S measures had forced the U-boat Command to move the boats from the vicinity of the English coast westwards into the Atlantic. Here we had insufficient boats for effective interception, and no aircraft of adequate range. Meanwhile, the increase in enemy convoy escorts had considerably reduced the effectiveness of our attacks.

There is no doubt that even an additional 30 boats-doubling the actual number-would have at least doubled the sinkings between July and November, 1940. Apart from their attacking value, the extra boats would have facilitated interception of convoys, and pack operations would not have been followed by empty periods in the Atlantic. In August, 1940, every additional boat had meant 20,000 tons of additional sinkings per month, by February, 1941, each boat accounted for only 16,000 tons, in April 13,500 tons, and from July onwards only 3,700 tons, or about one-sixth of the monthly figure per boat in 1940. There is no justification for the belief that the successes of 1940 were due only to the skill of such men as Prien, Kretschmer

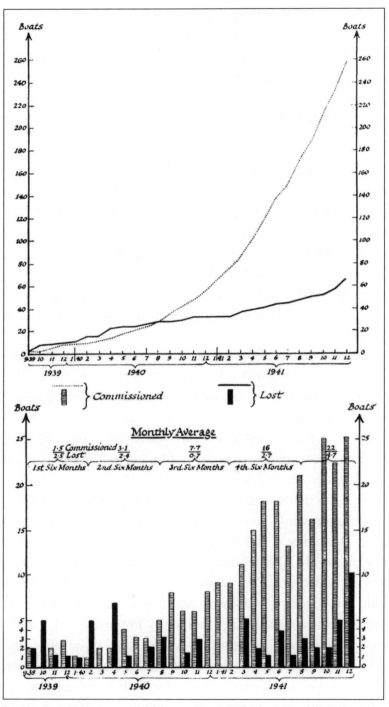

U-boats commissioned and lost from the outbreak of war to December, 1941

and Schepke, for there were equally competent commanders in 1941, who however had to contend with much greater difficulties. It is clear that the race between U-boat construction and the British A/S organisation had reached a turning-point.

119. Reason for the Move to the West

From February to April, 1941, there had been a gradual extension of operations westwards, which marked the beginning of a new phase, covering the whole North Atlantic.

The area between Britain and 20° West was too vast for stationary operations, and here it was doubtful whether single boats could penetrate the strong enemy escorts. Many convoys had up to eight and more escorting destroyers, and even beyond 20° West constant air cover had often been observed ... Chance successes by single U-boats remained few. The only course was to select an area where they would be able to act as a group on receipt of enemy sighting reports. The enemy had at last learned how to keep his convoys clear of the U-boat. All our efforts to discover their periodicity and routes were unavailing. From time to time enemy traffic was diverted north, but normally the convoys still seemed to use the whole area from Iceland to North Channel/Porcupine Bank, the largest scattering between Britain and America occurring between the meridians of 20° and 30° West.

The U-boats had to find an area where traffic was more concentrated. For reasons already mentioned they could not return east towards the North Channel. Alternatively, the heaviest concentration of traffic was to be found off the Newfoundland Bank. By the time eastbound convoys reached 35° West, they were less heavily protected, so that boats between there and 25° West could operate freely over long periods. This allowed distant boats to be concentrated for attack.

Information on the general situation in the vicinity of the British coast was still provided by air reconnaissance. There was no prospect of useful co-operation from the Italian U-boats in their new western zone, so they were allocated to the area between 47° 30' North to

165

57° 30' North and 15° to 25° West, where they would not prejudice German operations. Here-even if they were only sighted-they might assist the German boats by causing traffic to move into the German zone.

120. Westward to Greenland

On 8th May, 1941, the German boats were ordered to proceed westwards. Of the five boats south of Iceland, four were already pursuing OB 318 in a westerly direction. This convoy had been sighted by U.ll0 on 7th May. The boats closed in from some distance and one was lost in encounters with the escort. The boats reported sinking nine ships and damaging three. British figures give nine ships sunk and two damaged.

After the operation these boats and others-seven in all-were formed into a "western group" 350 miles southeast of Cape Farewell. Each boat had a depth of sweep of 20 miles. The formation remained there, maintaining radio silence, for one week only. On 15th May they were sent 240 miles to the southwest where they formed an open patrol line. The new area was expected to contain plenty of traffic, and was no further from the Biscay bases-the nearest refuelling point.

This new patrol line produced results. On 19th May HX 126 ran into its western flank. The convoy took evasive action to the northwest, but the boats lying to the south came up and on the second night-before the arrival of escort reinforcements-were able to attack successfully. Contact was then lost. The U-boats reported nine ships sunk and one damaged, and the British records confirm these figures. The boats had now reached the area east of Cape Farewell, and some returned home while the others proceeded to the southwest, where it was intended to form a new pack.

121. *Bismarck*

On the morning of 24th May, 1941, *Bismarck* - (with the Commander-in-Chief, Fleet) - and *Prinz Eugen* attempted to break through via Denmark Strait, where they encountered and sank H.M.S. *Hood*. No direct co-operation had been planned between the U-boats and the surface ships. On 8th April the Commander-in-Chief, Fleet had met F.O. U-boats in Paris, when they discussed the possibilities of U-boat support for the battleship operation. It was decided that the boats were to be disposed according to the normal requirements of U-boat warfare, and that any opportunities of co-operation with the surface ships were to be fully exploited. An experienced U-boat officer was embarked in *Bismarck*, and the flagship kept watch on the U-boat wave so as to know the boats' positions and the intentions of F.O. U-boats (70).

The western group of U-boats was only a hundred or two miles from *Bismarck*. Independent action by F.O. U-boats to bring them nearer was pointless until the Commander-in-Chief's plans were known. But on this occasion Dönitz suspended operations against shipping and placed all available boats unreservedly at the disposal of Admiral Saalwachter, Commander of Naval Group West, who was in control of German surface ship operations in the Atlantic.

On 24th May the Commander-in-Chief, Fleet requested the western U-boat group to assemble in a narrow patrol line 60 miles broad and 280 miles south of Cape Farewell. He intended to lure his persistent shadowers across this line on the morning of 25th May. But the patrol line was cancelled on the evening of 24th May when it was learned that the Commander-in-Chief had changed his plans. It seemed that *Bismarck* was returning to St. Nazaire, while *Prinz Eugen* would proceed independently to the southwest. On the order of Naval Group West the boats proceeded to a new patrol line 240 miles wide and 300 miles southeast of Cape Farewell.

The assumption that *Bismarck* would return to St. Nazaire gained in probability when on the night of 24th/25th May it was learned that she had been torpedoed by carrier-borne aircraft. The primary task now was to protect the returning ship. Group West ordered the western U-boat group to proceed eastwards at 12 knots to intercept heavy units pursuing *Bismarck*. The speed of the surface forces, the slowness of the U-boats and the uncertainty as to Bismdrrck's position and intentions made contact problematical. When in the evening it could be assumed that *Bismarck* and her pursuers had left that area, the boats were ordered to return to their former positions. They had insufficient speed for the southeasterly pursuit.

The second measure was the attempt to help the damaged ship in the Bay of Biscay. In anticipation of her return, all homeward and outward bound boats had been ordered on 24th May to assemble in an area 450 miles west of St. Nazaire, in latitude 47° 20' North, between 12° and 15° West. There were six boats in all, VAS, U.73, U.74, U97, U.9S and U.556. Three of these could be used only for reconnaissance. In the forenoon of 25th Mayall were ordered to form a northwest-southeast patrol line towards Cape Ortegal. If *Bismarck* were steering a southeasterly course, she would be able to draw her pursuers and shadowers across this formation. Apart from its reconnaissance value, the disposition would be practically useless against enemy ships coming from the north or south. But a heavy storm prevented the boats from reaching their positions until 26th May.

As expected, *Bismarck* approached the northwest flank of the patrol line. At 1844 on 26th May she reported her position and course of 115°, which meant that she would proceed parallel to and slightly east of the patrol line. At 2010 U.556 reported that *Bismarck*'s pursuers were hot on her heels. This U-boat under her outstanding commander, Lt. Wohlfahrt, was without torpedoes. Shortage of fuel had prevented her from taking up position as the second boat from the northern end of the patrol line, and she was still SO miles further north. Lt. Wohlfahrt commented in his War Diary:

"... 26th May, 1941:

Position: 640 miles west of Land's End. Wind: northwest, force 6-7, sea 5; weather clear, partly overcast; visibility moderate to good.

1531 Submerged because of aircraft. Heard several explosions like gunfire.

1948 Alarm. A battleship of King George class and an aircraft carrier, probably Ark Royal, suddenly sighted astern emerging from the mist at high speed. Inclination 170° right. If only I had torpedoes now! I should not even have to approach, as I am in exactly the right position for firing. No destroyers and no zig-zagging! I could get between them and finish them both off. The carrier has torpedo-bombers on board. I might have been able to help *Bismarck*.

2039 Surfaced. Sent signal: 'Enemy sighted: one battleship, one aircraft carrier, course 115°, high speed in 4So 20' North 16° 20' West. Vp to 2206 sent further signals on loss of contact, giving hydrophone bearings. I shall use the last of my fuel in an attempt to pursue them. Dive to listen, report hydrophone bearings and send homing signals.'…"

Bismarck was unable to proceed along the patrol line as intended. She encountered torpedo bombers, and at 2100 gave her position as 47° 20' North 14° 50' West, that is, SO miles east of the left flank of the patrol line. The ship was out of control. At 2142 a radio message of top priority ordered all boats with torpedoes to proceed directly towards her at maximum speed, but heavy weather prevented this. The boats battled against a sea of force 6 in their attempt to find her. U.73, which had torpedoes, made temporary contact with enemy forces between 0000 and 0230 on 27th May, but lost it in the squalls, despite the flashes of heavy guns. Only U.556 managed to remain in the vicinity for a few hours:

"… 26th May, 1941: Position: 420 miles west of Brest.

2330 Alarm. Destroyer suddenly approaching out of the mist. I am at 30 metres when she passes above. We can hear her screws. A narrow escape. No depth charges.

27th May:

0000 Northwest wind, force 5; sea 5, rain squalls, moderate visibility, very dark. Surfaced. What can I do for *Bismarck*? I can see her starshells and gun flashes. Sudden bursts of gunfire. It is an awful feeling to be so near, yet unable to help. I can only continue to reconnoitre and guide the U-boats that still have torpedoes. I maintain contact at the limit of visual range, report position and send homing signals to bring the other boats up.

0352 I proceed southwards on the eastern side. Fuel shortage will soon force me to return.

0400 Sea is increasing constantly. *Bismarck* is still fighting. Reported weather for aircraft and at 0630 sent my last shadowing report. Sighted U.74 and turned over to her by visual signal the duty of shadowing. I can still remain here by using my motors at dead slow. If I use Diesels, I will run out of fuel..."

The pitching boats could not take accurate bearings on the homing signals sent during the night by U.556 and *Bismarck*, and they were thus deprived of their only means of finding her, for the position she gave at 2100 was much further southeast than her true position. Even if the U-boats had reached her, it is doubtful whether in the prevailing weather they could have been useful.

About 0700 on 27th May, 1941, the Commander-in-Chief requested that a U-boat be sent to fetch his War Diary. Lt. Wohlfahrt was detailed, but did not receive the order until 1000 as enemy aircraft had forced him to submerge. *Bismarck* sank at about this time. The boats carefully searched the area up to 31st May, but picked up only three survivors.

122. South of Newfoundland Bank and back East

In connection with the *Bismarck* operation there were several German supply tankers in the North Atlantic which were also equipped for supplying the U-boats. U.lll and U.557 refuelled from the tanker Belchen in a position 120 miles southwest of Cape Farewell on 25th May and 2nd June respectively. While the tanker was supplying U.93 on 3rd June, she was sunk by a British destroyer. This put an end to the intended replenishment of all the western U-boat group. It was not known whether the sinking resulted from normal enemy search for German supply ships, or if the tanker's position had been betrayed by careless use of radio. U.93 embarked 50 survivors from the tanker and commenced to return. It was unfortunate that thus handicapped she chanced upon a convoy.

As no other boat had encountered targets since 22nd May, it seemed advisable to continue the move westwards towards the busy traffic area off Newfoundland Bank. On 1st June the western group was ordered to proceed a further 250 miles south. Their presence east of Newfoundland Bank seemed to be known, as U-boats arriving in the area sighted enemy ships at the southeast end of our patrol line and further south. It seemed therefore that shipping was making a southerly detour to avoid the boats. The traffic would probably be unable to circumvent the boats to the north via Newfoundland Bank, because of fog and ice. To check this, a U-boat was sent to Cape Race and Belle Isle Strait. On 6th June the patrol line was transferred 180 miles further south, and again on 13th June to the area southeast of Newfoundland Bank. The boats had never before been so far west, but again they failed to sight the enemy. Dönitz wrote in his War Diary of 20th June, 1941:

"... I had hoped to intercept convoys by concentrating the boats in what I thought to be a busy area. There are three possible reasons why no sightings were made:

(a) Ships may be using the waters around Newfoundland-despite the dangers from ice and fog-to avoid exposing themselves to attack.

(b) They may have gone south of the patrol line into the zone of the German surface raiders, where .U-boats do not operate.

(c) They may have broken through the patrol line under cover of fog, helped by their radar, which has considerable range.

"If either (a) or (b) should be the case, this shows that the enemy can disperse his convoy routes considerably, even as far west as Newfoundland, and therefore if our boats wish to find the nodal points of shipping they will have to operate west of 50° West, that is, off the Canadian and American ports of departure. But at present political considerations preclude this. Hence I have decided to evacuate the zone south of Newfoundland Bank, which offers only one type of shipping, namely the North-East traffic, and to station the U-boats in the narrowest part to the southeast of Greenland up to the edge of the zone reserved for our surface ships. The boats will be widely spaced in width and depth, which gives them as much chance of finding traffic as they would have on a patrol line."

On 20th June, the boats began to move northeast to take up this disposition, in which each would. have a depth of sweep of 100 miles. En route, U.203 encountered HX 133 some 450 miles south of Cape Farewell. Apparently this convoy *had* proceeded via Newfoundland Bank. In the next few days ten boats were involved in the action against it. Far apart and with their speed of advance sometimes limited by thick fog, the boats were slow in closing. This gave the enemy time to gather additional escort vessels, which sank the last two shadowers in 29° West and 18° West. The boats reported sinking six ships and damaging one. British records show that a further ship was damaged.

While pursuing HX 133, U.203 came upon and attacked a southbound OS convoy. Five more boats in the southeast tried to close the convoy, but increasing fog in the vicinity of Newfoundland Bank saved it from further attack.

The boats mentioned were now ordered to return to the east, and on 29th June, with five others, they were directed towards a convoy believed to be steering southwest. It had first been sighted by an aircraft some 300 miles west of Ireland, and reconnaissance aircraft again spotted it on 30th June and 1st July. This was the first instance where several boats succeeded in taking bearings of the homing signals by the shadowing aircraft, and in plotting a fairly accurate position of the target. But poor visibility and fog prevented the boats from reaching it. They also lost a northbound convoy which had been sighted for a short time on 2nd July. After this unsuccessful operation there was an uneventful period. From eight to twelve boats were stationed between Greenland and the Azores up to 15th July, but in this vast area they failed to encounter shipping. Operations at the end of June had shown how difficult it was, with such widely dispersed boats, to maintain contact and to close a sufficient number of U-boats for the attack. Closer dispositions would be more effective once a sighting had been made. On 14th July it was decided to close the boats up (71).

Most of the boats were now ordered to close in towards Britain in a northeasterly movement. On 17th July, before the move was completed, air reconnaissance sighted an outward bound convoy 60 miles south of Rockall Bank. Despite the decision in March that air sighting reports alone were not to govern the movements of boats, it was thought that something must be done to make up for all the recent failures to locate shipping. The air reports of 17th and 18th July, the bearings taken by the boats, and the convoy's aircraft warning reports picked up by our Radio Intercept Service all indicated that the convoy was steering a southwesterly course. Accordingly F.O. U-boats on the 19th drew up the five nearest boats in a patrol line across the estimated line of advance of the convoy, but on this vital day the two aircraft on reconnaissance failed to locate it. All available boats were formed into another long patrol line on the morning of the 20th. This the enemy by-passed. With no air reconnaissance to indicate which way the convoy had been deflected J there was no point in continuing the operation.

The boats did not return to the west. F.O. U-boats had come to the conclusion that without air reconnaissance in this large mid-Atlantic area results would not be forthcoming until more boats were available.

"... The attempt to intercept traffic in the west, where routes converge, has been fruitless. Fog and bad weather are largely to blame. From 21st July we shall attempt to locate shipping nearer the English coast. In this area the lengthening nights will help the boats to evade pursuit, and renewed attempts at direct co-operation with air reconnaissance will be possible..." (72).

This marked the end of the first searching movement across the Atlantic and back.

123. Operations against Russia

The small-scale U-boat operations in the initial stages of the Russian campaign are of only slight interest compared with Atlantic operations, though much later developments in the Baltic were to have a serious effect on the U-boat arm. The Supreme Command directive for operation "Barbarossa" states: "... Even in the event of an eastern campaign, Britain will remain the main objective of naval operations..." In accordance with this principle, the German Admiralty aimed at maintaining, and if possible increasing, pressure against Britain in the Atlantic. The preparatory order of 6th June, 1941, to the various naval headquarters stated that the U-boat campaign was to be continued (73). More single boats were to be sent to mid-Atlantic, so as to disperse enemy AIS forces. Some boats were to be ready to operate from Norwegian bases against any possible British action in the Norwegian area in support of Russia (74).

U-boat training in the Baltic would have to be severely curtailed because of the Baltic operations. As many training units as possible were to be transferred to Trondheim and the western Baltic. Any training boats which could not be used as such were to operate against Britain and, in the eastern Baltic, against Russia. Though F.O. U-boats insisted on the minimum interruption to training, it was agreed to place eight training U-boats on an operational basis. Five of these under F.O. Baltic were used for patrols near the Gulf of Riga and the Gulf of Finland, while the other three layoff Helsingor, ready to act in the event of British action in the Baltic entrances or off the Norwegian coast. Two small U-boats also were sent north of the Shetlands.

The five boats operating in the Baltic encountered few targets. They destroyed three Russian submarines and carried out valuable reconnaissance. Resulting from their observation of Russian return routes from Dago, E-boats were able to lay three TMB minefields, which were later effective. One of these U-boats was lost by mining. The others were not relinquished for training until the end of August.

FAILURE TO INTERCEPT

124. Own Radio under Suspicion
When, at the end of April, 1941, F.O. U-boats informed the Naval

Staff of his decision to dispose the U-boats further west, he ventured the opinion that the few convoy sightings in April were due not only to inherent factors such as the dispersion of routes in a vast area and the few U-boats, but also to a temporary reduction in or stoppage of enemy traffic. The Naval Staff's investigations did not bear this out. Neither the information gained by the Radio Intercept Service nor any other clues indicated a drop in traffic. Britain had to maintain a steady stream of imports, which could not be stopped or reduced for long, no matter how high her shipping losses might be. It was more likely that convoys might be systematically by-passing the U-boat formations (75).

The Naval Staff investigated this possibility and concluded that radio transmission by the boats had enabled the enemy to locate and avoid them. Analysing our own radio traffic, it seemed that the convoy SC 2 could have evaded us at the end of April. It was therefore decided to restrict the use of radio as far as possible. At the same time, radio deception was to be employed and a Radio Intelligence officer at the headquarters of F.O. U-boats was to make a comprehensive evaluation of the enemy Situation. This decision again raised in an acute form the question of the advantages and perils of radio in controlled operations.

125. Danger of Location by D/F

It had been known in peace-time that the British Navy had always devoted much attention to its D/F and location service. With stations from Land's End to the Shetlands, the base provided angles of intersection adequate for fixing all traffic east of the 35th meridian. IfBritish DjF stations were set up in Iceland, Greenland, Newfoundland, Spain and the Azores, this would allow fixes to be obtained by cross-bearings in the whole of the North Atlantic. It was certain that a D/F station in Iceland had been working for the British from 21st April, 1941, and further developments could be expected.

When Brest was occupied, the French Admiralty's radio messages were found almost intact, including a collection of short-wave bearings taken on U-boats by British and French DjF stations.

When the British submarine Seal was captured in May, 1940, an examination of her radio messages showed that during the Norwegian campaign the British Admiralty had several times supplied warships with short-wave bearings of U-boats and that British submarines had orders to maintain the strictest radio silence, because of the danger of being located.

In the first few months of the war careful examination of the enemy's use of DjF and his countermeasures had given no cause for alarm. The U-boat commanders reported that the enemy certainly obtained fixes on the boats. But his DjF system did not appear to be very accurate, according to the War Diary for 23rd January, 1940:

"... As far as can be ascertained, the enemy's errors in fixing by direction finding vary with the range from his coast. At 300 miles, the average error is 60 to 80 miles. Hitherto the best fix, immediately off the west coast of France, was 30 miles out. The worst error amounted to 320 miles at a range of 600 miles..."

The enemy rapidly improved his technique, for after the middle of 1940 the few instances of enemy direction finding picked up by our Radio Intercept Service were much more accurate. In October V,47 and other meteorological boats reported that even up to longitude 250 West they were nearly always pursued by enemy forces within one or two hours of making short signal weather reports. Our countermeasures-greater radio discipline, changing of frequencies and extensive adoption of " short signals" procedure-seemed unavailing against the efficient British DjF technique. We had to assume that all our radio messages and short signals would be fixed and probably exploited.

126. Possible Enemy Sources of Intelligence

Measures were taken to ascertain whether the enemy's diversion of traffic was the direct result of his own Radio Intelligence. The Naval Staff appointed a Radio Intelligence officer to the Staff of F.O. U-boats. In the past, insufficient attention had been paid to this subject by the U-boat Command. Now all available details of naval and merchant traffic collected from the U-boat reports, air reconnaissance, German Signals Intelligence, agents, meteorological trawlers and other German and Italian units were entered on a large map. The map also showed all information the enemy could possibly possess on U-boat positions derived from torpedoed ships, SSS reports, U-boat warning reports, sighting reports made by his aircraft, and U-boat radio messages, including short signals-presuming these to have been fixed by D/F. It was assumed that the enemy knew the exact number of boats leaving Germany and the French ports.

To check the accuracy of British D/F, the U-boats' position reports were taken from their War Diaries on their return, and compared with the decrypted British transmission of D/F bearings. All additional information on convoy routes from subsequently decrypted signals and other sources was entered in the evaluation maps. Independently and on a much larger scale, specialists of the main Radio Intelligence Centre at the German Admiralty also evaluated the enemy situation. F.O. U-boats utilised their analyses in conjunction with the U-boat commanders' reports (76).

On 7th June, 1941, a comparison between the investigations by F.O. U-boats and those of the Radio Intelligence Centre seemed to show that enemy reactions had not been the result of the boats' use of radio, but were due to sightings, attacks by U-boats and navigational and tactical data. It was shown that despite radio transmission by the boats, and sinkings and convoy battles in the area under examination, the enemy had often continued to run his single ships or convoys through that area. It was not clear why the British Commander-in-Chief Western Approaches, who was in charge of the routing, followed this procedure.

The following conclusions were drawn:

- the enemy obtained fairly accurate fixes of all our radio transmissions;
- every use of radio helped to complete the enemy's picture of the situation and might lead to by-passing the boats;
- the investigation failed to discover whether and how the enemy reacted, and this uncertainty would continue.

127. Control of Radio Traffic

F.O. U-boats now devised methods which would eliminate the less important radio messages. The principles were given in Standing Order No. 243 of 9th June, 1941:

"In the attack area: Radio is to be used only for messages of tactical importance or on request from the Command, or if the enemy is already aware of the boats' positions.

On passage: As above. Occasional transmission of less important information may be made if it is certain that succeeding boats or those already in the area concerned will not be endangered.

Technical: Wavelengths are to be changed frequently; additional channels to be introduced; new radio procedure to make it difficult for the enemy to take bearings."

These instructions did not result in any marked reduction in the use of radio, for the passing of "messages of tactical importance" still involved frequent transmission.

128. Radio Deception

Since it was found impossible to reduce the radio traffic substantially without sacrificing sinkings, measures had to be adopted-such as synchronisation or separation of the time and areas for transmission of messages-to make it harder for the enemy to deduce the true situation. Indispensable transmissions included the following: entering or leaving Biscay, commencement of homeward journey, weather, fuel remaining. The Naval Staff's proposal to use radio deception evoked this comment from F.O. U-boats:

"... The employment of radio deception for the purpose of simulating that certain areas are occupied and others unoccupied by U-boats seems admirable in theory, but in practice it is extremely complicated. The experts on the problem are faced with the difficulty of following the thought processes of the enemy. There is also the danger of inaccurate D/F bearings by the enemy, which might defeat the purpose of the scheme..."

However, small-scale deception schemes were tried out. On 29th June, 1941, several homeward-bound boats were ordered to transmit while southwest of Ireland in order to dissuade a convoy, sighted by the *Luftwaffe* 300 miles west of Ireland, from evading to the south.

With many more U-boats at sea it would perhaps be possible, by means of carefully planned transmissions schedules from all boats-whether on passage or on operations-to give the Command a complete picture of the situation while at the same time confusing the enemy as to the true location of the attacking formations. But this idea was never put into practice, and F.O. U-boats had to base his decisions on the few radio messages that the boats could safely send. This handicapped operational control, particularly in 1941, when there was so little help from air reconnaissance.

129. Questions of the Betrayal of U-boat Positions

During investigations early in 1941 on certain minor operational failures, a suspicion arose that the enemy had further unknown sources of information on U-boat dispositions. This suspicion was first mentioned in the War Diary on 18th April, 1941 ;

"Outside her attack area, U.94 at times encountered heavy north-south traffic about 240 miles east of Greenland. U.101 had a similar experience in the same locality, also outside her attack area. These observations give the impression that British traffic had been diverted around our attacking formations because the enemy had learned of their location from an unknown source. This might explain the failure of the convoy operation in co-operation with the *Luftwaffe* on 4th March. The convoy should have been intercepted that day by a reconnaissance line (of U-boats) and on 5th March by a patrol line. It was first reported steering a westerly course. After the first reconnaissance line had been directed into position, the convoy deviated far to the . north, thus avoiding the second patrol line which would otherwise have been in a favourable position for attack.

"Although much of this is conjecture, every possibility of security leakage must be obviated at all costs. Within the U-boat service I have ordered that as few people as possible should have knowledge of the boats' operations. For the same reason I have cancelled the daily position reports to Group West, Air Commander Atlantic, and

Liaison Officer, Bordeaux. Outside the U-boat service, Commander-in-Chief Navy has restricted to the minimum the stations which may tune to the U-boat wavelength, thus eliminating unauthorised use. All offices which, for operational or technical reasons, must use the U-boat wavelength have been informed of this suspected leakage of information and have been ordered to preserve absolute secrecy and severely restrict the number of persons who have access. The Commander in-Chief Navy has also approved my request for the introduction of a special cypher for U-boats."

This cypher-introduced in the summer of 1941-prevented unauthorised persons from knowing about the operations. It was supplied only to offices concerned with U-boat communications. Under the new arrangement the *Fliegerführer* Atlantic and the liaison officer with the Italians at Bordeaux received only occasional reviews of the U-boat situation, while Naval Group West no longer received the U-boat signals by land-line, but tuned in to the radio frequencies used by the boats.

The danger of leakage was greater in the German Admiralty. Vp to May, 1941, the practice here had been to make copies of the plotting-room chart of dispositions, which were available to a small number of staff officers. The dispositions were also sent daily by teleprinter to the German Admiral in the Balkans and to the German Naval Command in Italy, though there was no real reason why they should have this information (77). This practice was perhaps typical of the German inclination to pass on secrets to other authorities, which may well have been accessible to enemy agents at some point along the route. Whereas F.O. U-boats had already restricted access in his own service, he had been unaware until now of this wider distribution to outside authorities.

A further step towards security was taken on 9th September, 1941, when it was decided to encode the naval grid squares, before passing the en clair texts to the cypher office. Using a bigram code which changed at irregular intervals, all grid squares in the North Atlantic were encoded. The system was not infallible, but served the purpose of concealing the actual positions of U-boats from communications personnel and others who were not allowed access to the map room.

JULY - SEPTEMBER, 1941
RETURN TO THE EASTERN ATLANTIC

130. Air Reconnaissance

For ten weeks the Eastern Atlantic had been unoccupied by our boats, because of enemy patrols which restricted their freedom of movement. During this period conditions had not improved, and it now seemed necessary to accept these difficult conditions rather than to operate in less dangerous areas where traffic could not be located. The boats would be helped by the time of year, when the longer nights made it easier for them to evade pursuit. By returning to the east, another attempt could be made at direct co-operation with air reconnaissance. With more aircraft available, two to three could be expected for daily reconnaissance. Meanwhile, at the instigation of the *Luftwaffe*, IjK.G.40 had been transferred from F.O. U-boats to the command of Colonel Harlinghausen, *Fliegerführer* Atlantic, who ensured smooth co-operation. F.O. U-boats attributed the resulting improvement to' the anxiety of the German Air Force and perhaps of Goring himself to prove that direct subordination of this unit to the U-boat Command was not the best arrangement. As an expert, the *Fliegerführer* could naturally get better results from the Geschwader than any outsider. To the credit of his crews it must be said that they carried out their assignment enthusiastically and courageously.

Only four days after the new easterly disposition of the U-boats, the first convoy battle began. Among the many joint actions, the operations against OG 69, SL 81, HG 69, OG 71 and OS 4 are worthy of mention. In all cases strong formations of U-boats and aircraft were involved. The targets were Gibraltar and SL convoys, which for a large part of their voyage often came within range of the aircraft based at Bordeaux.

The part played by the Radio Intelligence Service during these weeks was appreciable. Their information was derived not only from cryptography, but mainly from an analysis of the intercepted radio traffic, which was heavy. The concentration of U-boats just off England forced the British Commander-in-Chief, Western Approaches, to transmit many instructions to his convoys and stragglers. Between July and the beginning of September many convoy positions were so promptly decrypted that the boats were able to take action. But in only two cases, against OG 69 and SL 81, were the boats able to act on sighting reports from aircraft to intercept and attack successfully. Contrary to expectations, the aircraft proved valuable, less in intercepting the convoys-only OG 71 was sighted by an aircraft-than in homing successive boats towards the convoys. This enabled convoy battles to be protracted up to eight days, often exposing the crews and particularly the commanders to great physical and mental strain.

131. Exaggerated Reports of Sinkings

Sinkings from January to June, 1941, were mostly accurately reported, but from July onwards figures were inexact and often greatly exaggerated, especially as regards Gibraltar convoys. The boats often reported the sinking of vessels which did not belong to the convoy concerned, but which were proceeding independently, or had become separated from other convoys. They also over-estimated the size of ships, particularly in the Gibraltar convoys.

The commanders were so convinced that their estimates were correct that F.O. U-boats was induced to believe them. In the case of sinkings from OG 71, an average size of ship of 5,0006,000 tons was claimed, whereas the true size was 1,500-2,000 tons. It was believed at Headquarters that in OG 71, apart from the rather small ships identified by name, there had been a number of larger ships unknown to our agents in Spain (77a). The tendency to overestimataion by U-boat Commanders is shown in the following table:

Convoy	U-boat Reports	British Admiralty Figures
OG 69	Sunk: 13 ships, totalling 71,000 tons	9 ships, totalling 25,000 tons
	Damaged: 3 ships	
SL 81	Sunk: 4 ships, totalling 24,500 tons	6 ships, totalling 27,500 tons
	Damaged: 6 ships	
OG 71	Sunk: 15 ships, totalling 90,000 tons	8 ships, totalling 13,000 tons
	Damaged: 5 ships	
OS 4	Sunk: 5 ships	5 ships, totalling 30,000 tons

132. Homing Signals Procedure

In January, 1941, the U-boats had made the first attempt to take bearings on homing signals sent by an aircraft. after further attempts during the first phase of air co-operation had failed, all U-boats and aircraft were given general instructions for homing procedure. On sighting a convoy, an aircraft, using trailing aerial, sent long-wave homing signals which the boats picked up and re-transmitted by short signal to F.O. U-boats. The pilot then shadowed in or above the clouds at the limit of visual range, avoiding enemy aircraft and anti-aircraft defences in order to continue transmission as long as possible.

While the U-boat commanders, acting on the homing signals, adjusted their course and speed to intercept the convoy the various U-boat positions and bearings of homing signals were plotted at Headquarters. Within a few minutes-after elimination of errors in bearings and dead reckoning and differences in reckoning between the aircraft and the convoy-Headquarters transmitted to the boats a corrected convoy position.

As the convoys hauled well to the west, lack of fuel often

prevented the aircraft from shadowing and sending homing signals for more than a few minutes. The boats could only utilise these signals if they had been warned of the DjF wave and the time of arrival of the aircraft in the convoy area, to give them time to set up their DjF frames and tune their receivers. It was also important to ensure rapid transmission of this warning. It took five to ten minutes from the aircraft via Air Commander Atlantic and F.O. U-boats to the boats themselves. For various technical reasons Ruch as lack of sets and personnel, and differences in radio procedure there could be no direct radio contact between the aircraft and the boats.

It was now possible to check the aircraft's convoy sighting reports by comparing them with positions obtained by cross-bearings. In many cases the errors were so great that the boats would have been unable to find the convoy without the homing signals. The sending of the aircraft's homing signals thus took precedence over reporting the position, and aircraft observers were ordered to report information in the following sequence: sighting of the convoy, warning of homing signals, sending of homing signals, fixing own position and then a report of the convoy's estimated position.

Owing to shortage of aircraft it was seldom possible to provide reliefs for shadowers. If two or three aircraft were in readiness, they took off at specified intervals, so that their homing signals would be sent over a slightly longer period.

The reverse procedure of the boats leading the aircraft on to a convoy by homing signals was again tried out in August, 1941. A homeward-bound boat was ordered to take up position as a radio beacon on the route of a convoy presumed making for Bordeaux. This allowed the aircraft under cloud cover to check their dead-reckoning position with the more accurate U-boat position. Normally however this procedure was not practicable. There was no certain means of identifying the nationality of a distant aircraft, and the boats could not be expected to remain on the surface as an aircraft approached.

133. Northwest of the North Channel
Unsuccessful Operation without Air Support

As the boats were all stationed between the west of Ireland and Gibraltar, the more northerly shipping could avoid the dangerous area. Increased radio traffic in the area south of Iceland at the beginning of August seemed to indicate that this was in fact happening. F.O. U-boats therefore decided to draw up a pack in that area also, composed mainly of boats on their first operation. Shortage of aircraft precluded support by air reconnaissance, but it was hoped that by luring the enemy's A/S forces to the area west of Ireland, the now greater number of boats in the north would have some freedom of movement for interception.

This expectation was not realised. No traffic was found, apart from three convoys sighted simultaneously on 10th and 11th August, by the boats while they were proceeding to their operational area. The attempt in the north persisted for three weeks. Changes were made in the formations, the distances between the boats, the depth of sweep and the orders on procedure; all without success. Even attempts to operate on convoys whose positions were reported by Radio Intelligence were frustrated owing to the strong air patrol, presumably based in Iceland.

It was astonishing to find this seemingly ubiquitous air patrol. The U-boat Command took a long time to realise that the increased effectiveness of the air patrol was not due to more enemy aircraft but to their radar equipment (AS V Mark 2).

134. Enemy Radar and Escorts

Fighting conditions became much more difficult as a result of radar equipment carried by enemy aircraft and destroyers. During the unsuccessful attack on HG 69, F.O. U-boats commented in his War Diary on 13th August:

"... Although this time we have managed to come very close to the enemy and several boats must be in the immediate vicinity, no enemy reports have been received up to the afternoon. It must be assumed that the enemy's destroyers are using radar to force the

U-boats to withdraw before they can make contact. The U-boats have been instructed on the best ways of evading this surface location. According to air reconnaissance, there is a cruiser in the convoy's escort: possibly she is employing radar to direct the other escorts. At any rate it seems that the shadowing of this convoy is proving exceptionally difficult..."

On 20th August, F.O. U-boats wrote:

"... The Greenland group has made no contact with the enemy. As the number of boats was sufficient to expect interception it may be that shipping in this area has been r.educed. It is suspected that the convoys may be taking diversionary action with the help of long-range radar, but even so in the prevailing good visibility the masts of the leading ships or destroyers should have been sighted..."

At this time it was only suspected that the larger escort vessels were able to locate U-boats at a great range. The incautious behaviour of many escort vessels, even during night convoy battles, seemed to indicate that in general they were still dependent on visual observation. The only course was to order the U-boats to look out for any signs of radar equipment and to report all their observations, which were passed on to the specialists' who had the task of evolving countermeasures. Perhaps we were too late in appreciating the momentous importance of this problem of radar (78).

Three weeks of battles against Gibraltar convoys showed that-apart from their greater effectiveness, probably owing to radar-enemy A/S forces had increased to an astonishing degree. Not only had the numbers of escort vessels and aircraft risen, but their methods of keeping the U-boats at a distance had improved. Where a few months ago one U-boat had been adequate for shadowing, a whole group was now required.

As far as the U-boat commanders and air observers could ascertain, the convoys had both inner and outer screens. The latter increased the difficulties of making contact, for the boats were kept at a distance from which they could not discover the position of the convoy in relation to the escorts. Even if they did find this out and prepared to attack, they had first to haul ahead, by-pass the escorts or proceed under them, which entailed a considerable loss of time and often meant losing the forward attacking position for which they had striven.

By day it was impossible to haul ahead inside the outer screen. At night these escort vessels usually closed in round the ships to increase the direct protection. To break up this defensive ring, F.O. U-boats decided to attempt a simultaneous night attack by a number of boats at a predetermined hour. Such a procedure was contrary to all pre-war experience. Its failure merely confirmed that it was impossible to achieve tactical control during an attack.

A further means of scattering the ring of escorts was to take offensive action against them. On 13th August the commanders were ordered in future to exploit every opportunity for attacking escort, vessels, and-even in unpromising circumstances-to fire a spread of torpedoes at them. The old procedure-to go for the shipping first and only attack escort vessels if they offered a "sitting shot" - was abandoned. In the long run, attack was the only means of compelling individual escort vessels to behave more cautiously. The best weapon against escorts, a homing torpedo (later named Zaunkonig), was still in the experimental stage.

Notwithstanding the difficulty of attacking the Gibraltar and SL convoys in face of the enemy's air and sea patrols, the results gave F.O. U-boats no immediate cause for concern. The young commanders-some on their first operation-succeeded in breaking through the convoy escorts to score successes. Moreover U-boat losses were surprisingly low. With the near prospect of many more boats, the impending introduction of the anti-destroyer torpedo, and the possibility of radar countermeasures, Dönitz was confident that his boats would prove equal to even harder conditions.

135. The Return to the West
Southwest of Ireland operations against convoys with the help of air reconnaissance continued into September, 1941. But despite many reports of convoys the past few weeks had brought only one large-

scale action. The group in this area was not kept up to strength, and operations were terminated on 12th September. Six boats having still sufficient fuel were moved to the west and north of the Hebrides to expend their torpedoes during the new moon period.

In July and August sin kings had been slight. It was once more decided to alter the battle area. The War Diary of 16th September states:

"... U-boats should not be concentrated in areas normally covered by enemy air patrols, as the enemy is then able to divert his traffic round them. Only short-term concentration promises success in such areas, more especially if a specific target is expected. But if the boats have to wait for long periods before making contact, it seems right to dispatch them to distant areas where there will be no fear of their detection before they can strike."

Despite the unsatisfactory results of the first search across the Atlantic in June; a second westward thrust could now be risked, particularly as the number of available boats had greatly increased.

The next few months saw only occasional operations in the Eastern Atlantic. In accordance with the policy decided on 16th September, the boats did not attack convoys here except when their numbers and relative positions at the moment of sighting offered favourable prospects.

SEPTEMBER -NOVEMBER, 1941
OPERATIONS COVER THE WHOLE
NORTH ATLANTIC

136. Mobile Groups

The need for a change of method was apparent. At first this took the form of a change of area, when the boats were sent to the west, while there was yet no thought of altering the form of tactics. The first westerly sweep from May to July, 1941, had failed owing to lack of boats. Another type of operation now evolved gradually. The whole area between Britain and Newfoundland, Greenland and the Azores was occupied by from two to four groups of boats, which were kept moving more rapidly over greater areas. Patrol lines, regarded as the most suitable means of interception and attack, were extensively used. The pack system remained in force.

It should be emphasised that neither the Staff of the U-boat Command nor the Naval Staff was conscious at the time of the individual phases which marked the almost complete transition in 1941 to a new method of operation. Fundamental conditions remained constant; the fighting efficiency of the boats was unchanged with few boats in vast areas, German air reconnaissance was inadequate while strong enemy air and naval patrols were encountered. It was extremely difficult to establish clear conceptions for a change in methods and tactics. We had to adapt ourselves to the altering conditions which were imposed on us.

In describing this period it is necessary to abandon chronological presentation and to furnish a clear survey from the point of view of the operations of the individual U-boat groups. Several successive large-scale movements can be recognised.

Movement No.1: From southwest of Iceland in a westerly direction via the southern tip of Greenland and Belle Isle Strait to Cape Race.

Movement No.2: From west of the North Channel to mid-Atlantic, eastwards to meet an ON convoy and westwards as far as Newfoundland Bank with this convoy. The group dissolved here.

Movement No.3: From west of Ireland, northwest as far as 300 miles south of Greenland, then towards Newfoundland Bank, northwards with SC 42 and further to the south coast of Greenland. From here, southeast to mid-Atlantic.

Movement No.4: From southwest of Ireland, southwards as far as east of the Azores, then northwest to mid-Atlantic. Here joined up with Movement No.3.

Two smaller movements: From southwest of Ireland, southwards with OG convoys and northwards with HG convoys.

137. Movement No.1

Movement No.1 began on 6th September, when the boats in close formation southwest of Iceland assumed a spread disposition between Iceland and the east coast of Greenland. The suspicion was confirmed that homeward-bound traffic was being diverted to the northwest. SC 42 was intercepted just off Greenland. The distances between individual boats prevented some of them from reaching the convoy, but the others attacked in succession with very good results, claiming the sinking of 20 ships. According to British records the number was sixteen. The sinking figures would have been even higher if fog had not descended on the night of 12th/13th October, hindering the boats' approach and making it more difficult to regain contact. In spite of the distance from the Iceland bases, the convoy's escort was surprisingly strong, and for the first time included air escort at night.

Most of the boats which took part in the action against SC 42 returned to base. The others formed a patrol line in a southeasterly direction from the southern tip of Greenland. This move was successful. On 18th October they made contact with SC 44. Throughout the ensuing operation the boats were at a disadvantage in that atmospherics interfered with radio reception to such an extent that Command Headquarters received no shadowing reports, while the boats picked up only corrupt messages, so that only five of them learned of the presence of the target. Again, heavy fog and mist from 20th October onwards caused loss of contact. The U-boats reported sinking seven ships. British figures mention only four.

The patrol line had become so short on 26th September that it was advisable to dissolve it. The commanders had more freedom of movement in long north-south sectors north of 54° North. Here they operated until the end of the month, when they were ordered to proceed in a southeasterly direction. The intention was not to evacuate the area, but only to leave it for a short time until, with the help of further approaching boats, a strong group could be formed on 10th October. This plan did not mature, for the first wave of boats to leave Biscay towards Cape Farewell was directed against OG 75 on 2nd October, while on 15th October a second wave was drawn into the operation against SC 48, sighted by the boat on the south flank of the patrol line . Thus by the middle of October there were only four boats southeast of Cape Farewell-too few for interception and attack. As it had long been intended to investigate the traffic situation off Belle Isle Strait, F.O. U-boats sent the boats to that area.

Apart from this watching task, the boats were to act as reconnaissance for two fairly large patrol lines, which had been formed with the boats of Movements 2 and 3. They lay between Greenland and Newfoundland, covering a large part of the convoy route from Cape Race to Greenland and from Cape Race .to the North Channel. Apparently no traffic ran through Belle Isle Strait. The boats therefore continued south to within 100 miles of Cape Race. The scouting task was successful. One boat sighted SC 52 some 80 miles east of St. John's. While this shadower proceeded north with the convoy, the other three boats remained as long as fuel permitted off Newfoundland Bank and then returned to base, sighting little traffic and sinking only two ships.

138. Movement No. 2

Movement No.2 began on 10th October. This second wave en route for Greenland had already become engaged with SC 48. The boats maintained contact with this convoy, running northeast at first and later east. Finally they were involved in a fierce battle with the strengthened naval escorts and with some Sunderland aircraft which appeared at 26° West. The U-boats reported nine ships sunk, and these figures are confirmed.

After the action it was decided to combine this movement with the next wave (Movement No.3) for operations against eastbound traffic from Cape Race. However, they did not join up, for the boats of Movement No.3 were delayed west of Ireland by small-scale operations which brought no particular results.

Movement No.2 proceeded to the patrol line as ordered and on 26th October, was sent further south where our Radio Intelligence estimated they would find a westbound convoy. On 27th October a boat of Movement No.3 (U.74) sighted a westbound convoy 300 miles west of Ireland. This may have been the ON convoy expected from Radio Intelligence, and Movement No.2 proceeded east at maximum speed to intercept it, then turned west and pursued it, at times in bad weather, for nearly 800 miles. The skilled handling of the escorts and, even more, the high convoy speed of 10-11 knots, kept the attackers at a distance, or at least prevented them from gaining a forward attacking position, so that the convoy escaped with only one ship sunk.

That was the end of Movement No.2. Most of the boats had expended their fuel in the long, fast chase. On their return passage three were able to join up with Movement No.4 against a southbound convoy.

139. Movement No. 3

A wave of boats, which left harbour almost simultaneously, was intended to assume the patrol line between Cape Race and Greenland, but became temporarily involved in two small-scale operations 350 miles west of Fastnet Rock. On 20th and 21st October, they attacked a homeward-bound formation of four large, fast ships, sinking the British transport Aurania. On 21st and 22nd October they operated against a homeward-bound convoy, but in the bad weather only two ships were torpedoed. Thereafter this group proceeded to the intended patrol line, leaving this on 30th October to move towards Newfoundland Bank and the mass of traffic off Cape Race.

On 1st November, as already mentioned, a scout (from Movement No.1) sighted SC 52. Movement No.3, favourably situated for an operation against it, proceeded at maxim urn speed so as to intercept on convoy courses between 020° and 070°. Contact was made and lost in the intermittent fog. Again atmospherics interfered with radio traffic, so that the Command was unable to assist with directions. A convoy was sighted in fog on 3rd November, but it was not clear whether this was a succeeding one following the same route. In the opinion of the searching boats the first convoy had made a deviation into Belle Isle Strait. Although many boats took part in the search, the fog prevented location and the operation was abandoned on 4th November. Good prospects had again been spoiled by the weather. Three ships were reported sunk and three damaged. The British Admiralty gives a total of four ships and one straggler sunk. Those boats of Movement No.3 having adequate fuel continued far north to form a patrol line southeast of Cape Farewell. Those with less fuel remained in the area off St. John's and Cape Race. For several days the patrol line failed to intercept the enemy and on 10th November, the boats were directed to proceed southeastwards. On 12th November they joined the boats of Movement No.4 in mid-Atlantic, where they operated unsuccessfully against several convoys including ONS 33. The only information on the latter convoy was a position derived from Radio Intelligence on 11th November.

140. Movement No.4

Another wave of boats which left port almost simultaneously was ordered on 31st October, while crossing the Bay of Biscay, to intercept a south-bound convoy originally sighted by an outward bound boat 500 miles west of Ireland. Coming in successively from great distances, the boats were unable to maintain contact long enough to achieve the necessary concentration for attack. German aircraft were only just able to reach the convoy on 2nd November. Further take-offs could not be made owing to ground fog at the Bordeaux airport. For four days the boats searched to the south between 21° and 24° West; they were joined by three large boats returning from the Freetown area. On 5th November the search was abandoned and a patrol line formed to search for an HG convoy which had put out from Gibraltar on 1st November.

For a week the various patrol lines searched the area northeast of the Azores for an HG convoy, SL 91 (reported by Radio Intelligence) and OG convoys. In spite of air support-on one day six aircraft were on reconnaissance-all measures were unavailing. On 10th November the group was directed to proceed northwest to mid-Atlantic. Here they continued with Movement No.3 from

Greenland to search for ONS 11 and other England-U.S. convoys. These measures were terminated with the formation of a patrol line almost 500 miles broad between Ireland and the Azores to intercept Gibraltar and SL convoys. As this formation was also unsuccessful, the Command concluded that at this stage of the war the patrol line was unsuitable as a method of interception, and decided to change over to smaller, looser groups. The new disposition of four small groups was ordered on 19th November but never formed, for on 22nd November the Naval Staff ordered U-boat operations to be concentrated in the Mediterranean and off Gibraltar. The resulting evacuation of the main battle area in the North Atlantic and the interruption in the controlled operations against U.S.-England convoys lasted until January, 1942. This order also affected a new group of boats off Newfoundland, which was to attempt to penetrate the harbours of St. John's and Conception Bay. On 23rd November it was ordered to proceed towards Gibraltar.

141. Attacks on Gibraltar Convoys
Independently of these four large-scale movements, two smaller actions were fought against Gibraltar convoys. The experiences of July and August had shown that it was useless to expect results against these convoys unless they had first been tracked by air reconnaissance or by a shadowing boat. From September, 1941, operational procedure was adjusted accordingly; in two cases the boats left the Bay of Biscay, went south for an operation against an OG convoy and returned to the north with an HG convoy-South with OG 74 and OG 75, north with HG 73 and HG 75.

OG 74 was sighted by an outward-bound boat on 20th September. One other boat took part in the pursuit. The U-boats correctly reported five ships sunk. After losing contact, both boats continued southwards where a homeward-bound Gibraltar convoy, HG 73, had been sighted by Italian boats. The Italian boat J.8 re-intercepted the convoy on 23rd September and provided data for air reconnaissance, whose homing signals led the boats to their target on 25th September. Two more boats joined in the operation, which had to be abandoned

194

after six days when the ships approached land. The boats reported sinking 18 ships, but nine only are given in British records.

OG 75 was sighted by a reconnaissance aircraft west of the North Channel on 2nd October and air contact was renewed on two more days. No boat sighted the convoy until the sixth day of the operation. Visibility was at times unfavourable and a strong head sea persisted while the boats pursued the enemy for eleven days as far as west of Gibraltar. On an average, air reconnaissance sighted the convoy only for a limited period every second day, and it was necessary to open out the boats for search purposes. But this meant that when the convoy was again found by air reconnaissance, the boats took too long to close, so that the necessary concentration was not achieved, and no attacks materialised. Owing to underestimation of the convoy's speed by the Command, the boats were behind the convoy for several days and on 13th October they abandoned the chase, which had lasted eleven days without result.

From previous experience it was anticipated that our agents in Spain would promptly furnish information on the next HG convoy from Gibraltar. The boats were therefore given waiting positions west of the Strait. The sailing of the convoy was delayed for four days, presumably because the enemy had knowledge of the boats' presence. The boats clung to the convoy from the day of sailing until 29th October, reporting six ships sunk and eight damaged. British Admiralty figures give four sunk.

142. The Patrol Line Formation proves Ineffective

On 19th November the long patrol line was abandoned in favour of small groups . F.O. U-boats gave the following reasons for this measure:

"... The patrol line, which, during the last few days, has been operating against an OG convoy and an expected SL convoy, brought no success and has been dissolved. Theoretically a narrow patrol line has more chance of intercepting enemy traffic than a wide formation of single boats. In practice, however, single boats have found convoys, whereas with one exception, no patrol line has located the enemy without the help of a previous sighting report from a detached boat. Why this should be is not clear. It cannot depend on chance, because chance does not always favour the one side, and this state of affairs will soon have existed for more than nine months. It is possible that from some source or other the British obtain information on our concentrated formations, and take diversionary measures which occasionally lead them into the path of detached boats. Their information might be gained:

(a) As a result of treachery: We have done everything to obviate this possibility, by encoding the naval grid square reference numbers, by limiting the users of the radio frequency and by adopting our own U-boat cypher. The circle of informed personnel is so restricted that it is difficult to see where the leakages could occur.

(b) By decrypting our radio messages: the Naval Staff continually checks. up on this possibility, but regards it as out if the question.

(c) By co-ordinating radio traffic analysis and sighting reports: We cannot judge this as we do not know how much information the enemy gains from sighting reports and radio traffic, or how accurate is his DjF organisation. F.O. U-boats has this question constantly in mind. In many cases we have observed that the enemy has not drawn the expected conclusions from information known to be in his possession. That may be because his giant organisation is too cumbersome for quick reaction or, on the other hand, because his conclusions are derived from further data of which. we are ignorant. At any rate, we have so far found it impossible to understand the enemy's thought processes and conclusions, although efforts are constantly made to do so.

Closer co-operation with our Radio Intelligence Service might be helpful in this problem. I intend to achieve this by requesting the appointment to my staff of an experienced Signals Intelligence Officer. This should help to establish further means of probing into the enemy's intentions.

(d) By radar: This may be helping the enemy to take avoiding action, but so far we have no confirmation.

"All these possibilities are not enough to explain the failure of our concentrated formations, and it has' therefore been decided to employ another method. The boats will be formed into several groups, not too far apart, so that if any boat sights a convoy, the others will be able to come up relatively quickly. I do not intend these groups to be stationary, but to move about constantly, to make it more difficult for the enemy to escape..."

But the crisis in the Mediterranean led to a suspension of operations in the Atlantic, so that these plans for new operational dispositions were not realised.

143. Consideration for U.S.A. causes Restriction in Attacks

The original boundary of the blockade area around Britain, announced by the German Government on 17th August, 1940, had been extended to the west and north on 1st April, 1941, when it transpired that Iceland was being used as a British naval base. The new boundary ran from a point 45° North 20° West in a northwesterly direction to 59° North 38° West, then along the three-mile limit off Greenland, enclosing the whole area around Iceland.

Directions for the conduct of the war against shipping had changed only slightly since August, 1940. U.S. ships were still in a privileged category. To avoid incidents with the U.S.A. their ships, even if carrying contraband, could not be taken in prize or sunk outside the blockade area. Indeed they could not even be stopped, and the special clause in the Prize Regulations-allowing the sinking of neutral ships which passed information to the enemy-did not apply to U.S. ships.

In the spring of 1940 this attitude towards the U.S.A. had for the first time interfered with operations, when for political reasons a joint minelaying operation off Halifax by aU-boat and an auxiliary cruiser had to be abandoned. In June 1941, during the first U-boat sweep across the Atlantic, the same reasons prevented the boats from penetrating west of Newfoundland Bank (80). The cancellation of this operational plan was more serious. West of Newfoundland Bank, off the southern estuary of the St. Lawrence River and off Halifax, lay the second main area of concentrated British convoy traffic.

Being less strictly patrolled, it offered more chances of interception and attack than mid-Atlantic or the Eastern Atlantic.

In April, 1941, the U.S.A. had begun to establish forces in Greenland. This increased the chances of encountering U.S: shipping and warships in the western North Atlantic. When iIi the middle of May they crossed the western boundary of the blockade area for the first time, the U-boats were again expressly directed to observe the regulations regarding attacks outside the "operational zone." They were forbidden to attack any independently routed warships, or warships acting as convoy escort, until it had been definitely established that they were enemy ships or unless they were darkened, or first opened fire.

Hitler believed that the war with Russia would be short, and once terminated, he thought he could continue to keep the U.S.A. out of the war. Incidents at sea which might lead to a deterioration of the political situation had to be avoided at all costs. That such incidents could occur very easily was shown by a report from U.203 on 20th June, 1941, two days before" Barbarossa." On this day the boat had sighted the U.S. battleship *Texas* inside the blockade area and in accordance with existing orders had attempted to attack her. As a result, the following order was issued to the Atlantic boats on 21st June, 1941:

"... The *Führer* has ordered that during the next few weeks all incidents with the U. S .A. are to be avoided. Procedure is to conform to this order in every conceivable case. Until further notice, only clearly identifiable enemy cruisers, battleships and aircraft carriers may be attacked. Should darkened warships be sighted, this is no proof that they are hostile" (81).

This was a very unwelcome order, for it meant that the U-boats could no longer attack their worst enemies, destroyers, frigates and corvettes, even in convoy battles. Freedom of attack was even more restricted than it had been against French ships during the first few weeks of the war, which was an unparalleled situation.

F.O. U-boats and the Naval Staff thoroughly understood the

difficult position of the U-boats and did everything in their power to have the order amended. Early in July, after Roosevelt's statement on the occupation of Iceland by U.S. troops, Raeder unsuccessfully petitioned the *Führer* for the cancellation of the order. Wishing to avoid all incidents with the U.S.A., Hitler further decreed that U.S. merchant ships were not to be attacked even within the blockade area (82). But the onus of establishing nationality before attacking could not be accepted, for in practice this would mean the suspension of all attacks by U-boats.

By an amendment issued in August, attacks were permitted on all destroyers and smaller warships provided they were within the old German blockade area, declared on 17th August, 1940, whose boundary coincided with the U.S.A. zone along the 20th meridian. Outside this area, that is, within the new blockade area of 1st April, 1941, all clearly identifiable enemy warships might be attacked. But at night the nationality of darkened ships could not be established, and so in practice warships with convoys, single destroyers and AIS vessels could not be attacked.

The *Greer* incident of 7th September, 1941, caused the Naval Staff to approach the Supreme Command once more with a view to having this order relaxed. On 4th September U.652 had been attacked with depth-charges by a U.S. destroyer some 180 miles southwest of Reykjavik. In self-defence she had fired two torpedoes at the destroyer. Hitler approved the action of the U-boat commander, but orders were issued to all boats that even if attacked, they were not free to take offensive action by way of retaliation (83).

On 12th July, 1941, President Roosevelt had permitted U.S. Naval forces to attack U-boats, and on the 29th a U.S. patrol vessel east of Greenland attacked one boat. There were further incidents on 18th October (U.S.S. Kearney) and on 29th October Mr. Knox, Secretary of the Navy, released details to the press about actions against U-boats. Despite these hostile acts, the German order forbidding attacks on darkened ships remained in force until the U.S.A. entered the war on 11th December, 1941. All this greatly increased the boats' difficulties in their attempts to sink British merchant ships. The author, whose boat, U.107, took part in the attack on SL 87 west of the Canary Islands from 20th to 24th September, 1941, can well remember cursing the order forbidding attacks on darkened ships-particularly on the last dark night, when he located destroyers several times and need only have fired his torpedoes at close range in order to strike the convoy (79).

SECONDARY TASKS PREJUDICE ATLANTIC OPERATIONS

144. F.O. U-boats Objects

No senior officer of the German Navy was more emphatic than Dönitz that the issue of the war depended on sinking as much enemy shipping as possible with the U-boat as the principal weapon, and that everything must be subordinated to this aim.

Consequently Dönitz was strongly opposed to any demands for U-boats to carry out any tasks which involved splitting up his forces. He made every effort to accelerate new construction, equipment and training, and to put the available boats to more effective use by employing air reconnaissance, by improving the dockyard situation, and by improving weapons (84).

The Naval Staff made every effort to weigh the advantages and disadvantages of the auxiliary tasks requested of the U-boats, but too often circumstances such as *Führer*'s orders, requests from the Supreme Command, crises in the various theatres of war, fear of landings, etc., forced them to act. The following is a short survey of these secondary tasks and the efforts of F.O. U-boats to prevent the splitting-up of his forces.

145. U-boats as Weather Ships

In Section 96 it was mentioned that after the outbreak of war the German Meteorological Service rarely received weather forecasts from the U.S.A. or the Atlantic. They therefore found it difficult to forecast weather conditions for *Luftwaffe* raids on Britain. At the request of the Commander-in-Chief *Luftwaffe*, the Naval Staff at the end of August, 1940, ordered that two U-boats were to act as weather ships, reporting from the Atlantic two or three times each day. F.O. U-boats appreciated the value of these reports, but at the same time feared that this secondary task would prejudice the main operations. One boat was to report from between 20° and 25° West and could not therefore be considered as operational. The other had to proceed cautiously between 10° and 15° West, otherwise her presence might cause the enemy to by-pass the operational U-boat group.

At the end of October, 1940, two to four of the boats in the operational area were employed on this secondary duty. F.O. U-boats made every effort to get rid of this task, but his attempts were unsuccessful and boats continued to carry out meteorological reconnaissance until 1944. In 1942 all commanders were ordered to add a short weather report (temperature, wind, sea and cloud) to each radio message. The occasional laying of weather buoys near Rockall Bank and Porcupine Bank, which automatically transmitted two or three times a day, also added to the weather data.

146. U-Boats as Escorts

From May, 1941, onwards British patrols managed to intercept and destroy increasing numbers of German auxiliary cruisers, blockade runners, supply ships and prize ships in all parts of the Atlantic (85). To afford the ships a certain amount of protection in the first (or last) part of the route from Bordeaux to the Azores the Naval Staff allocated U-boats to defend the ships against surface forces, for no fast escort cruisers were available. F.O. U-boats considered that the U-boat was ill-suited for such tasks. At best, a U-boat escort maintained the morale of the merchant seamen, who could expect to be rescued if their ship were sunk. But the escorting tasks ordered by the Naval Staff had to be carried out. "… For the general conduct of the war and the continuance of the U-boat campaign, safe passage of the prize ships and blockade runners is vital. Every security measure is therefore justified even if the escort can be only of slight use…" (86).

The following escort duties were performed:

Month	Homeward-Bound	Outward-Bound
May 1941	Steamer *Lech* (eastwards from Rio)	
August 1941	*Ship 36* (2 U-boats) *Anneliese Essenberger* (1 U-boat)	
September 1941		*Rio Grande* (2 U-boats) *Kota Penang* (1 U-boat)
November 1941	*Ship 45* (2 U-boats)	
November 1941	*Silva Plana* (1 U-boat)	

Of these ships, the supply ship *Kota Penang*, equipped and intended for replenishing U-boats and auxiliary cruisers in the Atlantic and the Indian Oceans, was destroyed by long range gunfire from a British cruiser as she was proceeding north of the Azores. [34]The crew was picked up by the U-boat and transferred to a Spanish tug off the port of EI Ferrol. Neither in this case nor in later cases in 1942/43 did the escorting U-boat manage to repel the attack or protect the ship under escort. In November, 1941, the Naval Staff required six boats for escort duties.

147. Operations for "Barbarossa"

As mentioned in Section 123, U-boat operations for " Barbarossa" had only an indirect influence on Atlantic warfare, for they retarded the training and readiness of new boats. During the first few weeks careful organisation and temporary transfer of training units did not affect the training activity, but on 31st July (87) and again on 15th August (88), F.O. U-boats had to request the Naval Staff and Group North to return eight boats to resume training duties. They were not returned to him until September, 1941, when the situation in the

---

34 H.M.S. *Kenya* on 3rd October, 1941.

Baltic had become easier. Their slight achievements in the Eastern Baltic had been no compensation for the delays caused in training.

148. Boats in the Arctic and the Mediterranean

In June, 1941, the outbreak of war with Russia brought a new theatre into naval warfare, the Arctic. There was little point in operating in this area unless Britain supported her new ally by sending supplies by the northern route. Against this eventuality two U-boats had been sent north by Raeder in July, 1941, followed in September by two others. As no repairs could be carried out in the north, some four to six boats had to be held available for these duties, and were lost to the Atlantic force. Sinkings by these first boats in 1941 were negligible, for Allied supplies to Russia had barely started. Seeing hIs Atlantic operations weakened by w.hat he then considered a useless diversion of his forces, F.O. U-boats objected repeatedly.

"... Hitherto the sinkings by these boats have been of no consequence. This is because their targets were very small ships against which torpedo attacks are not promising... The war will ultimately be decided by attacks on Britain's imports, which are the main objective. The war against Russia will be decided on land and U-boats can play only a secondary role in the campaign..." (89).

These objections, justified in 1941, were not upheld by the Naval Staff.

149. Reconnaissance for Surface Ships

Group North was the command responsible for the passage of surface forces to the Atlantic. Prior to the sailing of Scheer at the end of October, the Group requested reconnaissance by U-boats of both sea routes concerned. For this purpose one boat was sent on ice reconnaissance through the Denmark Strait, and four boats from Germany were to be sent to reconnoitre certain areas south of Iceland where they would remain while Scheer was proceeding. As reliable weather forecasts were extremely important for her sailing, four more boats, one of them off Jan Mayen, were to be employed at the same time to send weather reports (90). F.O. U-boats raised objections to these plans. "… The sailing of one surface ship is seriously interfering with U-boat operations. Eight boats are already employed in this connection, even before the ship has sailed. If she does sail it is obvious, in view of the present situation in the Atlantic and the fate of *Bismarck*, that more boats will be demanded for the task, thus diverting them from their true purpose. The sailing of Scheer will not provide any relief for the U-boat campaign, but, on the contrary, will weaken it. It is hardly likely that this weakness will be made good by the ship's achievements…" (91). However, *Scheer* did not sail.

150. More Secondary Tasks in November, 1941

By the beginning of November the Naval Staff had requested U-boats for the following duties, to be carried out in the course of the month:-six boats for escort duty, four for special reconnaissance for Group North, four in the Arctic Ocean and a reinforcement of six for the Mediterranean. This left only five to ten boats for Atlantic interception, and operations there came to a standstill by the second half of the month. Again F.O. U-boats protested, this time at a Berlin conference with the Commander-in-Chief Navy on 8th November, 1941. On this occasion he also expressed anxiety about the repair situation and new construction. "… Britain will welcome the (resulting) cessation of Atlantic operations over a period of weeks. Since for political and strategic reasons we have already had to send part of our U-boat force to the Mediterranean, I consider that any further diversion of forces for secondary tasks must be avoided…" (92 and 93).

The Axis situation in the Mediterranean now led to several weeks' suspension of Atlantic operations in favour of a concentration in the Mediterranean and off Gibraltar.

It was not until he became Commander-in-Chief of the Navy in January, 1943, that Dönitz was able to prevent this dispersion of forces. By then, however, he had to face even graver problems affecting the conduct of U-boat warfare.

NOVEMBER AND DECEMBER, 1941
FOCUS ON THE MEDITERRANEAN

151. Urgency of the Mediterranean Situation

The transfer of U-boats to the Mediterranean in 1941 will be reviewed here only as it affected Atlantic warfare. The Mediterranean operations will be described in a later volume.

On 16th April, 1941, and again in June (94) the Naval Staff had asked Dönitz to comment on the proposed dispatch of U-boats to the Mediterranean, on the latter occasion having regard to the *Führer*'s request for naval support in that area. The Commander-in-Chief Navy reiterated that the dispatch of the boats would not vitally affect the main objective-operations against British merchant shipping-and he persuaded the *Führer* accordingly (95).

Developments in the Mediterranean that summer required every possible support from the German Navy. It was on 7th September that the Naval Staff ordered F.O. U-boats to be ready to send U-boats to be based on Salamis under Group Command South, to operate against British supply traffic along the North African coast. In the second half of the month a group of six boats sailed, proceeding on the surface without incident via the Strait of Gibraltar to their new operational area. This caused a reduction of more than a quarter in the average number of 20 boats hitherto in the Atlantic.

In October conditions in the Mediterranean had deteriorated with the crisis in the transport situation resulting from the inadequacy of the Italian Navy and imminent major land operations made further immediate reinforcements necessary. On 4th November, the Naval Staff decided that a second wave of six boats was to be sent to the Western Mediterranean at once, six further boats being held ready in the French Atlantic bases to act as reliefs for these (96).

Four boats of the second wave entered the Mediterranean, and on 13th November two of these (U.205 and U.Sl) attacked and sank Ark Royal. It was also reported by U.Sl that she had torpedoed *Malaya*.[35]

---

[35] Ark Royal torpedoed and sunk by a U-boat on 13th November, 1941, in 36° 03' N. 4° 45' W. while returning from operation "Perpetual", in company with *Malaya, Argus,*

A third wave sailed for the Mediterranean on 16th November. Meanwhile in the Eastern Mediterranean a German S.O. of U-boats formed his organisation, which came under the control of the German Naval Command in Italy.

On 22nd November the Naval Staff decided that "The British North African offensive[36] and the reports of intended Anglo-French landings in French North Africa constitute a grave threat to the Mediterranean and to Italy. In so far as our Navy can influence the situation, the area round Gibraltar now becomes vitally important. The strategic importance of holding our position in the Mediterranean compels us to concentrate the main operational strength of the U-boats in the Gibraltar area until the situation improves" (97).

152. Concentration off Gibraltar

To prevent enemy shipping assembled at Gibraltar from moving in either direction would require a large number of boats on both sides of the Strait. Those available in French ports were insufficient, and it was necessary to divert many more from the Atlantic. By order of the Naval Staff the boats operating in and en route for mid-Atlantic were instructed by radio on 22nd November to break off operations. The Newfoundland group received similar orders on 23rd November. Those boats which had adequate fuel made for Gibraltar to operate in the Mediterranean or west of the Strait. Boats short of fuel returned to their bases to be fitted out for the Mediterranean. At the same time arrangements were made to allow a considerable number of boats to refuel in the Spanish ports of Vigo and Cadiz.

While making for Gibraltar a boat of the Newfoundland group sighted a south-bound convoy north of the Azores. F.O. U-boats believed it to be a WS convoy as it included a ship laden with ammunition which had exploded on being torpedoed, endangering the attacking U-boat. Attacks on such convoys with supplies for the Mediterranean were entirely suitable to the new objective. Other

---

Hermione and seven destroyers. *Malaya* was not hit.
36 The second British Western Desert Offensive began on 18th November, 1941, when the Eight Army advanced into Cyrenaica.

boats were ordered to concentrate for the attack, but they failed due to the inexperience of some commanders. Misled by neutral ships and by a detached enemy vessel, they made inappropriate sighting reports which drew most of the boats in the wrong direction. After this action the boats proceeded further east in a scouting formation along the supposed convoy routes, hoping to intercept shipping coming from the west. More boats had meanwhile arrived west of Gibraltar, taking up positions in the Strait and east of Cape Sf: Vincent. The most suitable formation here was an east-west patrol line, which allowed the commanders on fine moonlight nights to push eastwards as far as Tarifa, or in bad weather to withdraw to the west.

Their task was to attack enemy convoys entering the Mediterranean. Little traffic was found, but increasing enemy patrols were observed at the western entrance to the Strait, which compelled the boats to submerge for long periods, thus restricting their freedom of movement. Probably this was the cause of the few sightings. After long periods of uneventful waiting F.O. U-boats decided, with the approval of the Naval Staff, that the boats should abandon the search and attack a Britain-bound convoy, HG 76.

153. Failure against HG 76

For some time it had been expected that HG 76 would be sailing, and the delay was attributed by the Naval Staff to the presence of our U-boats west of Gibraltar. F.O. U-boats had anticipated a particularly. strong escort for this convoy, but its actual strength was a surprise. According to British figures it consisted of 16 escort vessels and an escort carrier, Audacity. This time the weather was too calm for the U-boats, but the chief reason for their serious failure was the extremely skillful handling of the A/S forces. Two ships and the carrier were sunk, against a loss of five U-boats-the highest loss so far in any single operation.

F. O. U-boats gave his views on the action in *"Reports on convoy operations"* - a series circulated fir the instruction of all U-boat commanders and training centres (98):

"… Experience shows that Gibraltar convoys are more difficult to attack than the Atlantic convoys. This is because of the relatively short distance from Gibraltar to Britain, which enables the enemy to concentrate his available AIS forces. For this reason operations against Gibraltar convoys have generally been avoided unless the U-boats were already in the area as a result of other operations.

"In the case of HG 76 particularly strong escorting and AIS forces were to be expected. (Contact with this convoy was gained on 14th December.) Both during and after the operation the prevalent good weather did not help the U-boats. The complete calm particularly favoured the enemy's use of radar and asdic. The U-boats maneuvering·for attack could be heard plainly, while their bow waves were easily identifiable, particularly from the air (99). On the other hand the nights were so dark that the boats were frequently unable to detect destroyers and patrol vessels until it was too late to evade them unnoticed. Moreover, the boats had to run close in to the convoy in order to see their targets.

"The worst feature was the presence of the aircraft carrier. Small, fast, maneuverable aircraft circled the convoy continuously, so that when it was sighted the boats were repeatedly forced to submerge or withdraw. The presence of enemy aircraft also prevented any protracted shadowing or homing procedure by German Aircraft. The sinking of the aircraft carrier is therefore of particular importance not only in this case but also in every future convoy action…

"… On learning the extent of the first losses, the Command was faced with the problem of whether to continue the operation, for they could not know how adversely the weather and the aircraft carrier had affected the U-boats. F.O. U-boats therefore decided to send three more boats-U.567, U.71 and U.751-into the battle. It was thought that with their experienced commanders they would be able to cope with the difficult conditions. This step resulted in the sinking of the aircraft carrier. Contact was lost in the deteriorating conditions and the operation was abandoned on 23rd December. Three boats still had torpedoes but two of them had been holding on to the convoy since 14th December, and were bound to be exhausted and no longer fit for operations."

154. The Gibraltar "Mouse Trap"

On 29th November the Naval Staff had ordered that until further notice ten boats were to be constantly on operations in the Eastern Mediterranean and 15 in the area east and west of the Strait of Gibraltar. The sailing of reliefs was to be arranged so that whenever possible the relieving boats should reach the operational area before the others left it. The number of boats operating inside the Mediterranean-amounting to 18-was not to be reduced.

Since 10th November three boats had been lost trying to enter the Mediterranean, while others, incurring bomb damage, had abandoned the attempt. In order to build up the necessary strength as quickly as possible, F.O. U-boats was therefore forced to send through the Strait boats which had been on their first Atlantic operation, and some of them carried only general charts of the Mediterranean.

Because of their susceptibility to depth-charges and bombs, and their liability to location, Type IX boats were ill-suited to operations in the Mediterranean. In these restricted waters they were unable to make full use of their high fuel and torpedo capacity. On the advice of F.O. U-boats, the Naval Staff agreed to use them west of Gibraltar.

Since 15th November all boats at readiness in the Biscay bases had proceeded to the Gibraltar area by the shortest route. There were not enough boats to ensure that the numbers ordered by the Naval Staff would be maintained despite losses. Therefore all the boats leaving the home ports for their first operation were ordered to proceed round England to the Atlantic bases, where they were replenished and fitted out and received instructions on the conditions to be expected on passage to the Mediterranean.

The British had very quickly detected the withdrawal from the Atlantic to the new battle area west of Gibraltar, and had concentrated light naval forces in the new operational area probably at the expense of escorts for the Britain-U.S.A. convoys. These additional forces particularly the dangerous and continuous air patrol, even at night-made it increasingly difficult for the U-boats to break into the Mediterranean. The first two waves of boats had managed to pass quickly through the Strait. The third had a tedious passage, sometimes hugging the coast as far as Cape Spartel and Cape Trafalgar, then surfacing under cover of darkness to dash through the most dangerous part of the Strait. At the full moon period it was impossible to pass submerged through the Strait without proceeding very close to the land. The standing patrols on both sides of tQe Strait forced the boats to remain submerged for some 40 miles, a distance which the medium boats could not achieve. Even short stretches were difficult for them if caught in underwater currents, which put a heavy strain on their batteries. At certain depths the current ran eastwards at two to four knots, which shortened the danger period. But the same current seriously impeded the return passage, while enemy patrols east of Gibraltar were so attentive that a return to the Atlantic became most difficult. As Italian bases had inadequate repair facilities it had been planned to send Mediterranean boats after their operations back to St. Nazaire and Brest for overhaul, but this plan had to be abandoned. Once inside the Mediterranean, the boats were in a trap. The first wave had no losses. In the second wave, one boat was lost. Of the next large wave of 24 boats, three were lost and five had to return to Biscay because of bomb damage. The losses among these boats amounted to 33 per cent of the total and this rate of loss was expected to continue.

155. Effect on Atlantic Operations

The concentration of the boats in the Mediterranean had brought our Atlantic operations almost to a standstill. F.o. U-boats stated on 22nd November: "… Regrettable as this may be it is obviously necessary to do everything to retrieve the situation in the Mediterranean."

Though agreeing with the Naval Staff as to the need, he did not believe the reports of AngloFrench landing intentions at Oran and Algiers, for he considered that after the sinking of Ark Royal and the damage to *Malaya*[37], Force H at Gibraltar lacked the power to

---

37 See Section 151

undertake this action. In his opinion the assembly of many merchant ships (at Gibraltar) was no sign of an impending landing, or indicative of increased shipments to the east. He thought that British supplies were being carried in WS convoys around the Cape and through the Suez Canal to North Africa. He therefore proposed that boats be concentrated in the Eastern Mediterranean, while reducing the numbers in the Gibraltar area where the risk was excessive. But still fearing the Anglo-French landings, the Naval Staff rejected this proposal at the end of November.

The absence of boats in the Atlantic, the high casualties near Gibraltar and their ultimate effect on Atlantic operations were viewed with increasing anxiety by F.O. U-boats. On 10th December[38] the general position was as follows:

There were in all 86 boats in operational commission. Four boats were operating in the Eastern Mediterranean, five in the Western Mediterranean, and five West of Gibraltar. Four were in Salamis, two in Spezia. Another sixteen boats were on their way or under orders to proceed to the Mediterranean and Gibraltar areas, making a total of 36. A further 14 boats were needed to keep up operational strength in these areas and these were detailed. Thus fifty boats in all had been diverted, leaving only 36 for all other purposes. Of these, three boats were in the Arctic, five boats were returning from the South Atlantic, and most of the others were in dockyard hands or resting.

Ever since the beginning of December Dönitz had pressed for a resumption of Atlantic operations. He regarded the Gibraltar activity as wasteful and detrimental to the U-boat campaign as a whole (100). By 30th December the Naval Staff considered that:

"... Owing to the recent favourable developments in Libya, the U-boat successes in the Mediterranean, the successful minelaying off Tripoli, the results to be expected from the mines laid by E-boats

38 The immediate repercussion of Pearl Harbour (7th December, 1941) on future U-boat dispositions is not mentioned here. Germany and Italy declared war on U.S. on 11th December. While 12 large U-boats were got ready for a sudden descent on shipping in the Caribbean, the policy of maintaining a minimum of 25 medium U-boats in the Mediterranean continued into 1942.

off Malta, and the intensified German air operations in the south of Italy, the whole situation in the Mediterranean has so improved since last month that it is no longer vital to block the stream of enemy traffic through the Strait of Gibraltar..." (101).

The Naval Staff decided to send only three more boats into the Mediterranean, and to stop operations west of Gibraltar. The senior Officer in the Mediterranean was to use his boats in concentrated operations in the Eastern and Central part. They were to make occasional thrusts from the east as far as the Strait, and three Atlantic boats were to operate temporarily west of Gibraltar as far as the Azores, in order to mislead the enemy as to the change of dispositions.

This marked the end of seven weeks' inactivity in the Atlantic. The influence of the U-boats on the situation in the Mediterranean will not be examined here.

It was now up to the U-boat Command to combat the new enemy, the U.S.A., as effectively as possible with the boats that remained.

THE CENTRAL AND SOUTH ATLANTIC

156. Factors governing Southern Operations
In July, 1940, the first Central Atlantic operation had been performed by VA, which proceeded to Freetown. U.SS was active in the same area in November and December, 1940. After many months, the area off the African coast around Freetown was again occupied in force at the beginning of March 1941. As the first two southern operations had been extremely successful, it may be wondered why the interval was so long. Sinkings per boat while in the operational area were greater off Freetown than off Ireland, and this applied for the last six months of 1940. But owing to the length and time of the journey to and from Freetown the overall performance of the boats in this area compared unfavourably with that of the northern boats. Until the spring of 1941, the shortage of boats made interception difficult,

and any reduction of numbers in the main operational area-the North Atlantic-resulted in a proportionately greater reduction in overall sinkings: "… Harassing of the enemy in other areas and diversionary movements are in themselves desirable. They can bring relief to the main theatre of war, but do not have a decisive effect on the enemy…" (102).

Moreover, it was not at all certain that the enemy's A/S forces and traffic would react in the desired way. It must be admitted that in 1940 the enemy had accurate information on the numbers of large U-boats available for southern operations. He could estimate the probable maximum sinkings there, and continue without large-scale countermeasures as long as the losses were not excessive. Not until the winter of 1940/41, when conditions in the northern area were deteriorating, was it decided to send more boats to the south.

157. Endurance of Type IX Boats

With three exceptions, only boats of the improved Type IX (IXb and IXc) were used in southern Atlantic operations. The range of Type IXb boats allowed them, while outward-bound, to proceed as far west as 250 West, remain four to five weeks off Freetown and return by the direct route. Type IXc, carrying 50-60 tons more fuel, were able to reach the Guinea coast by the same long approach route. The boats were directed to proceed at economical speed to avoid refuelling during the operation.

Until the first southern operations the technical experts and engineers of the U-boat arm had no precise knowledge of the radius of action of these boats, for there had been no time before the war to carry out long endurance trials. It was left to the initiative of the boats' engineers to work out the best speeds and settings to save fuel. They discovered that diesel-electric propulsion proved to be the most economical method. For instance, the starboard screw was coupled to diesel, while the battery was charged using the starboard motor as dynamo, with revolutions for approximately half speed. The port screw was coupled to the motor with current from the battery; motor revolutions approximately slow to half speed. With this arrangement the greatest range could be covered while proceeding at approximately seven knots.

158. Replenishing during Operations

Before the big radius of action of the boats had been realized, the U-boat Command believed that refuelling would be needed during the operations, and the first series of operations in March had been planned on the understanding that the Naval Staff would make auxiliary cruisers or supply ships available for this purpose.

The boats carried fourteen torpedoes below decks, and four to six in sealed tubes on the upper deck, outside the pressure hull. Special transporting gear was used to transfer torpedoes outboard through the water and place them in the bow or stern torpedo compartments. During the summer and in calm weather this method was often used when replenishing the boats from auxiliary cruisers or supply ships. It enabled the boats to carry out successive operations, saving some 4,000 miles of passage-time.

At first the boats could avail themselves of shore supply facilities or they could refuel at sea. For shore supplies, they could call at Las Palmas (Canary Islands) on their way south, where the German supply ships Charlotte Schliemann (code name " Culler") and Coronets (code name " Lima ") had been since September, 1939. With the connivance of the Spanish authorities the boats put in at night, fuelled and sailed again before daylight. Despite the strictest security measures the presence of these supply ships became known to local British agents. This led to a British protest to the Spanish Government, which in July, 1941, withdrew these facilities:

Replenishing at sea took place either by day or night from German auxiliary cruisers or supply ships. These vessels were under the control of the Naval Staff Operations Division, and were ordered by radio to certain areas as required by F.O. U-boats (103). In the summer of 1941 preference was given to the area north of St. Paul between 280 and 350 West, which was sufficiently remote from the British base at Freetown and from the Brazilian coast. But it was not beyond the reach of British patrols, as was shown on 8th May,

1941, when an Italian U-boat sighted an aircraft carrier south of the Cape Verde Islands. The supply areas were designated by radio, using certain reference points known only to the southern U-boats and the supply ships (for example: Points Schwarz and Rot, areas Kleiderstoffe and Getriinke). This security measure avoided the need for including latitude and longitude in the radio messages.

In March, 1941, the auxiliary cruiser Ship 41 was available for replenishment duties, while in April and May the fast tanker Nordmark was used. The latter also worked with the German auxiliary cruisers, blockade runners and prize ships in the Central and South Atlantic. The first supply ship exclusively for U-boats-the Egerland which carried a large number of torpedoes, arrived in the Central Atlantic in the middle of May, 1941, but was sunk by enemy forces at supply point Rot (north of St. Paul's Rock) at the beginning of June.[39] The next ship, Lotharingen, met the same fate before she had even arrived in the replenishment area.

As five supply ships (Belchen, Egerland, Lotharingen, Esso and Gedania) were destroyed by enemy search forces in various parts of the Atlantic during the first weeks of June, it was decided to abandon the use of ships for refuelling boats at sea." The Naval Staff then endeavored to obtain permission to use Dakar for German replenishment ships. They negotiated with the French Government through the Franco-German Armistice Commission (104). The supply ships *Kota Penang* and *Python* were quickly fitted out, and the former was to be available in Dakar from 15th July. The negotiations opened promisingly but were gradually prolonged and finally collapsed due to the attitude of the French commission. Consequently from July to November there were no facilities for replenishing U-boats in the Central Atlantic.

At the beginning of October, 1941, in a new effort to refuel the boats at sea, the Naval Staff sent *Kota Penang* to sea under U-boat escort. She was sunk on her outward passage. *Python* sailed at the beginning of November and managed to reach the South Atlantic. On

---

39 *Egerland* was intercepted by *London* and sunk by *Brilliant* on 5th June, 1941, in 7° N. 31° W.

1st December, while refuelling her third U-boat, she was destroyed 780 miles south of St. Helena by a British cruiser.[40] A few days earlier the auxiliary cruiser Ship 16, also in process of refuelling a U-boat, had been sunk north of Ascension. These disasters finally terminated the replenishment of U-boats from surface ships in the Atlantic.

159. March to July, 1941-Successful Period using Supply Ships

The successes of the first four months' operations in the Central Atlantic were due to the extremely favourable traffic situation-almost up to pre-war volume-off Freetown, and to the abundant facilities for refuelling during this period. Freetown was the most important British port of transshipment for traffic running from the Cape and from South America to Britain. It was the only Central Atlantic port where ships could be assembled to form convoys. According to the enemy shipping section of our Naval Intelligence Division (105) slow north-bound ships ran from Freetown in convoys between 19° and 22° West, while fast ships proceeded independently on very varying routes. Some of the slow ships from Britain travelled in convoy as far as Freetown; some joined OG and ON convoys and, after leaving the U-boat zone west of England, proceeded independently.

From the beginning of March, 1941, the general rule was that all slow ships travelled in convoys, while all fast ships proceeded further west using variable routes. It was known from captured documents and from Radio Intelligence that all vessels carried directions for a diversionary route, which came into use by radio order in the event of danger from U-boats. Ships approaching Freetown from the south and west had so far always been sighted singly.

The southern operations planned from the end of February, 1941, aimed at attacks on traffic running to and from Freetown. The U-boats were to be stationed close to this port. In the hope of finding targets during their long approach, the boats were routed southwards along certain meridians, sometimes hauling further west when the Naval Staff provided fresh information on shipping movements. U.lOS, U.124, and U.106 were on the 20th, 21st and 22nd meridians, U.107

---

40 H.M.S. *Devonshire*.

on the 24th and 25th meridians, and U.103, U.38 and U.A. between the 20th meridian and the African coast at different dates in March and April.

This outward routing proved very successful. The first three boats attacked two convoys, SL 67 and SL 68, while U.107 came upon a promising artery of traffic at 24° West, where she found ships of a dispersed southbound convoy and fast single ships.

SL 67 was sighted on 7th March, 300 miles northeast of Cape Verde by the battleships *Gneisenau* and *Scharnhorst*, which were operating in the Central Atlantic. The U-boats were informed and those in the vicinity, U.lOS and U.124, came up quickly to score successes. They reported five ships sunk, and these figures are corroborated by the British Admiralty.

A week later, in the area southwest of Dakar, U.106 intercepted the next north-bound Freetown convoy, SL 68, and led in U.lOS by shadowing reports. In a perfect example of mutual co-operation in leading-in and taking over the shadowing, the two boats maintained contact for seven days, although the convoy had made many attempts to shake them off, including a sharp deviation to the west. In dangerous attacking conditions, U.lOS scored a hit on the battleship *Malaya*[41] without knowing it. Our Radio Intelligence learned of the torpedoing, which the U-boat commander was able to confirm in a later reconstruction of the action. Ten ships were reported sunk. British Admiralty figures give seven.

The climax of the operations off the port of Freetown came between the end of April and the middle of July. During this period an average of six to seven boats operated in the Central Atlantic, of which three were usually in the actual zone of sinkings, while the others were proceeding to and from the replenishment areas.

As the first two convoy battles had been very successful with only two boats, F.O. U-boats ordered a disposition from which the boats would be able to intercept outward-bound convoys soon after they left Freetown. This step brought no success however, and

---

41 *Malaya*, acting as ocean escort for SL 68, was torpedoed on 20th March, 1941, some 255 miles N.N.W. of Cape Verde Islands. Damage was not serious.

the boats were drawn up to intercept single vessels approaching Freetown from the south and west. Thanks to what we regarded as unexpectedly uniform and ineffective routing of traffic and control of times of arrival, and owing to the consistently inadequate escorts, this operation against single ships was outstandingly successful. The following numbers of ships were sunk or torpedoed by the first seven boats; the numbers include the results against SL 67 and SL 68:

U.106 - 10 ships
U.105 - 12 ships
U.124 - 12 ships
U.107 - 14 ships
U.103 - 12 ships
U.38 - 8 ships
U.69 - 6 ships + results from minelaying
U.A. - 7 ships

During this successful period, the first long-distance minelaying operation was carried out by U.69 (Type VII) off Lagos and Takoradi on the Guinea coast. The commander succeeded in laying seven ground mines in each harbour entrance, forcing the Admiralty to close them temporarily.

During the early months-when F.O. U-boats wished to exploit the favourable conditions quickly with all available forces-the prospects were jeopardised by an escort task. The Naval Staff required two boats to escort the German ship Lech with an important cargo from Rio as far as the eastern boundary of the U.S. neutrality zone. Apart from the negligible value of a U-boat escort, F.O. U-boats regarded this particular task as useless. What were the boats to do if, for example, a U.S. cruiser shadowed the German ship and reported her position? No action could be taken against U.S. forces. Out of regard for the U.S.A., the boats were not even allowed to operate against shipping within the new neutrality zone.

On 7th April F.O. U-boats ordered U.lOS and U.106 to proceed to Rio for this task, As Lech's sailing was delayed, one boat was later released from this duty and was able to proceed to the replenishment area. U.100 waited until the end of the month when she escorted the ship to the eastern boundary of the zone without incident. U.106 had sacrificed seven weeks, U.10S almost two weeks of valuable operations to this secondary task.

160. July and August, 1941 - Scattering of Traffic and Lack of Supply Facilities interrupt the Southern Operations

Lack of supply facilities as a result of the loss of the tankers Egerland and Lothringen soon affected the situation in the south. U.38, U.107, U.69 and U.103, which, after replenishing, should have continued to operate in the Freetown area, had to return. One of them could not reach western France without refuelling, and proceeded to Las Palmas, to fuel from Charlotte Schliemann. On 27th June, 300 miles southwest of the Canary Islands, she came upon SL 76, making a successful surprise attack. A few hours later, after replenishing at Las Palmas, U.123 also made contact. Her energetic commander, Lt. Hardegen, pursued the convoy alone for three days. Five ships were reported sunk and one-Rio Azul-probably sunk. British records show two ships in convoy and two stragglers sunk. U.123 continued to Freetown. Here conditions had greatly altered in the last few weeks. At the end of June, when over 30 ships had been sunk near the base, the enemy had finally instituted effective dispersion and control of traffic. There were no longer any single ships and even the incoming traffic from the south seemed to be in convoy. Only increased A/S patrols and numerous U.S. ships were seen entering or leaving - a sign that the U.S.A. had begun openly to support Great Britain. In view of the embargo on attacks on U.S. ships, there was no point in remaining. In addition, there were signs - confirmed in the following months by Radio Intelligence - that much traffic had been diverted from Freetown (106). The only ships which still called there were those in urgent need of coal. Much of the traffic, particularly the faster ships, passed to the west of the U-boat area, that is, west of the 30th meridian, mostly proceeding from the South Atlantic to the Pan-American safety area. The U-boats were forbidden to attack in this area, as it was the route of the German prize ships and blockade runners. As these ships often travelled under camouflage and the Naval Staff was not always exactly informed as to their positions, there was a danger of mistaking them for enemy ships. F.O. U-boats made several requests for freedom of attack west of 30° West, and even proposed altering the prize routes, but the Naval Staff regarded this as impracticable and the area west of 30° West remained forbidden to the U-boats (107).

Anticipating that supply facilities would soon be available in Dakar, four boats had been despatched southward at the beginning of July. In view of the unfavourable traffic situation off Freetown, they were now ordered to carry out a broad sweep to the south, starting at 35° North, and combing the area between 25° and 30° West-that is, as far west as possible. The War Diary of 21st July, 1941, states:

"... These boats will comb the western edge of the permitted operational area. A negative result will indicate that all single ship traffic has been diverted west of 30° West, in which case there is no point in pursuing operations in this vast southern area..."

The boats were unsuccessful and on 30th July F.O. U-boats decided to stop the southern operations. The 4 boats were directed to turn about and, from 3rd August, to proceed in a reconnaissance sweep towards Gibraltar. Here they joined the northern boats in an unsuccessful operation against HG 69, after which they returned to base.

161. September and October, 1941 - Operations mainly Unsuccessful

After attacks had become permissible to the west of 30° West, and when boats could be refuelled at sea by the supply ship *Kota Penang* and later by *Python*, the southern operations were resumed.

The first wave proceeded south on 24th August, 1941, to comb the area between 30° and 35° West and then remained on either side of and south of St. Paul's Rock, where-according to decryptions of routing instructions to British ships-there should be a fair amount of traffic. But no traffic was found and the boats were sent towards Freetown to take up positions with a second wave.

The first boat of the second wave, U.107, which had been at sea since the beginning of September, met SL 87 on the 21st. Although the others were still anything up to 1,200 miles off, they closed the Gonvoy. The boats reported sinking nine ships and damaging two. British Admiralty figures show seven ships sunk.

Both waves operated off Freetown, adjusting their positions as necessary for intercepting outward-bound convoys. Here three uneventful weeks were followed by an order on 16th October to search northwards between the 17th and 23rd meridians, where SL convoys had been observed. After remaining several days between the Azores and the Canary Islands, the boats operated-while fuel lasted-with another lot of boats northeast of the Azores. After the action against SL 87 they had no further opportunities for attack.

Two boats remained in the Central Atlantic. U.68 had by order of F.O. U-boats taken over torpedoes from the returning U.1ll in the secluded bay of Tarafal, in St. Antao Island, Cape Verde Islands, where strangely the boats encountered a British submarine. A third German boat, U.67, was damaged in an attempt to ram the British submarine[42] and she also had to return to base. U.68 took over U.67's remaining fuel and was now able to operate for a long period. She was ordered to thrust via Ascension to St. Helena and then to Walvis Bay. En route she sank a British naval tanker in the harbour of St. Helena and two independent ships making for Walvis Bay. The other U-boat remained off Freetown, and later off the coast of Guinea.

The German auxiliary cruiser Ship 16 was then in the South Atlantic as supply ship for both boats. U.68 embarked supplies on 13th November in the area south of St. Helena, while U.126 was ordered to a rendezvous northwest of Ascension on 22nd November.

162. November and December, 1941 - Failure of First Thrust to Capetown

Two more boats, U.124 and U.129, had meanwhile arrived in the South Atlantic. They had left western France at about the same time as the supply ship *Python* and were to refuel from her while

---

42 H.M.S./M. *Clyde* had been sent to intercept the U-boats. She was slightly damaged and returned to Gibralter.

on the way south, and then continue to Capetown. They replenished according to plan on 20th November to the southwest of Cape Verde. The voyage to Capetown was cancelled on 22nd November, when U.126 reported by radio that Ship 16 had been sunk by a British cruiser in the replenishment area northwest of Ascension[43]. U.l24 and U.l29 were ordered to proceed to the place of sinking. En route, U.l24 sank the British light cruiser *Dunedin* 240 miles northeast of St. Paul's Rock[44]. *Python* had meanwhile been ordered by the Naval Staff to take over the survivors of Ship 16 from U.126. This she did on 24th/25th November.

There were still five U-boats in the South Atlantic, four of which could continue to operate. F.O. U-boats decided to take advantage of the supply facilities and to dispose the boats in close formation off Capetown. They were to be replenished between 30th November and 4th December, 780 miles south of St. Helena, almost 1,700 miles from the place of sinking of Ship 16. In this new supply area, *Python* was sunk by a British cruiser[45] on 1st December and the Capetown operation had therefore to be cancelled.

The survivors of both ships were towed north in lifeboats. When U.124 and U.129 arrived the rescued crews were divided among the four U-boats, which under extremely difficult conditions, with up to 150 men on board, commenced the return passage to Germany. Arrangements were made for them to be met 300 miles north of Cape Verdes by four Italian U-boats (*Torelli*, *Finzi*, *Tazzoli* and *Calvi*), which embarked half of the survivors. By the end of the year all the survivors had reached the Biscay ports, thus ending a rescue action unique in the history of U-boat warfare. The survivors had been brought over a distance of more than 5,000 miles.

The War Diary of F.O. U-boats stated on 1st December, 1941:

"... The sinking of *Python* means that there is no longer any possibility of refuelling in the Atlantic. Supplying from surface ships will not be resumed. The time for such operations has passed..."

---

43 Sunk by Devonshire in 4° 2' S. 18° 29' W.
44 *Dunedin* sunk by U-boat on 24th November, 1941, while on patrol in the South Atlantic.
45 H.M.S. *Dorsetshire*

163. Suspected Leakage of Information

How had the British found the two replenishment ships? Since May, 1941, the security of U-boat movements had been under constant review. Among several more or less suspicious cases of leakage, the incident in Tarafal Bay on 28th September was outstanding. On this night U.67 was to meet U.111 to take over torpedoes, while on the following night U.67 was to transfer a sick man to U.lll. After the torpedo transfer, the boats were surprised by a British *Clyde* class submarine, which had apparently attacked them with torpedoes, but missed, for two loud explosions were heard on land. U.67, which had proceeded to the rendezvous on the first night, rammed the British submarine under cover of darkness at the entrance to the bay, but the latter was able to make off at high speed. What was the explanation of the sudden appearance of the British submarine?

"… Either our cyphers have been compromised or it is a case of leakage. A British submarine does not appear by chance in such a remote part of the ocean. The Naval Staff is requested to take the necessary measures to safeguard the cypher system…" (108).

Subsequent investigations of this and other suspicious incidents, completed at the end of October by Rear-Admiral Maertens, Chief of the Communications Service, led to the following official prognosis:

"There is no real basis for acute anxiety as regards any compromise of operational security. In the last few weeks there has been no evidence of leakage either through cypher material which we had previously lost, or through espionage. But for operational security it seems important to make every effort to restrict the circle of personnel having access to the secret material, and thereby reduce the chances of betrayal. The more important cyphers do not seem to have been compromised, despite their constant heavy use and occasional loss" (109).

In these circumstances, how could the British warships' appearance in these remote places be explained? The German authorities could provide no satisfactory answer.

AUTHOR'S NOTES AND LIST OF SOURCES

SECTION		NUMBER OF REFERENCE IN TEXT
1	Files of F.O. U-boats (*Akte B.d.U.*), Orders and intentions from page 5 onwards, PG 32419a	(1)
4	War Diary of S.O. U-boats (*KTB F.d.U.*) of 21st August, 1939, *Survey of the situation*, paragraph 3 ..	(2)
5	The War Diary of S.O. U-boats contains no *Survey of the situation* at the outbreak of war. This passage compiled from notes and comments entered in the War Diary of S.O. U-boats during the emergency period and in the first days of hostilities	(3)
5	*OKM B Nr. 734/38 KIU, 19th September, 1938*, contains *Discussions on types of U-boats to be built*, PG 34179 and PG 34180	(4)
6	*See* (1)	(5)
6	This is the opinion of all responsible officers of the former German U-boat arm, who were much impressed by his personal influence over officers and men, particularly at critical periods in the war ..	(6)
8	War Diary of S.O. U-boats of 7th September, 1939	(7)
9	Quotation from War Diary of S.O. U-boats of 7th September, 1939..	(8)
10	*Inter alia, see* War Diary of S.O. U-boats of 9th October, 1939 ..	(9)
10	A principle repeatedly stressed by Dönitz at later dates	(10)
12	U-boat warfare: *Survey of the situation*, PG 33352, page 2 and following ..	(11)
15	U-boat warfare: *Survey of the situation*, PG 33352	(12)
15	From the operational order for Atlantic U-boats (North Sea) contained in " *Group West U-boat operations*," PG 37896	(13)
16	Typical of problems due to initial inadequacy of U-boat force	(14)
18	The *Athenia* incident and all important questions of naval–political development in U-boat warfare are dealt with in Sections 74–84. In the chronological presentation of events the various stages are mentioned only when they bear on operational planning and U-boat operations	(15)
19	This exercise with the German fleet during the spring training cruise of 1939 was designed to test the convoy attack procedure and to train the U-boat personnel in operating and attacking under Atlantic conditions	(15a)
27	From *Operational Orders Atlantic Number 23* contained in *F.O. U-boats— Orders and intentions*, PG 32419a, page 197	(16)
29	Preference for minelaying is mentioned several times in the War Diary for this period	(17)
30	Memorandum by Captain Assmann, War Diary of Naval War Staff, Part C 40, 1940 (*KTB Skl. Teil C*), PG 32011	(18)
33, 35	*F.O. U-boats—Orders and intentions*, PG 32419a, page 248 and following ..	(19)
36	U-boat warfare: *Survey of the situation, 14th to 20th March, 1940, Section III*, PG 33352	(20)
38	Full details of the torpedo catastrophe are omitted. There were numerous amendments to torpedo orders for the U-boats	(21)
38	War Diary of F.O. U-boats of 19th April, 1940	(22)
39	From U.47's Short Report contained in files *Torpedo Short Reports*, PG 32107	(23)

40   From War Diary of F.O. U-boats of 19th April, 1940   ..   ..   ..   (24)

40   *See* (24) ..   ..   (25)

40   Dönitz understood this reaction perfectly, despite his insistence that commanders should show an offensive spirit   ..   ..   (26)

44   (*a*) *Report to Commander-in-Chief Navy, 29th April, 1940, (Prof. Cornelius, Serial Number 301 CO*) contained in files *Torpedoes*, PG 33322, page 254. (*Appendix 2* is not comprehensive.)

(*b*) *Boats' reports* contained in files *U-boat Short Reports*, PG 32207.

(*c*) Teleprinter message *F.O. U-boats, Top Secret 670, 17th April, 1940*, PG 33322, page 184.

(*d*) Notes on individual commanders' reports, in War Diary of F.O. U-boats.

(*e*) Exact details cannot be given because the actual firing records are no longer available. If a boat repeated an attack on a target after a torpedo failure, the second attempt was counted as a fresh opportunity to attack. This was likely when a large convoy was met. Sometimes in such cases the boats, having expended all torpedoes, were still in a suitable position for attack   ..   ..   (27)

44   From U.47's Short Report contained in file *Torpedoes*, PG 33322, page 195 ..   (28)

45   All these commanders were decorated with oak leaves (*Eichenlaub*) for sinking more than 200,000 G.R.T. Prien also received the crossed swords (*Schwerter*)   ..   ..   (29)

45   The Norwegian charts, which as regards soundings were sometimes very incomplete, created difficulties in the fjords. Several boats grounded or failed in attacks due to being in the wrong position   ..   ..   ..   (30)

45   *See* (22)   ..   ..   (31)

45   Quotation from War Diary of 30th April, 1940   ..   ..   ..   (32)

46   *See* (27) ..   ..   (33)

47   *Torpedoes 1915/40, Top Secret, 20th April, 1940*, contained in files *Torpedoes*, PG 33322 from page 219   ..   ..   (34)

47   *Commander-in-Chief Navy. Serial Number 261/40, Top Secret, 23rd July, 1940. Section II* contained in War Diary of Naval Staff, Part C, April, 1940, PG 32011 ..   ..   (35)

47   (*a*) A proposal by Prof. Cornelius to Commander-in-Chief Navy for the reorganisation of the Torpedo Service, dated 8th June, 1940, *Serial Number 481/CO/NA/620/A* contained in files *Torpedoes*, PG 33322, page 239.

(*b*) Teleprinter message : *F.O. U-boats, Serial Number 685, Top Secret to Commander-in-Chief Navy, 20th April, 1940, Section III*, PG 33322, page 190.

(*c*) The author recalls that the considerable deep running of the torpedoes was later found to be due to leakage in the glands of the horizontal rudder rods, which admitted the abnormal internal pressure of the U-boat into the balance-chamber of the torpedo, affecting the depth-keeping mechanism. The normal zero position was graduated for a pressure of 760 millibars, and the false zero gave a deeper setting. During the Norwegian operations the boats were forced to remain submerged for long periods because of the strong patrols and light nights, and the abnormal pressure due to leakage was sometimes considerable. The author could find no documentary data on this subject in the available files, and has therefore omitted these facts from the text. He understands however that the packing gland (through which the horizontal rudder rod enters the pressure chamber) was later modified   ..   ..   (36)

47   War Diary of F.O. U-boats of 15th May, 1940, *Consultation with Prof. Cornelius* .. .. (37)

47   Files *Torpedo development*, PG 33322, page 338 .. .. (38)

47   From a report made to Commander-in-Chief Navy on 7th June, 1940, by Prof. Cornelius, *465/CO*, PG 33322, page 231, Section II .. .. .. (39)

57   War Diary of S.O. U-boats West of 29th October, 1939 .. .. .. (40)

60   Two days after the loss Daventry announced that a U-boat had been wrecked on Goodwin Sands, and that there had been a thick fog in that area during the previous two days. An attempt by German bombers to destroy the wreck —so that the enemy could not use it for research purposes—failed. Despite the good visibility the wreck was not located .. .. (41)

62   Quotation from War Diary of F.O. U-boats of 30th November, 1939 .. (42)

64   War Diary of S.O. U-boats West of 25th December, 1939 .. .. .. (43)

65   Quotation from War Diary of S.O. U-boats West of 25th December, 1939 .. (44)

65   Although this point is not clearly indicated in the War Diary, the author believes he is justified in drawing this conclusion from examination of the effects of the danger area, as far as this is possible from the War Diary .. (45)

66   U.23 was a typical " burrower " (*Lochkriecher*). Besides penetrating to the Moray Firth to lay mines off Cromarty, on the three operations mentioned she searched 10 to 15 bays for warships and merchant shipping. Net barrages sometimes prevented her from approaching these targets (Sullom Voe) .. (46)

66   The percentage is probably higher. There were about 20 per cent prematures alone .. .. (47)

75   War Diary of Naval War Staff Part A of 31st August, 1939. From *the first directive of the Supreme Command of the Armed Forces* .. .. .. (48)

75   War Diary of F.O. U-boats of 21st September, 1939 .. .. (49)

76   Before all the files of F.O. U-boats were destroyed at the beginning of February, 1940, in the Staff H.Q. (*Koralle*) near Berlin, the author was able to see a specially restricted secret document containing details of the *Athenia* incident, which are missing from the War Diary of F.O. U-boats and of U.30. The facts given are based on that information .. .. (50)

79   War Diary of U.3 of 30th September, 1939, War Diary of S.O. U-boats West of 3rd October, 1939 .. .. (51)

86   U-boat reports : Files *Torpedo sinkings by U-boats* February, 1940, to May, 1942, PG 30956. The author had to compile the lists for the period September, 1939, to January, 1940, from a rough *sinkings* curve, and the tonnage is therefore approximate. Figures of German Naval Intelligence Division *Enemy merchant shipping losses*, PG 49391. British Admiralty figures : From Director of Trade Division, B.R. 1337 (1945) and *Ships of the Royal Navy, Statement of losses during the Second World War*, H.M. Stationery Office, 1947 .. (52)

88   Designation of the convoys. *See* page 104 .. .. (53)

89   Only those convoy battles have been described in which four or more U-boats participated, and which were of particular interest. There were of course other attacks by single boats and many unsuccessful attacks by groups of boats. To preserve clarity, these have been omitted from Diagrams 9–14 .. (54)

90   Examination of the successes of Lt. Schepke for the first year of the war showed that he often considerably overestimated the tonnage of the ships he sank. He was reproved by F.O. U-boats, while the attention of the other commanders was drawn to his exaggerations. During the war the term *Schepke-tonnage* was often used cynically to infer that claims had been exaggerated .. (55)

226

GERMAN U-BOAT BUILDING POLICY, 1922—1945

The following data, obtained from the German Naval Archives, give the principal stages in the development of the U-boat arm.

1922—1939

Note.—Those items which were secret at the time are indented.

By the Treaty of Versailles Germany was denied the right to build or acquire submarines.

1922

In 1922 German Building yards, with the approval of Admiral Behnke, C.-in-C., Navy, founded in the Hague a German Submarine Construction Office under cover of a Dutch firm " Ingenieurkantoor voor Scheepsbouw " (I.v.S., Ltd.). This office, directed by a former Chief Constructor at the Germaniawerft, Kiel, with a German naval representative, was to provide an efficient U-Boat Construction Staff to keep abreast of all technical developments by means of practical work for foreign navies. " Mentor Bilanz, Ltd.," a secret Berlin company, provided the link between I.v.S., Ltd., and the German Admiralty.

1927

In 1927 a technical department was set up in Mentor Bilanz, Ltd., staffed by personnel from the Admiralty Construction Office. This became the Admiralty's secret U-boat

1928

technical section. Mentor Bilanz, Ltd., was liquidated in 1928 for internal political reasons and a new company " Igewit, Ltd." (Ingenieurburo für Wirtschaft und Tecknik) was formed to make preparations for a speedy and effective rebuilding of the German U-boat arm—in such a way that the Navy and Government would not be compromised. U-boat constructional drawings were prepared there in accordance with German Navy specifications. Data in respect of submarine development outside Germany were supplied

October, 1924

by I.v.S., Ltd., The Hague, and German Naval Advisers abroad.

October, 1928

In October, 1924, Admiral Zenker replaced Admiral Behnke as C.-in-C., Navy. He was in turn succeeded by Admiral Raeder in October, 1928.

November, 1932

On 15th November, 1932—before the National Socialists came into power—*Reichswehrminister* von Schleicher had approved a plan for rebuilding the German Navy. This included 16 U-boats to be built in three stages up to and after 1938. Von Schleicher stipulated, however, that no U-boats were to be purchased or commenced until he considered the political situation favourable.

1933 January

The National Socialists came into power on 30th January, 1933. General Blomberg subsequently replaced von Schleicher as *Reichswehrminister*.

March

Prime Minister Macdonald presented his general Disarmament Plan at the Disarmament Conference in Geneva in March, 1933. This called for cessation of all naval construction until 1936.

October

On 13th October, 1933 the German Admiralty discussed a programme, known as New Construction Plan A, for the rebuilding of the German Navy, and it was decided that the U-boats already planned should be built. In addition, large U-boats were to be built as far as the available dockyard capacity allowed. A target of six small U-boats a month was to be reached as soon as the necessary facilities could be provided.

1927

Germany had already built and tested the prototypes of the U-boats now scheduled to be constructed. In 1927 an agreement had been concluded with the King of Spain for the technical section of Mentor Bilanz to build a 750-ton U-boat in Cadiz. After thorough trials this boat was sold to Turkey at the end of 1931. Under Plan A two U-boats of

1930

this type were to be built. A small 250-ton U-boat built in Finland in 1930 with the permission of the Finnish Government was the prototype for the first 25 German coastal U-boats to be constructed. This prototype was also used in 1933/34 to give practical

1935 March

experience to a number of German naval officers.

June

On 16th March, 1935, Germany repudiated the Treaty of Versailles, announcing her intention of building up her Air Force. Three months later, on 18th June, she voluntarily entered into a Naval Agreement with Britain, undertaking to restrict her naval tonnage in the ratio of 35 to 100 to the aggregate naval tonnage of the British Commonwealth. This was to apply to all categories of ships with the exception of submarines, in which Germany was given the right to possess a tonnage equal to that of Britain. She agreed, however, not to build beyond 45 per cent. of British submarine tonnage unless special circumstances arose. (The increased tonnage allowed in the category " submarines " was to be compensated by a corresponding reduction in tonnage of other categories of vessels, so that the overall ratio of German tonnage to British remained at 35 to 100.)

Preliminary work on U-boat construction was so far advanced that eleven days after the Agreement had been signed, that is on 29th June, Germany commissioned her first U-boat since 1918, in Kiel.

By the end of 1935 fourteen U-boats had been commissioned.

July

On 22nd July, 1935, the German Admiralty laid before von Blomberg a proposal for a U-boat building programme covering up to October, 1939. This read as follows :—

COMMENCING DATES FOR BUILDING	NO. OF BOATS	ANTICIPATED DATES OF COMPLETION	NO. OF BOATS
February, 1935/March, 1936 ..	36	June, 1935/March, 1936 ..	19
April, 1936	4	April/November, 1936 ..	17
April, 1937	4	October, 1937	4
April, 1938	4	October, 1938	4
		October, 1939	4
TOTAL	48	TOTAL	48

During November, 1935, budget difficulties necessitated deferment of eight boats of the 1935 programme, but in the 1936 and 1937 programmes this reduction was eliminated and one boat added to the 1937 programme—so that the total number of boats intended to be in commission by October, 1939, was raised to 49.

Germany entered into a second Naval Agreement with Great Britain on 17th July, 1937, which stipulated, *inter alia*, that no submarine built was to exceed 2,000 tons (2,032 metric tons) in standard displacement or carry a gun in excess of 5·1 in. (130 mm.) in calibre. The Signatory Powers also undertook to exchange information regarding their annual building programmes, and affirmed that all matters relating to submarines were governed exclusively by the Agreement of 18th June, 1935.

But in the German Navy Estimates for the year 1938 allowance was made for the fact that the U-boat fleet might have to be increased to parity with the British. This would require the raising of the U-boat tonnage from 22,000 tons to 70,000 tons. By May, 1938, Hitler had decided that France and Britain must be regarded as potential opponents of Germany. He therefore instructed Raeder on 27th May to take all measures for bringing the German U-boat fleet up to parity with that of Britain. Raeder informed him that preliminary orders to achieve this had already been placed. A review of U-boat con-

struction issued on 19th September, 1938, gave the position as follows :—

39 U-boats had been completed and 33 were building. The total of these (72 boats) represented 45 per cent of the British submarine tonnage. In addition, between May and August, 1938, contracts had been placed for a further 25 boats, drawings and preparations completed for 26 boats and six had been projected. The overall figure of 129 U-boats thus built, building or planned corresponded to 100 per cent of the British tonnage.

Although these detailed plans had been made by September, 1938, it was not until 7th November that Raeder informed Keitel (Chief of Staff, Supreme Command) of them, requesting him to arrange to notify the British Government accordingly.

On 12th December, 1938, the German Government notified the British Government of their intention to exercise their treaty rights and increase their U-boat tonnage to 100 per cent of that of Britain. A British Mission, led by Vice-Admiral A. B. Cunningham, left London for Berlin on 28th December to discuss matters arising from the above notification. The discussions were very friendly, but from the German point of view a mere formality, as the decision to achieve parity had already been taken and Germany had no intention either of withdrawing or excusing it. British public opinion, while deploring the German decision, recognised that it was nevertheless permissible by the terms of the Anglo-German Naval Agreement of 18th June, 1935.

In view of the international situation in the latter part of 1938 (Czechoslovakian crisis, Munich Agreement, 29th September, 1938, etc.) the German Admiralty had on 24th November reviewed the possibility of expanding their entire building programme. As a result of these deliberations a plan, known as the " Z " plan, was drawn up on 16th December, provisionally approved by Raeder on 31st December as the basis for all further expansion of the Navy, and circulated in the German Admiralty on 6th January, 1939. In this plan it was proposed that by 1943 the German U-boat fleet should number 162 boats, by 1945—230 boats, and by 1948—247 boats. By 10th March, 1939, 72 U-boats had been built or were building ; of these, 48 were in commission. Of the 175 further U-boats required to complete the " Z " plan, contracts had been placed for 46.

On 28th April, 1939, Hitler denounced the Anglo-German Naval Agreements in the Reichstag. He stated that he had been prompted to enter into and observe the Agreements by a feeling of friendliness towards England, but he now maintained that Britain's attitude to Germany —both in the Press and officially—was one of active hostility. Alleging that the basis of mutual confidence upon which the Agreements were built had been undermined by England, he now resolved to terminate the Agreements. A Note to this effect was sent to the British Government on 29th April, 1939.

1939—1945

When war commenced Germany had 46 U-boats ready for operations, while ten more were in commission and being prepared for active service.

A New Construction Plan resulting from the outbreak of war was approved by Hitler on 7th September, 1939. The following increases were to be made in the U-boat building programme already in force :—

In 1939 (that is, from September) seven additional boats were to be laid down. The figure for 1940 was to be raised by about 46 boats, while the target for 1941 was an increase of ten boats a month over the number previously scheduled for the period. Raeder, discussing the programme with Hitler on 23rd September, pointed out that as by the Autumn of 1940 Britain would have had time to build up strong A.A. defences for her harbours, the main burden of the attack on her Navy would have to be borne by U-boats. The increases allowed in the plan of 7th September, far from being adequate for this task, would barely cover anticipated losses. Hitler agreed, and ordered an extension of the U-boat building programme—even at the expense of the Ju.88 (aircraft) programme.

Accordingly on 6th October the Naval Construction Office made a plan for the building of U-boats up to U.850. Its ultimate aim was a monthly output of 29½ boats. When Raeder discussed the plan with Hitler on 10th October he urged that it should be given priority allocations of labour and materials—but though Hitler approved the plan, he refused to sanction absolute priority, since he was at that time more concerned with ensuring that all

Army requirements were met. Raeder stated on 1st November that the inadequate quota of steel made its completion impossible. On 8th and 11th November he again drew the attention of Hitler and Keitel to this fact and at a further meeting on 30th December he requested authority to begin drawing on stocks of certain materials—particularly tin—which were being held in reserve for the Navy's use in the next few years. This would allow a *modified* programme which would produce, by 1st January, 1942, 316 U-boats above the existing strength of 56 (that is, a total of 372). A decision as to whether this modified programme could be carried out or whether even it would have to be reduced could wait until May/June, 1940.

1940
May
June

By June, 1940, however, matters were still unsettled. Despite promises from Hitler on 21st May and 4th June that as soon as the operations in France had been completed he would issue priority orders for the U-boat and Ju.88 programmes, Raeder was forced to point out on 20th June that shortages of men and materials were delaying even the modified programme of 30th December, 1939. On 28th June, 1940, six days after the armistice with France had been signed, Raeder wrote to Keitel reviewing the U-boat building situation. The modified programme of 30th December was running fairly satisfactorily, despite some hold-ups in labour and materials. But, unless there were an immediate allocation of additional labour and materials, a most unwelcome interruption of U-boat building would occur after January, 1942, when the modified plan was completed.

July

On 10th July Hitler ordered immediate measures for completing the modified programme. When by 21st July he had given no ruling about the continuation of U-boat building beyond 1st January, 1942, Raeder gave orders that ten more boats of the modified programme were to be constructed to avoid any break in production.

August

But on 31st July Hitler cancelled all restrictions on materials for U-boat building ; whereupon on 3rd August Raeder ordered contracts to be placed immediately—and thereafter as required —for as many boats as would maintain the highest monthly output for 1941 (that is, 24 boats rising to 25 as soon as possible). This corresponded to the proposal he had made to Keitel in his letter of 28th June, 1940. On 19th August the Naval Construction Office reported that in addition to the 316 boats of the modified programme contracts had been placed for a further 120. It was intended to complete these during 1942.

November
December

Once again, however, U-boat building was destined to be held up by shortages. On 14th November and again on 27th December Raeder complained that too many types of armaments were being given priority while U-boats were being neglected. The output for 1941 would be 37 less than projected. The monthly output up to November, 1940, had been only seven. On 27th December he informed Hitler that the maximum possible monthly output with the number of workers then available was 18 boats—which was inadequate. While agreeing that the current rate was too low, Hitler stated that in view of the political situation (that is, of Russia's interference in the Balkans), all army requirements must be met before further priority could be given to speeding up U-boat production.

1941
January
March

On 8th January, 1941, the Naval Construction Office produced a schedule for the period December, 1940–December, 1941, which provided for 205 new boats. But, by 18th March, Raeder was again compelled to inform Hitler that unless the demands for additional workers were conceded production figures would decline. The monthly output for the second quarter of 1941 would be 18 U-boats, but it would afterwards drop to 15. If, on the other hand, the demands were met, the rate could be increased to 20 a month by the end of 1941 and to 24 a month in 1942. A report on 23rd July, 1941, giving figures up to 15th June, gave the total number of contracts placed as 787. Of these, 189 had been completed, 216 were building and 382 had not yet been started. Included in the 189 completed were : Losses 40 boats, completing trials 22 boats, for training purposes 50 boats. Thus on 15th June, 1941, the operational strength was only 77 boats.

June

On 30th June, 1941, Raeder urgently represented to Keitel that the Naval building programme should be given equal priority with the Air Force programme and that both should take precedence over all other types of armament. He asked Keitel to confirm the Führer directive of 27th December, 1940, promising priority to the Navy and Air Force programmes as soon as the Army had been fully equipped for the Russian campaign. But Hitler's directive of 14th July, while confirming the continuation of the U-boat programme, gave the Air Force programme, augmented at his instructions, absolute priority. Yet on 25th July he emphasised that the U-boat target of 25 boats per month was not to be reduced. This is an example of uncoordinated planning, and reflects on the higher direction of the war.

July

September

On 11th September Hitler followed up his directive of 14th July by ordering all three services to collaborate in adapting their armaments demands to the prevailing industrial potential, Keitel being given full powers to inaugurate the appropriate measures. On 29th November all three services were told that their allocations of raw materials must be cut. For the Navy this entailed an immediate reduction of 1–2 U-boats a month. It was consequently estimated that the monthly output for 1942 would be about 19–20 boats.

November

1942
March

When, on 5th March, Keitel notified the Navy that the allocation of raw materials for the second quarter of 1942 would be considerably smaller than for the first, it was estimated that the maximum monthly output of U-boats would fall to 15. Discussing the problem of raw materials with Hitler on 12th March, Raeder pointed out that from 1944 onwards it would be impossible to produce more than 15 boats a month. If the Navy received only the allocation announced on 5th March, the U-boat war would gradually come to a standstill. The metal most urgently required was copper, but Hitler said that no further supplies were available. On 13th April Raeder again pleaded for more extensive U-boat building. Hitler agreed in principle, but the Naval Staff realised that there was no point in demanding supplementary labour for U-boat building until the vital question of the copper supply had been solved.

April

December

In December, 1942, Raeder decided that in view of further large reductions in the allocation of raw materials he must make severe cuts in the production of all types of warships, except U-boats, and he informed Hitler accordingly. His aim once again was to achieve a production rate of 25 U-boats a month.

1943 January	As a direct result of the unsuccessful action off the North Cape by *Hipper* and *Lützow* on 31st December, 1942, Hitler began to consider de-commissioning the big ships and asked Raeder on 6th January, 1943, what effect this would have on accelerating U-boat building. Raeder's written reply of 10th January emphatically advocated the retention of the big ships, arguing that de-commissioning them would have little effect on U-boat production. Despite this, Hitler on 26th January ordered these ships to be de-commissioned, hoping that the dock-yard capacity thus made available could be utilised for U-boat building. Actually, however, the order was never implemented on the scale originally intended, though it was the direct cause of Raeder's resignation. Dönitz, who succeeded him as C.-in-C. Navy on 30th January, 1943, modified the order, so that only *Hipper, Koeln* and *Leipzig* paid off for a limited period.
March	The records show that by the end of March Dönitz had succeeded in getting approval for building 30 boats a month. An increased allocation of raw materials was sanctioned by Hitler
April	on 11th April.
May	But on 31st May Dönitz was forced to tell Hitler that the U-boat war had reached a critical stage, where even 30 new boats a month would be inadequate. In April, 1943, losses had risen to 30 per cent of the total number of boats on operations. In 1940 the average tonnage sunk per day at sea per U-boat had been 1,000 tons, but by the end of 1942 the figure had dropped to 200 tons. He had to have a target of 40 new boats per month. In the meantime he had, with the co-operation of Minister Speer, set the thirty-boat a month programme in motion. At this stage Hitler signed a directive authorising a building target of 40 U-boats a month.
June	But, on 6th June Dönitz informed his Naval Group Commanders that, although he was aiming at this large-scale building plan, he had no guarantee that either labour or materials would be forthcoming. The only hope for the Navy was to go on pressing its claims, otherwise it would obtain nothing at all. The situation as he saw it was one of living from hand to mouth. This was also Hitler's view when, approached by Dönitz on 15th June, he postponed a decision on the provision of personnel for new U-boats. Keitel was merely told to see that no one engaged on the naval building programme was drafted into the Armed Forces.
September **1944** February	After this period no further major alterations or decisions were made regarding U-boat building policy. The programme introduced by Dönitz on 31st May continued nominally until the end of the war—the large deviations from it being occasioned by the deterioration in the overall war situation. On 24th September, 1943, and again on 26th February, 1944, Hitler assured Dönitz that any measures taken to expedite the production of the new types of boats (types XXI and XXIII) would receive his full support. But by this time the problem of finding labour and materials had been overshadowed by the difficulty of maintaining production under the constant threat of concentrated Allied air attacks. By February, 1944, there was a delay
April	of one to two months in the programme. The delay was increased when, in April, absolute priority was given to the construction of fighter aircraft, for Hitler reasoned that without this additional fighter protection all German industry, including U-boat building, must come to a complete standstill.
May	In an attempt to accelerate U-boat building a system of mass-production of individual U-boat sections had been adopted. By May, 1944, only eight yards were engaged on U-boat construction, with the result that at times there were more than 30 U-boats together on the slips waiting to be assembled and 30–40 sections under construction on the same site. Under such conditions whole batches of U-boats were in danger of being eliminated by one heavy air raid.
October	It became imperative to provide heavy shelters for building, but in October, 1944, the question of starting on these in the Spring of 1945 was still being discussed. On 13th October, Dönitz informed Hitler that he hoped to have the first of the new U-boats (type XXIII) ready for operations in January, 1945, and 40 of type XXI in February. In November he reported
November	that the U-boat output had fallen far below schedule as a result of shortages of materials, and of bombing attacks. The appalling delays are shown by the fact that in January, 1944, it had been intended to complete by October 150 boats of type XXI, and 140 boats of type XXIII. Actual delivery had been only 40 boats of type XXI and 25 of type XXIII.
1945 January	On 26th January, 1945, Dönitz informed Hitler that in the event of the industrial area of Upper Silesia being lost—which he anticipated—it would still be possible to complete 170 U-boats of type XXI and 70 of type XXIII (this figure included those boats already delivered). Hitler agreed that building should proceed and approved Dönitz's request that the programme be given
February	the same priority classification as the Emergency Armaments Programme. On 15th February Dönitz reported that the then total of 450 U-boats in commission was the highest Germany had ever had. Of these, 237 (111 old-type U-boats, 84 of type XXI and 42 of type XXIII) were in various stages of preparation for operational service. It was expected that from then on 60 additional U-boats would become available each month.
April	The last entry in the German naval records states that between 30th March and 10th April, 1945, 24 U-boats had been destroyed and 12 damaged through air raids on the building yards.
	It is a most eloquent tribute to the progressive efficiency of Allied Anti-Submarine technique that at the final stage of the war, with a potential strength of 450 U-boats still available, Germany could achieve so little with them.

- A P P E N D I X   2   -

TYPES AND SPECIFICATIONS OF U-BOATS

TYPES AND "U" NUMBERS OF GERMAN U-BOATS COMMISSIONED IN THE SECOND WORLD WAR

TYPE		"U" NUMBERS			WHEN COMMISSIONED	TOTAL
IA	Pre-war Atlantic U-boat	25	to	26	1936	2
IIA	250 to 300-ton coastal U-boat	1	to	6	1935	6
IIB	250 to 300-ton coastal U-boat	7	to	24	1935	
		120	to	121	1940	20
IIC	250 to 300-ton coastal U-boat	56	to	63	1938–1940	
		137			1940	9
IID	250 to 300-ton coastal U-boat	138	to	152	1940–1941	15
VII	625-ton Atlantic U-boat	27	to	36	1936–1937	10
VIIB	750-ton Atlantic U-boat	45	to	55	1938–1939	
		73	to	76	1940	
		83	to	87	1941–1942	
		99	to	102	1940	24
VIIC	770-ton Atlantic U-boat	69	to	72	1940–1941	
		77	to	82	1941	
		88	to	98	1941–1942	
		132	to	136	1941	
		201	to	212	1941–1942	
		221	to	232	1942	
		235	to	291	1942–1943	
		301	to	316	1942–1943	
		331	to	394	1941–1944	
		396	to	458	1941–1944	
		465	to	473	1942–1944	
		475	to	486	1942–1944	
		551	to	683	1940–1944	
		701	to	722	1941–1943	
		731	to	768	1942–1944	
		771	to	779	1943–1944	
		821	to	822	1943–1945	
		825	to	826	1944	
		901			1944	
		903	to	907	1943–1944	
		921	to	928	1943–1944	
		951	to	994	1942–1943	
		1051	to	1058	1944	
		1131	to	1132	1944	
		1161	to	1162	1943	
		1191	to	1210	1943–1944	567
VIIC/41	770-ton Atlantic U-boat	292	to	300	1943	
		317	to	329	1943–1944	
		827	to	828	1944	
		929	to	930	1944–1945	
		995			1943	
		997	to	1010	1943–1944	
		1013	to	1025	1943–1944	
		1063	to	1065	1944	
		1103	to	1110	1944	
		1163	to	1172	1943–1944	
		1271	to	1279	1944–1945	
		1301	to	1308	1944–1945	92
VIIC/42	1,080-ton Atlantic U-boat	1101	to	1102	1943	2
VIID	960-ton minelaying U-boat	213	to	218	1941–1942	6
VIIF	Torpedo transport U-boat	1059	to	1062	1943	4
IX	1,030-ton Atlantic U-boat	37	to	44	1938–1939	8

TYPE				"U" NUMBERS			WHEN COMMISSIONED	TOTAL
IXB	1,050-ton Atlantic U-boat	..	..	64	to	65	1939–1940	
				103	to	111	1940	
				122	to	124	1940	14
IXC	1,120-ton Atlantic U-boat	..	..	66	to	68	1941	
				125	to	131	1941	
				153	to	160	1941	
				161	to	166	1941–1943	
				171	to	176	1941	30
IXC/40	1,140-ton Atlantic U-boat	..	..	167	to	170	1941–1943	
				183	to	194	1942	
				501	to	550	1941–1943	
				801	to	806	1943–1945	
				841	to	846	1943	
				853	to	858	1943	
				865	to	870	1943	
				877	to	881	1944	
				889			1944	
				1221	to	1235	1943–1945	111
IXD/41	1,600-ton U-cruiser	..	.. ..	180			1942	
				195			1942	2
IXD/42	1,600-ton U-cruiser	..	..	177	to	179	1942	
				181	to	182	1942	
				196	to	200	1942	
				847	to	852	1943	
				859	to	864	1943	
				871	to	876	1943–1944	
				883			1944	29
XB	1,760-ton minelaying U-boat		..	116	to	119	1941–1942	
				219	to	220	1942–1943	
				233	to	234	1943	8
XIV	1,690-ton supply U-boat	..	..	459	to	464	1941–1942	
				487	to	490	1942–1943	10

PREFABRICATED U-BOATS

(a) Type XXI Atlantic U-boat

NUMBERS BUILT BY THE END OF THE WAR	NUMBERS COMMISSIONED BY THE END OF 1944
U.2501 to 2546	U.2501 to 2519
2548 to 2552	2521 to 2522
3001 to 3041	2524
3044	2529
3501 to 3530	2534
	2540
Total 123	3001 to 3010
	3013
	3017
	3030
	3032
	3035
	3041
	3501 to 3508
	3510 to 3512
	3514 to 3515
	3523
	Total 55

Type XXIII Coastal U-boat

NUMBERS BUILT BY THE END OF THE WAR	NUMBERS COMMISSIONED BY THE END OF 1944
U.2321 to 2371	U.2321 to 2332
4701 to 4707	2334 to 2346
4710	2348
	2350 to 2351
Total 59	2353 to 2354
	2356
	2359
	2361
	2363
	4706
	Total 35

N.B.—The German record of U-boats commissioned in 1945 is incomplete, but the number is estimated to be approximately 65.

" WALTER " TYPE U-BOATS

A number of " Walter " type U-boats were built, but were still undergoing trials at the end of the war. They comprised :—

Type XVII B	300 ton coastal U-boat	..	..	U.1405 to 1407	Built 1944–1945
Type Wa 201	250 ton experimental U-boat		..	792 to 793	Built 1943–1944
Type Wk 202	250 ton experimental U-boat		..	794 to 795	Built 1943–1944
		Total 7			

SUMMARY

TYPE				BUILT	COMMISSIONED
IA	..	..	..	2	2
IIA	..	..	..	6	6
IIB	..	..	..	20	20
IIC	..	..	..	9	9
IID	..	..	..	15	15
VII	..	..	..	10	10
VIIB	..	..	..	24	24
VIIC	..	..	..	567	567
VIIC/41 ..	..	..	..	92	92
VIIC/42 ..	..	..	..	2	2
VIID	..	..	..	6	6
VIIF	..	..	..	4	4
IX	..	..	..	8	8
IXB	..	..	..	14	14
IXC	..	..	..	30	30
IXC/40 ..	..	..	..	111	111
IXD/41 ..	..	..	..	2	2
IXD/42 ..	..	..	..	29	29
XB	..	..	..	8	8
XIV	..	..	..	10	10
XXI	..	..	..	123	55 (to the end of 1944)
XXIII	..	..	..	59	35 (to the end of 1944)
" Walter " type U-boats		..		7	7
Estimated number of U-boats commissioned in 1945					65
				1,158	1,131

QUARTERLY STATE OF U-BOATS FROM SEPTEMBER, 1939—JANUARY, 1945

DATE	OPERATIONAL	TRAINING AND TRIALS	TOTAL	COMMISSIONED DURING THE PREVIOUS QUARTER
September, 1939 ..	49	8	57	
January, 1940 ..	32	24	56	7
April, 1940 ..	46	6	52	4
July, 1940 ..	28	23	51	9
October, 1940 ..	27	37	64	15
January, 1941 ..	22	67	89	22
April, 1941 ..	32	81	113	30
July, 1941 ..	65	93	158	47
October, 1941 ..	80	118	198	53
January, 1942 ..	91	158	249	69
April, 1942 ..	121	164	285	49
July, 1942 ..	140	191	331	59
October, 1942 ..	196	169	365	61
January, 1943 ..	212	181	393	69
April, 1943 ..	240	185	425	69
July, 1943 ..	207	208	415	71
October, 1943 ..	175	237	412	61
January, 1944 ..	168	268	436	78
April, 1944 ..	166	278	444	62
July, 1944 ..	188	246	434	53
October, 1944 ..	141	260	401	49
January, 1945 ..	144	281	425	65

FOREIGN SUBMARINES WHICH WERE REQUISITIONED OR CAPTURED AND USED BY GERMANY

GERMAN NUMBER	ORIGINAL NAME	NATIONALITY
UA ..	ex-Batiray* ..	Turkish
UB ..	ex-Seal ..	British
UC 1 ..	ex-B.5 ..	Norwegian
UC 2 ..	ex-B.6 ..	Norwegian
UD 1 ..	ex-O.8 ..	Dutch
UD 2 ..	ex-O.12 ..	Dutch
UD 3 ..	ex-O.25 ..	Dutch
UD 4 ..	ex-O.26 ..	Dutch
UD 5 ..	ex-O.27 ..	Dutch
UF 1 ..	ex-L'Africaine ..	French
UF 2 ..	ex-La Favorite ..	French
UF 3 ..	ex-L'Astrie ..	French
? ..	ex-La Martinique ..	French

* Built in Germany.

236

Type IA

Length ..	..	238·88 feet
Beam ..	..	20·49 feet
Draught (average) ..		13·94 feet
Displacement :		
surfaced ..	..	862 tons
submerged	..	983 tons
form* ..	..	1,200 tons (approx.)
Speed (laden) :		
surfaced ..	..	18·6 knots (maximum)
surfaced ..	..	17·75 knots (maximum sustained)
submerged	..	8·3 knots (for one hour)
Endurance :		
surfaced :		
8,100 miles at		10 knots (Diesel-electric)
7,900 miles at		10 knots (cruising)
6,700 miles at		12 knots (cruising)
3,300 miles at		17·75 knots (maximum sustained)
submerged :		
136 miles at		2 knots
78 miles at		4 knots
Diving depth	..	330 feet
Armament :		
torpedo tubes	..	4 bow, 2 stern
outfit ..	..	14 torpedoes (normal)
	or	4 torpedoes plus 16 TMA mines
	or	4 torpedoes plus 24 TMB mines
	or	4 torpedoes plus 10 TMA and 9 TMB mines
	or	28 TMA mines
	or	42 TMB mines
guns ..	..	1—10·5 cm. SKC/36 with 150 rounds of ammunition.
		1—20 mm. Flak single with 2,000 rounds of ammunition
Crew ..	..	43

Type IIA

Length ..	..	134·97 feet
Beam ..	..	13·467 feet
Draught (average) ..		12·639 feet
Displacement :		
surfaced ..	..	253·8 tons
submerged	..	303·1 tons
form ..	..	381 tons
Speed (laden) :		
surfaced ..	..	13 knots
submerged	..	6·9 knots (for one hour)
Endurance :		
surfaced :		
2,000 miles at		8 knots (Diesel-electric)
1,600 miles at		8 knots (cruising)
1,500 miles at		10 knots (cruising)
1,050 miles at		12 knots (cruising)
950 miles at		13 knots (maximum sustained)

Type IIA—cont.

Endurance—cont.		
submerged :		
71 miles at		2 knots
35 miles at		4 knots
Diving depth	..	330 feet
Armament :		
torpedo tubes	..	3 bow
outfit ..	..	5 torpedoes (normal)
		6 torpedoes (maximum)
	or	1 torpedo plus 8 TMA mines
	or	1 torpedo plus 10 TMB mines
	or	1 torpedo plus 4 TMA and 6 TMB mines
	or	12 TMA mines
	or	18 TMB mines
guns ..	..	1—20 mm. Flak twin with about 850 rounds of ammunition
Crew ..	..	25

Type IIB

Length ..	..	140 feet
Beam ..	..	13·467 feet
Draught (average) ..		12·87 feet
Displacement :		
surfaced ..	..	278·9 tons
submerged	..	328·5 tons
form ..	..	414 tons
Speed (laden) :		
surfaced ..	..	13 knots
submerged	..	7 knots (for one hour)
Endurance :		
surfaced :		
3,900 miles at		8 knots (Diesel-electric)
3,100 miles at		8 knots (cruising)
2,700 miles at		10 knots (cruising)
1,800 miles at		12 knots (cruising)
1,300 miles at		13 knots (maximum sustained)
submerged :		
71 miles at		2 knots (MAK battery)†
35 miles at		4 knots (MAK battery)†
83 miles at		2 knots (MAL battery)†
43 miles at		4 knots (MAL battery)†
Diving depth	..	330 feet
Armament :		
torpedo tubes	..	As for type IIA
outfit ..	..	As for type IIA
guns ..	..	1—20 mm. Flak twin with 1,000 rounds of ammunition
	or	1—20 mm. Flak twin and 1—20 mm. Flak single with 1,800 rounds of ammunition (Black Sea boats)
Crew ..	..	25

* form displacement = total submerged displacement including free flooding spaces
† MAK = Pre-1938 design of U-boat battery
  MAL = An improved design of the MAK, introduced in 1938, in which the number of plates was increased and the thickness of the grids reduced to give a higher battery rate performance

237

Type IIC

Length	.. ..	144·87 feet
Beam	..	13·467 feet
Draught (average) ..		12·616 feet
Displacement :		
surfaced ..	..	291 tons
submerged	..	341 tons
form	..	435 tons (approx.)
Speed (laden) :		
surfaced ..	..	12 knots
submerged	..	7 knots (for one hour)
Endurance :		
surfaced :		
4,200 miles at		8 knots (Diesel-electric)
3,800 miles at		8 knots (cruising)
2,900 miles at		10 knots (cruising)
1,900 miles at		12 knots (maximum sustained)
submerged :		
71 miles at		2 knots (MAK battery)
35 miles at		4 knots (MAK battery)
81 miles at		2 knots (MAL battery)
42 miles at		4 knots (MAL battery)
Diving depth	..	330 feet
Armament :		
torpedo tubes	..	As for type IIA
outfit	..	As for type IIA
guns	..	1—20 mm. Flak twin with 1,200 rounds of ammunition
Crew	.. ..	25

Type IID

Length	.. ..	145·1 feet
Beam	..	16·129 feet
Draught (average) ..		12·76 feet
Displacement :		
surfaced ..	..	314 tons
submerged	..	364 tons
form	..	460 tons
Speed (laden) :		
surfaced	..	12·7 knots
submerged	..	7·4 knots (for one hour)
Endurance :		
surfaced :		
5,650 miles at		8 knots (cruising)
4,400 miles at		10 knots (cruising)
3,450 miles at		12 knots (cruising)
3,200 miles at		12·7 knots (maximum sustained)
submerged :		
100 miles at		2 knots
56 miles at		4 knots
Diving depth	..	330 feet
Armament :		
torpedo tubes	..	As for type IIA
outfit	..	As for type IIA
guns	..	1—20 mm. Flak twin with 1,200 rounds of ammunition
Crew	.. ..	25

Type VII

Length	.. ..	212·88 feet
Beam	..	19·302 feet
Draught :		
light	..	14·404 feet
laden	..	?
Displacement :		
surfaced ..	..	626 tons
submerged	..	745 tons
form	..	915 tons
Speed (laden) :		
surfaced ..	..	17 knots (maximum)
surfaced ..	..	16 knots (maximum sustained)
submerged	..	8 knots (for one hour)
Endurance :		
surfaced :		
6,800 miles at		10 knots (Diesel-electric)
6,200 miles at		10 knots (cruising)
4,300 miles at		12 knots (cruising)
2,900 miles at		16 knots (maximum sustained)
submerged :		
130 miles at		2 knots (MAK battery)
73 miles at		4 knots (MAK battery)
146 miles at		2 knots (MAL battery)
90 miles at		4 knots (MAL battery)
Diving depth	..	309 feet
Armament :		
torpedo tubes	..	4 bow, 1 stern
outfit	..	11 torpedoes (maximum)
	or	3 torpedoes plus 12 TMA mines
	or	3 torpedoes plus 18 TMB mines
	or	3 torpedoes plus 8 TMA and 6 TMB mines
	or	22 TMA mines
	or	33 TMB mines
guns	..	1—37 mm. Flak with 1,195 rounds of ammunition
		2—20 mm. Flak twin with 4,380 rounds of ammunition
Crew	.. ..	44

Type VIIB

Length	.. ..	219·45 feet
Beam	..	20·47 feet
Draught :		
light	..	14·8 feet
laden	..	15·55 feet
Displacement :		
surfaced ..	..	753 tons
submerged	..	857 tons
form	..	1,040 tons
Speed (laden) :		
surfaced ..	..	17·9 knots (maximum)
surfaced ..	..	17·2 knots (maximum sustained)
submerged	..	8 knots (for one hour)

Type VIIB—cont.

Endurance :

surfaced :

9,400 miles at	10 knots (Diesel-electric) (with GW diesels)
8,700 miles at	10 knots (cruising) (with GW diesels)
6,500 miles at	12 knots (cruising) (with GW diesels)
3,850 miles at	17·2 knots (maximum sustained) (with GW diesels)
9,700 miles at	10 knots (Diesel-electric) (with MAN diesels)
9,100 miles at	10 knots (cruising) (with MAN diesels)
6,900 miles at	12 knots (cruising) (with MAN diesels)
4,000 miles at	17 knots (maximum sustained) (with MAN diesels)

submerged :

110 miles at	2 knots (MAK battery)
72 miles at	4 knots (MAK battery)
130 miles at	2 knots (MAL battery)
90 miles at	4 knots (MAL battery)
Diving depth ..	309 feet

Armament :

torpedo tubes ..	4 bow, 1 stern
outfit	14 torpedoes (maximum)
	12 torpedoes (normal)
or	4 torpedoes plus 16 TMA mines
or	3 torpedoes plus 24 TMB mines
or	4 torpedoes plus 10 TMA and 9 TMB mines
or	26 TMA mines
or	39 TMB mines
guns	As for type VII
Crew	44

Type VIIC

Length	221·43 feet
Beam	20·47 feet
Draught :	
light	14·86 feet
laden	15·62 feet
Displacement :	
surfaced	769 tons
submerged ..	871 tons
form	1,070 tons
Speed (laden) :	
surfaced	17·7 knots (maximum)
surfaced	17 knots (maximum sustained)
submerged ..	7·6 knots (for one hour)

Type VIIC—cont.

Endurance :

surfaced :

9,700 miles at	10 knots (Diesel-electric) (with MAN diesels)
8,850 miles at	10 knots (cruising) (with MAN diesels)
6,500 miles at	12 knots (cruising) (with MAN diesels)
3,450 miles at	17 knots (maximum sustained) (with MAN diesels)

submerged :

130 miles at	2 knots
80 miles at	4 knots
Diving depth ..	309 feet

Armament :

torpedo tubes ..	As for type VIIB
outfit	As for type VIIB
guns	As for type VII
Crew	44

Type VIIC 41

This boat was the same in all respects as the type VIIC with the exception of diving depth, which was 394 feet.

Type VIIC/42

This was virtually an expanded type VIIC, redesigned to meet the new tactical requirements brought about by the increase in convoy speeds, greater dispersal of convoy routes, and improved A/S methods. The diving depth was increased, and new diesels were installed which, at a speed of 10 knots, provided nearly double the range of the type VIIC.

The available specifications of the type VII C/42 are as follows :—

Length	225·49 feet
Beam	20·34 feet
Displacement :	
surfaced	1,084·5 tons
submerged ..	1,098·92 tons
form	1,362 tons
Speed (laden) :	
surfaced	18·6 knots (maximum)
submerged	?
Endurance :	
12,600 miles at ..	10 knots
Diving depth ..	394 feet
Armament	As for type VIIC except for reserve torpedoes

Type VIID

Length	.. ..	252·3 feet
Beam	.. ..	20·9 feet
Draught :		
light	.. ..	15·8 feet
laden	.. ..	16·4 feet
Displacement :		
surfaced ..		965 tons
submerged	..	1,080 tons
form	..	1,285 tons (approx.)
Speed (laden) :		
surfaced ..	..	16·7 knots (maximum)
surfaced ..	..	16 knots (maximum sustained)
submerged	..	7·3 knots (for one hour)
Endurance :		
surfaced :		
13,000 miles at		10 knots (Diesel-electric)
11,200 miles at		10 knots (cruising)
8,100 miles at		12 knots (cruising)
5,050 miles at		16 knots (maximum sustained)
submerged :		
127 miles at		2 knots
69 miles at		4 knots
Diving depth	..	330 feet
Armament :		
torpedo tubes	..	4 bow, 1 stern
		5 mine shafts
outfit	.. ..	12 torpedoes (normal)
	or	4 torpedoes plus 16 TMA and 15 SMA mines
	or	3 torpedoes plus 24 TMB and 15 SMA mines
	or	4 torpedoes plus 10 TMA, 9 TMB and 15 SMA mines
	or	14 torpedoes plus 15 SMA mines
	or	26 TMA and 15 SMA mines
	or	39 TMB and 15 SMA mines
guns	.. ..	1—37 mm. Flak with 1,995 rounds of ammunition
		2—20 mm. Flak twin with 4,380 rounds of ammunition
Crew	.. ..	44

Type VIIF

Length	.. ..	256·18 feet
Beam	.. ..	23·95 feet
Draught :		
light	.. ..	16·1 feet
laden	.. ..	?
Displacement :		
surfaced ..	..	1,084 tons
submerged	..	1,181 tons
form	..	1,345 tons
Speed (laden) :		
surfaced ..	..	17·6 knots (maximum)
surfaced ..	..	16·9 knots (maximum sustained)
submerged	..	7·9 knots (for one hour)

Type VIIF—*cont.*

Endurance :		
surfaced :		
13,950 miles at		10 knots (Diesel-electric)
14,700 miles at		10 knots (cruising)
9,500 miles at		12 knots (cruising)
5,350 miles at		16·9 knots (maximum sustained)
submerged :		
130 miles at		2 knots
75 miles at		4 knots
Diving depth	..	330 feet
Armament :		
torpedo tubes	..	4 bow, 1 stern
outfit	.. ..	39 torpedoes (normal and maximum)
guns	.. ..	As for type VIID
Crew	.. ..	46

Type IX

Length	.. ..	252·45 feet
Beam	.. ..	21·48 feet
Draught :		
light	.. ..	14·289 feet
laden	.. ..	15·51 feet
Displacement :		
surfaced ..	..	1,032 tons
submerged	..	1,153 tons
form	..	1,408 tons
Speed (laden) :		
surfaced ..	..	18·2 knots (maximum sustained)
submerged	..	7·7 knots (for one hour)
Endurance :		
surfaced :		
11,350 miles at		10 knots (Diesel-electric)
10,500 miles at		10 knots (cruising)
8,100 miles at		12 knots (cruising)
3,800 miles at		18·2 knots (maximum sustained)
submerged :		
128 miles at		2 knots (MAK battery)
65 miles at		4 knots (MAK battery)
152 miles at		2 knots (MAL battery)
82 miles at		4 knots (MAL battery)
Diving depth	..	330 feet
Armament :		
torpedo tubes	..	4 bow, 2 stern
outfit	.. ..	19 torpedoes (normal) (22 maximum)
	or	8 torpedoes plus 22 TMA mines
	or	8 torpedoes plus 33 TMB mines
	or	8 torpedoes plus 14 TMA and 12 TMB mines
	or	44 TMA mines
	or	66 TMB mines
guns	.. ..	1—37 mm. Flak with 2,625 rounds of ammunition
		2—20 mm. Flak twin with 8,500 rounds of ammunition
Crew	.. ..	48

Type IXB

Length	.. ..	252·45 feet
Beam	.. ..	22·308 feet
Draught :		
light	.. ..	14·322 feet
laden	.. ..	15·51 feet
Displacement :		
surfaced ..	..	1,051 tons
submerged	..	1,178 tons
form	..	1,430 tons
Speed (laden) :		
surfaced ..	..	18·2 knots (maximum sustained)
submerged	..	7·3 knots (for one hour)
Endurance :		
surfaced :		
12,400 miles at		10 knots (Diesel-electric)
12,000 miles at		10 knots (cruising)
8,700 miles at		12 knots (cruising)
3,800 miles at		18·2 knots (maximum sustained)
submerged :		
134 miles at		2 knots
64 miles at		4 knots
Diving depth	..	330 feet
Armament ..	..	As for type IX
Crew	.. ..	48

Type IXC

Length	.. ..	237·18 feet
Beam	.. ..	22·308 feet
Draught :		
light	.. ..	14·388 feet
laden	.. ..	15·411 feet
Displacement :		
surfaced ..	..	1,120 tons
submerged	..	1,232 tons
form	.. ..	1,540 tons
Speed (laden) :		
surfaced ..	..	18·3 knots (maximum sustained)
submerged	..	7·3 knots (for one hour)
Endurance :		
16,300 miles at		10 knots (Diesel-electric)
13,450 miles at		10 knots (cruising)
11,000 miles at		12 knots (cruising)
5,000 miles at		18·3 knots (maximum sustained)
submerged :		
128 miles at		2 knots
63 miles at		4 knots
Diving depth	..	330 feet
Armament ..	..	As for type IX
Crew	.. ..	48

Type IXC/40

Length	.. ..	237·18 feet
Beam	.. ..	22·688 feet
Draught :		
light	.. ..	14·27 feet
laden	.. ..	15·41 feet
Displacement :		
surfaced ..	..	1,144 tons
submerged	..	1,257 tons
form	..	1,545 tons
Speed (laden) :		
surfaced ..	..	18·3 knots (maximum sustained)
submerged	..	7·3 knots (for one hour)
Endurance :		
surfaced :		
16,800 miles at		10 knots (Diesel-electric)
13,850 miles at		10 knots (cruising)
11,400 miles at		12 knots (cruising)
5,100 miles at		18·3 knots (maximum sustained)
submerged :		
128 miles at		2 knots
63 miles at		4 knots
Diving depth	..	330 feet
Armament ..	..	As for type IX
Crew	.. ..	48

Type IXD/41

Length	.. ..	289·01 feet
Beam	.. ..	24·75 feet
Draught :		
light	.. ..	15·4 feet
laden	.. ..	18·249 feet
Displacement :		
surfaced ..	..	1,610 tons
submerged	..	1,799 tons
form	.. ..	2,150 tons
Speed (laden) :		
surfaced ..	..	16·5 knots (maximum)
surfaced ..	..	15·8 knots (maximum sustained)
submerged	..	6·9 knots (for one hour)
Endurance :		
surfaced :		
13,000 miles at		10 knots (Diesel-electric)
12,750 miles at		10 knots (cruising)
9,900 miles at		12 knots (cruising)
5,600 miles at		15·8 knots (maximum sustained)
submerged :		
254 miles at		2 knots
115 miles at		4 knots
Diving depth	..	330 feet
Armament :		
torpedo tubes ..		4 bow, 2 stern
outfit	..	24 torpedoes (maximum)
guns	.. ..	1—37 mm. Flak with 2,575 rounds of ammunition
		2—20 mm. Flak twins with 8,100 rounds of ammunition
Crew	.. ..	57

Type IXD/42

Length	.. ..	289·01 feet
Beam	.. ..	24·75 feet
Draught :		
light	.. ..	15·4 feet
laden	.. ..	18·249 feet
Displacement :		
surfaced ..	..	1,616 tons
submerged	..	1,804 tons
form	.. ..	2,150 tons
Speed (laden) :		
surfaced ..	..	19·2 knots (maximum)
surfaced ..	..	19·2 knots (maximum sustained)
submerged	..	6·9 knots (for one hour)
Endurance :		
surfaced :		
32,300 miles at		10 knots (Diesel-electric)
31,500 miles at		10 knots (cruising)
23,700 miles at		12 knots (cruising)
8,500 miles at		19·2 knots (maximum sustained)
submerged :		
121 miles at		2 knots
57 miles at		4 knots
Diving depth	..	330 feet
Armament :		
torpedo tubes	..	4 bow, 2 stern
outfit	.. ..	21 torpedoes (normal)
	or	8 torpedoes plus 26 TMA mines
	or	8 torpedoes plus 39 TMB mines
guns	.. ..	1—37 mm. Flak with 2,575 rounds of ammunition
		2—20 mm. Flak twins with 8,100 rounds of ammunition
Crew	.. ..	57

Type XB

Length	.. ..	296·34 feet
Beam	.. ..	30·36 feet
Draught :		
light	.. ..	15·114 feet
laden	.. ..	15·5 feet
Displacement :		
surfaced ..	..	1,763 tons
submerged	..	2,177 tons
form	.. ..	2,710 tons
Speed (laden) :		
surfaced ..	..	17 knots (maximum)
surfaced ..	..	16·4 knots (maximum sustained)
submerged	..	7 knots (for one hour)

Type XB—continued

Endurance :		
surfaced :		
21,000 miles at		10 knots (Diesel-electric)
18,450 miles at		10 knots (cruising)
14,450 miles at		12 knots (cruising)
6,750 miles at		16·4 knots (maximum sustained)
submerged :		
188 miles at		2 knots
93 miles at		4 knots
Diving depth	..	376 feet
Armament :		
mine shafts	..	30
torpedo tubes	..	2 stern
outfit	.. ..	15 torpedoes and 66 SMA mines
guns	.. ..	1—37 mm. Flak with 2,500 rounds of ammunition
		2—20 mm. Flak twins with 8,000 rounds of ammunition
Crew	.. ..	52

Type XIV

Length	.. ..	221·43 feet
Beam	.. ..	30·85 feet
Draught (average) ..		21·48 feet
Displacement :		
surfaced ..	..	1,688 tons
submerged	..	1,932 tons
form	.. ..	2,300 tons
Speed (laden) :		
surfaced ..	..	14·9 knots (maximum)
surfaced ..	..	14·4 knots (maximum sustained)
submerged	..	6·2 knots (for one hour)
Endurance :		
surfaced :		
12,300 miles at		10 knots (Diesel-electric)
12,350 miles at		10 knots (cruising)
9,300 miles at		12 knots (cruising)
5,500 miles at		14·4 knots (maximum sustained)
submerged :		
120 miles at		2 knots
55 miles at		4 knots
Diving depth	..	396 feet
Armament :		
torpedo tubes	..	none
torpedoes	..	none
guns	.. ..	1—37 mm. Flak with 2,500 rounds of ammunition
		2—20 mm. Flak twins with 8,000 rounds of ammunition
Capacity :		
Diesel oil	..	720 tons (approx.)
Lubricating oil ..		34 tons (approx.)
Fresh water	..	10·5 tons (approx.)
Distilled water ..		3 tons (approx.)
Crew	.. ..	53

Type XXI			Type XXIII		
Length	..	237 feet	Length	..	114·44 feet
Beam	..	21·78 feet	Beam	..	9·9 feet
Draught (average)	..	20·46 feet	Draught (average)	..	12·078 feet
Displacement :			Displacement :		
surfaced	..	1,621 tons	surfaced	..	232 tons
submerged	..	1,819 tons	submerged	..	256 tons
form	..	2,100 tons	form	..	274 tons
Speed (laden) :			Speed (laden) :		
surfaced	..	15·6 knots (maximum)	surfaced	..	9·75 knots (maximum)
surfaced	..	15·6 knots (maximum sustained)	surfaced	..	9·7 knots (maximum sustained)
submerged	..	*17·18 knots (for one hour)	submerged	..	†12·5 knots (for one hour)
Endurance :			Endurance :		
surfaced :			surfaced :		
15,500 miles at	10 knots (cruising)		4,300 miles at	6 knots (cruising)	
11,150 miles at	12 knots (cruising)		2,800 miles at	8 knots (cruising)	
5,100 miles at	15·6 knots (maximum sustained)		1,350 miles at	9·7 knots (maximum sustained)	
submerged :			submerged :		
365 miles at	5 knots		175 miles at	4 knots	
285 miles at	6 knots	(on electric motors)	113 miles at	6 knots	(on electric motors)
170 miles at	8 knots		70 miles at	8 knots	
110 miles at	10 knots		43 miles at	10 knots	
Diving depth	..	376 feet	Diving depth	..	330 feet
Armament :			Armament :		
torpedo tubes	..	6 bow	torpedo tubes	..	2 bow
outfit	..	20 torpedoes (maximum)	Outfit	..	2 torpedoes (maximum)
guns	..	2—30 mm. Flak in twin mounting with 3,800 rounds of ammunition	guns	..	none
Crew	..	57	Crew	..	14

* Trials carried out in the United States gave a maximum speed of 15·2 knots for 1·2 hours.

† Trials carried out in the United Kingdom gave a maximum speed of 11·14 knots for 1·27 hours.

MORE FROM THE SAME SERIES

Most books from the 'World War II from Original Sources' series are edited and endorsed by Emmy Award winning film maker and military historian Bob Carruthers, producer of Discovery Channel's Line of Fire and Weapons of War and BBC's Both Sides of the Line. Long experience and strong editorial control gives the military history enthusiast the ability to buy with confidence.

The series advisor is David McWhinnie, producer of the acclaimed Battlefield series for Discovery Channel. David and Bob have co-produced books and films with a wide variety of the UK's leading historians including Professor John Erickson and Dr David Chandler.

Where possible the books draw on rare primary sources to give the military enthusiast new insights into a fascinating subject.

For more information visit www.pen-and-sword.co.uk